Empowering Students

Empowering Students

A Contemporary and Essential Approach to Education

Elizabeth Quinn and John Scileppi, eds.

Washington DC

Copyright © 2016 by Elizabeth Quinn

New Academia Publishing, 2016

All rights reserved. No part of this book may be reproduced or transmitted in any form or by any means, electronic or mechanical, including photocopying, recording, or by any information storage and retrieval system.

Printed in the United States of America

Library of Congress Control Number: 2015960983
ISBN 978-0-9966484-5-5 paperback (alk. paper)

4401-A Connecticut Ave., NW #236 - Washington DC 20008
info@newacademia.com - www.newacademia.com

Contents

Acknowledgments   vii

Introduction
John Scileppi and Elizabeth Quinn   1

THEORETICAL PERSPECTIVES AFFECTING EDUCATION IN GENERAL

1. Personal and Social Empowerment in a Globalized World: How Empowering Subcultures Results in Flourishing Societies
Maurizio Geri   7

2. The Role of Language in Empowerment: How Toxic Language Leads to Negativity and Erroneous Cognition, and Numbs Creativity
Fabrizio Guarducci   33

3. The Power of Language to Make a Difference: How Educators' Words Impact Students Perceptions of Their own Competence
Ronald Cromwell, Debra Baird, Tedi Gordon, & Brandon Baird   59

4. Literacy Education: The Antidote to Oppression
Maureen Fitzgerald-Riker   81

5. Humanistic Education: How Teachers Empower Students to Collaborate in Their Own Learning Process
John Scileppi   95

6. Value Clarification: The Basis for Informed Life Choices
John Scileppi   127

SPECIFIC APPLICATIONS OF EMPOWERMENT THROUGH EDUCATION

7. Self-Management of Behavior: When We Know Better, We Do Better
   Elizabeth Quinn — 153

8. Gender Equity in Education: The Societal Benefits of Empowering Females
   Elizabeth Quinn — 173

9. Case Studies of Empowerment in Primary and Middle Schools
   Barbara Ruggiero & Linda Dixon-Dziedzic — 193

10. Improving Self-Efficacy Through Cultural Competence: The Role of International Study Abroad in Empowerment
    Gavin Webb and John Peters — 223

References — 249
List of Contributors — 266
Index — 271

Acknowledgments

We deeply and sincerely appreciate those in our personal lives who support, inspire, and encourage us, and those in our professional lives who edit, proofread, and critique our writing. Your contributions have improved our work. Thank you.

Introduction

John Scileppi and Elizabeth Quinn

If a man is hungry and you give him a fish, you fed him for one day; but if you teach him how to fish, you have fed him for the rest of his life. This paraphrase of Anne Thackeray Ritchie's (1885) famous quote (frequently misattributed to Confucius and many other notable thinkers) sums up one of the most important goals of education. Our role as educators is to empower our students enabling them to reach their goals in the context of contributing to society. As we all know, our educational system does not always achieve this goal, perhaps because social scientific research on empowerment has been long overlooked in the discussion and teaching of philosophies of education. Or perhaps because the system focuses on teaching and testing academic subjects and not intellectual skills such as innovation, creativity, curiosity, and a sense of intellectual adventure (Zakaria, 2015). The purpose of this book is to help teachers and parents become more aware of empowerment and to help transform school-aged youth into enthusiastic, intellectually curious, self-directed learners who are motivated toward academic success, self-discovery, and civic engagement.

This book is written for those who believe the role of education is to empower students. In researching this theme, we found there is no academic course in teacher preparation curricula anywhere in the United States that is dedicated to this role. Many publishers rejected the manuscript as they did not expect college teachers would adopt the book as, in one editor's opinion, the book might pertain to at most a two week segment in either a graduate or undergraduate teacher education course. Given that this perception is accurate, one wonders how a teacher in training might gain the necessary theory base and strategies needed to empower students. Thus this book helps to fill this need for prospective – and current – educators. Further, perhaps there *should be* courses dedicated to this theme. Thus this book is also useful for teacher educators and to those who create educational policy. A final audience includes those parents and concerned citizens who believe student empowerment should be a central goal in the national and state educational systems. Hopefully this book can provide a rationale for such advocacy. While the need for empowering students is important in the United States and in other developed nations, it is probably more imperative in the schools of developing countries. Empowering students in these latter societies will enable the youth to create their own goals and not merely replicate the beliefs and values of the formerly colonizing cultures.

This book addresses first some theoretical perspectives that can influence all levels of education. Maurizio Geri introduces what empowerment entails both at the individual and organizational levels. He notes that a social system will flourish if all of its subcultures are empowered. The empowerment movement of the past fifty years helps individuals realize their full human potentials. What follows are two chapters on the importance of language. Fabrizio Guarducci focuses on the role language plays in helping students structure their own ideas and feelings, symbolize their experiences and communicate them effectively. Guarducci discusses how mirror neurons enhance compassion and understanding others and how toxic language sometimes inappropriately used by teachers leads to negativity and aggression and numbs creativity. In the chapter on the power of language, Ron Cromwell and his colleagues show the effect of what educators say to their students on the students' belief in their own competence. Teaching the language of possibilities should be taught in every school as it helps students achieve success and frees them from distortions of reality. Educators need to listen to the voices of their students, and help youth to understand the social and political context which gives meaning to the words expressed. Maureen Fitzgerald-Riker points out the importance of teaching literacy as a basic right of all students to know how to read and to comprehend the meaning of what they are encountering. Literacy education is a political act and an effective means of confronting oppression against the poor. John Scileppi describes how John Dewey's theories guided the empowerment in education movement in order to transform students into productive and contributing members of a democratic society. He shows various examples of how teachers can respect their students and invite them to cooperate in the teaching-learning process. In the following chapter, Scileppi also describes how value clarification can assist students in enhancing their awareness of the priorities they hold. Frequently students need to bring into their consciousness what truly matters to them so that they can make informed career choices and other decisions that will affect their lives.

While the chapters in the theoretical perspectives section also give examples of how the principles can be applied, the second half of the book focuses on specific applications. Beth Quinn follows up on the last chapter in the first section by describing how educators can teach their students to take control of their own behavior. Once students know their values and priorities, they need to learn some concrete strategies to implement them in practice. Educators can encourage students to manage their own behavior so that they can effectively utilize their time and energy. Taken together these two chapters empower students to "pull their own strings" and accomplish the objectives they have for themselves. In the next chapter, Quinn points out how educators consciously or unconsciously can harm student achievement and motivation on the basis of their gender. Girls and later women often are the victims of gender discrimination relating to educational and professional opportunity, but boys and later men need greater sensitivity in this issue so as to be able to develop more holistic and egalitarian relationships respectful of the other. The next chapter focuses on primary education. Barbara Ruggiero describes an inner city private school serving the needs of young students from economically poor families. This school, in existence for over forty years and supported nearly completely by donations and a very low tuition, has the objective of empowering students in its mission statement. Because of the creative instructional strategies developed in this school (and reported in the chapter), the children attending The Children's Community School have achieved scores on standardized tests that exceed state averages. Many of the alumni have succeeded in diverse spheres of life in the community. To balance the chapter, Linda Dixon-Dziedzic, a school psychologist, describes the strategies to empower students in a more affluent suburban school district. This chapter brings home the fact that students coming from both poor and middle class families need to be taught by educators who use effective strategies to enhance empowerment. The book ends with a chapter by Gavin Webb and John Peters on how international study abroad can be very empowering if those running the program are aware of their role in achieving this objective. Given that the world is "shrinking" and today's students will need a greater level of cultural competence to effectively succeed in multi-national corporations and to interact meaningfully with individuals from other cultures, exposure to multiple cultures is becoming more and more essential. In addition, young people studying abroad face many new and unfamiliar situations, and mastering them enhances their feelings of self-efficacy and confidence. By broadening their perspectives, these students become more cosmopolitan and are better able to creatively deal with whatever conflicts and problems they may encounter. Returning home from successful study abroad activities enables the students to become citizens of the world, able to confront challenges creatively and effectively.

Theoretical Perspectives Affecting Education in General

1

Personal and Social Empowerment in a Globalized World:

How Empowering Subcultures Results in Flourishing Societies

Maurizio Geri

> Everyone is the maker of his own destiny
> —*Appio Claudio, Rome, I century BC*
>
> Be the change you want to see in the world
> —*Mohandas Karamchand Gandhi, India, XX century AD*

This chapter explores the concept of empowerment, in particular, personal and social empowerment, related to education. In this analysis, I draw upon my own observations and experiences in studying and working on peace and development in different countries of the world, and on theories of empowerment processes at different levels, with respect to the social relations, and the politics and the economics of a given society. The chapter begins with a general philosophical introduction on empowerment, followed by a more detailed analysis of the processes of social, political and economic empowerment, the influence of cultural dimensions on empowerment and concludes by analyzing how experiential learning experiences in peace building can represent empowerment tools for women and men around the planet. These experiential examples derive from an international studies program and women empowerment training workshop.

A philosophical Introduction

> Empowerment refers to increasing the spiritual, political, social, educational, gender or economic strength of individuals and communities. Sociological empowerment often addresses members of groups that social discrimination processes have excluded from decision-making processes through, for example, discrimination based on disability, race, ethnicity, religion, or gender.
> (Empowerment, n.d.).

This definition of empowerment can be found in Wikipedia, the free and collaborative encyclopedia freely written by women and men around the world a process which in itself is empowering.

But how can we really define empowerment? First of all we have to say the word "empowerment" nowadays can be defined and interpreted in a wide spectrum of meanings in different sociocultural and political contexts, and does not translate easily into all languages. However, at its heart we could agree it has an intrinsic and instrumental value that can be considered a basic tool for human evolution and growth, an instrument for the realization of individuals' potentials and a foundation for the social, economic and political improvement of a community. Before discussing the analysis of the forms empowerment can take and the areas in which it can be carried out with a strong or weak impact, I would like to make a short philosophical digression to introduce this concept that since the 1960s has been used in different ways and with different consequences and interpretations. Therefore a brief historical and philosophical review of literature of philosophers and scholars across cultures, continents, and time follows.

As the most recent scientific theories tell us, the entire universe never stopped expanding, and it evolves at an increasing rate since its day of birth[1]. It could even be said that human life, which is considered the leading edge of its evolution (or at least that on Planet Earth) is doing the same, as an integral part of the universe, following parallel laws. Since our species is an integral part of our ecosystem, we could say that human life evolved and keeps evolving faster and faster, and not only that but also by "self-gestation", thanks to its innate inner power, constantly "self-recreating" itself (as biologists teach us with the reproduction of the cells for themselves). Humberto Maturana, a famous biologist and philosopher from Chile, developed a few decades ago the theory of *autopoiesis*, to explain that every living system, from the human being to the universe, is a complex system in constant "redefinition", sustaining and reproducing "itself by itself" (Maturana and Varela, 1980). Similarly, Henry Bergson's (1911) "Élan Vital", the vital force that creates the evolution[2] or the "Omega Point" of Teilhard de Chardin (2004), tell us how the universe is constantly developing towards higher levels of complexity and consciousness).

So if we are able to think human life evolves thanks to its own inner power, innate in human beings as in every living being, and not from mysterious external forces that cannot be controlled, then the concept of empowerment represents a tool that may help human beings to become aware of their inner strengths, abilities and capacities, in order to use them for their growth and the growth of their communities. The "art" of empowerment could be defined then as the process of putting into practice our own thoughts, needs and goals to fulfill our lives and to improve as individuals and as part of a society, and to do this we should start by becoming aware of this power, instead of delegating it to the external systems that guided humankind since its birth. Obviously it is not enough for our inner consciousness to empower us but it represents the first step in the process. As Martin Luther King said we have to "take the first step in faith. We don't have to see the whole staircase, just take the first step" (Mirable & Mullins, 2009). And faith is not only something irrational but can be very rational. Erich Fromm (2004), explained to us in his masterpiece *The art of loving* how we have faith because we experience the growth of our own potentialities, the reality of the growth in ourselves and the strength of our own power.

So if empowerment can be defined as the ability to use our own power (and not the giving of it from the "powerful people" to the "powerless people", as sometimes could be erroneously interpreted in our societies) enabling us to achieve our full actualization and at the same time help others to do the same, in a personal and social path more satisfying for all, then we can affirm that empowerment is rooted, at least in some part, in humanism[3]. Humanism started as a cultural movement during the Renaissance, affirming the dignity of human beings as such, putting them at the center of the world, and considering reason, ethics, and justice as the basis for their evolution (while rejecting supernatural and religious ideas as the basis of morality and decision-making). Actually while in the medieval period people were trained mostly in logic, medicine, law or theology (in order to create doctors, lawyers and theologians) the renaissance humanists tried to teach grammar, history, rhetoric, poetry and moral philosophy, in order to foster citizens' ability to speak and write with eloquence and clarity. Citizens became more capable of engaging in the civic life of their communities, empowering them for more freedom and democracy.

Empowerment too puts human beings at the center of attention and ultimately seeks to help individuals to put in practice principles of self-guidance and self-realization, trying to realize what the Roman scholar and politician Appio Claudio was saying: "Everyone is the maker of his own destiny". Following the transformative learning theory[4] we could say empowerment needs the "expansion of consciousness, through the transformation of capacities of the self" in order to have a positive change in the lifestyle, for individuals and their communities.

If we agree empowerment starts with the awareness of our inner power, then this awareness must be developed through an educative process such as that used by Socrates called maieutics. Maieutics[5] is the idea that the truth is within us; we need not receive it from above or from outside ourselves. Interestingly, the word *education* comes from the Latin *e-ducere*, meaning "draw out, bring to light something that stays inside". Therefore education should have as its goal, first and foremost, to make people aware of their own inner truth and of the goals they want to fulfill in their lives. Guided by such awareness and with their own power, they are able to create their personal "story" and their mission, and be self-directed toward positive change and transformation. An educative process characterized by the maieutic method, for example, would implement experiential learning using empowering tools like narration of personal experiences, group activities to learn to dialogue, peer review to learn to analyze themselves, open space methodology to enable them to express their ideas and so on, instead of trying to pour into their minds some knowledge or notion. It would teach more how to learn instead of what to learn. This would be a tool that would allow students to become aware of all the knowledge that stays inside them, increase their ability to express this knowledge and make them able to put the knowledge at the service of their growth and the growth of their community[6].

Even if empowerment starts as an inner process though, in order to be fully realized it has to be shared with the others, at a communal and social level, as alone we are not capable of self-actualization (Maslow, 1970). We are social animals living only in the relation with our natural and social environment, we really exists as a whole (as *Ubuntu* philosophy also teach us[7]). That is, actualization is a synergistic, not a parallel process between the individual and his or her social environment. Koestler (1983) described this as the *"complex of yogi and commissar"* meaning we have to learn how to be at the same time *yogis* and *commissars*: change ourselves and change the world, otherwise we will always be "out of sync". In other words, if we imagine social and individual development as the two legs needed for moving forward and we don't use them together, we will be forever walking lame. So, once we understand that evolution is based on both levels at the same time, our systems should understand also the importance of dedicating time, space and efforts to the citizens for their "inner" growth and time, space and efforts for their "external" growth, with the consequent economic, political and social implications for our communities. As Hanna Arendt famously argued (1958) to have active citizenship we need a *vita activa* based on labor or work but also political and social action, that is the action of "great deeds and great words".

Concluding this brief philosophical excursion one could say that everyone can benefit from the empowerment process but in particular the youth, who have to find their own social and professional definition and their "place in the world". Empowerment can have a big impact also in the life of people who are discriminated against or are living in a "minor level of power" with respect to the mainstream (from gender to ethnic, religious or sexual orientation minorities). These people need to empower themselves in order to be at an equal status with the other actors of the society and be able to defend their rights against discrimination and oppression. But empowerment enables all citizens, not only the disenfranchised, to become active members of their society instead of maintaining passive roles. Active citizens are citizens who are able to influence their communities because they believe they have the right and the duty to participate and not only to observe what is happening around them. If I decide to avoid, for example, engaging in a problem of someone else, i.e. an accident or a fight on the street, I act as a passive citizen, who withdraws for fear or indifference, and that ultimately doesn't bring a contribution to the growth and welfare of the society. But if I decide to fully engage in what is happening around me, I become active and even freer, as I am able to influence with my thoughts and actions the events that are unfolding in front of me. So participation means finally freedom and evolution of all individuals, and these are the ultimate goals of empowerment. There is no empowered society without integration and solidarity, as Durkheim taught us.

The knowledge and study of empowerment processes would be useful then for educators, behavioral healthcare professionals, teachers and all the women and men who need to shape their abilities in order to support, in the process of growth, the people with whom they live or work. It can represent also a major force in developing future leaders as it grants individuals the permission to utilize their talents, skills, resources and experiences to make the right decisions to fulfill their career and become in this way a guiding example for the others, psychologically, socially, politically or economically. Ultimately we can say empowerment is a leading force that puts strong foundations for better future societies in all parts of our planet, regardless of their economic or social development, if we really take it as a strategy for the good of all.

But it has to be fulfilled taking into account several considerations; otherwise it would remain just a good intention, without a real impact.

Social, political and economic empowerment and the educative process

Amartya Sen, the famous Indian economist and Nobel Prize winner, conceived in the 1980s an approach to "welfare economics"[8] called the capability approach[9], defining what women and men are capable of doing in their societies. The approach emphasized functional capabilities (such as the ability to live to old age, engage in economic transactions, or participate in political activities) that were construed in terms of the "substantive freedoms" people have reason to value (like happiness, desire-fulfillment or free choice) instead of utility or access to resources (like income, commodities, and assets). Since the contribution of Sen, the welfare and development concepts have been considered complex and holistic issues and not only a unique path to follow, but also good for all. The human well-being started to be valued as something based on freedom of choice and respect for individual heterogeneity and not only as something based on production and consumption. This doesn't mean, however, that both development and welfare are seen in this way in the mainstream politics nowadays, at least the ones of western countries.

This short analysis on social, political and economic empowerment was begun by discussing Sen's contributions in economic theory because empowerment can be very much related to his insights and reflections in this area. Actually empowerment as a social theory since the 1990s has represented one of the principal paradigms of development, in particular for the "developing countries" or the so called "Global South". And even if there is not yet a clear definition universally accepted, scholars agree empowerment in the development process has social, political and economic implications, being something that can be connected with all sides of human life, but it is also a process based on individual learning and personal improvement. As was stated, in the empowerment process individuals have first to learn to raise their awareness and control over their decisions, before becoming able to understand what are their needs, interests and goals. After this they start transforming their life and their role in the society, with both inner analysis and external action, towards a full realization of themselves. And subsequently they can improve their ability to influence the power relations in the society and participate more in the decision making processes of the political and economic arena, showing in this way how empowerment requires the acquisition of personal skills and abilities but also the acquisition of social power to influence the objectives and the rules of the society itself, transforming the social system and fostering the full participation of everyone.

Going back to Sen's *capability approach,* we can say empowerment for holistic development implies in particular the building of the potentialities and the "capabilities" of women and men who are discriminated against or subordinated in their societies, the access of these people to the productive resources and the growing of their capacities of negotiation and influence in the relations and in the decisions that affect their lives. This process would allow the excluded to elevate their level of confidence, self-esteem and ability to address their own needs, in front of the structures of the society that many times oppress and subordinate them. Then, at the collective level, empowerment aiming at holistic developmental needs to facilitate the access of these individuals to the decision making process of the society, realizing their full participation in the social, political, economic and cultural structures and in the collective actions. And this has to be done through cooperation and collaboration among them, what is often called networking.

Actually the concept of cooperation and networking is very important in empowerment as it is based on the fact that vulnerable people have more ability to participate in and defend their rights when they are united with others to reach a common goal, than when they are divided or isolated from others. A demonstration of this can be seen when the strength of the grassroots movements improved because they were coordinated and organized instead of divided among themselves. We have many examples of this concept around the world among discriminated people or minorities: from the indigenous movements demanding respect for their rights and the ownership of their lands (as in Mexico with indigenous people from Chiapas or in Brazil with the *Movimento dos Trabalhadores Rurais Sem Terra*/*Movement of the rural workers without land*) to the defense of the environment in the case of natural resources exploitation (like in Papua New Guinea with people fighting against the mine exploitation). Other examples of the importance of networking in the empowerment of vulnerable people can be seen in the economic empowerment of the poor in a given society (like with the *Grameen Bank*[10] in Bangladesh) to the gender empowerment based on coordinated efforts of women's movements asking for improvements in women basic rights (like in many countries of central Africa or south Asia).

We can affirm than that empowerment requires the weakest parts of a society to obtain more power and more capacity of participation in the decision making processes in order to organize, mobilize and transform the relations, structures and institutions that limit their development and maintain their subordination. But this power needs to be a shared power otherwise it would not be strong enough to become a force for change. Kenneth Boulding (1989) (a famous English economist and philosopher, cofounder of the General Systems Theory[11]) defined the so called "integrative power" as a power which rests on relationships such as legitimacy, respect, community and identity. And this is actually the power that can represent the base of development and social empowerment, because it is the power without which the other two powers (as defined by this scholar the "threat power" (in the political arena) and the "economic power" (in the production arena) cannot be effective. So we can say empowerment needs relationships, needs network and community, without which it cannot really become a "transforming force" for the society.

But is empowerment a transforming force that defies the system, trying to create an alternative system, a different development with respect to the mainstream, or it is a force independent from it, able also to exist in parallel with the main system, and so is not interested in fighting the status quo? John Friedmann (1992), the Austrian/Canadian sociologist who wrote about empowerment as a development force, talks about it as an alternative force. He argued poverty should be seen not merely in material terms, but as social, political and psychological powerlessness, so, he stated, an "alternative development" should be committed to empowering poor people in their own communities, mobilizing them for political participation on a wider scale. In contrast to centralized development policies, implemented at the national and international level, Friedman described an alternative and sustainable development, that should restore first the initiative to those in need, on the grounds that unless people have an active role in directing their own destinies, long-term progress will not be achieved.

In history there have always been "alternative powers" to those of the *Prince* and this allowed the progress of ideas, social mobility and political changes. Just to remember few examples from the Global South during the last century, which can be defined as empowerment processes that changed the status quo, we can mention the Independence Movement in India, the Anti-Apartheid Movement in South Africa or the People's Power Revolution in the Philippines. But also in the "Global North" there have been many experiences related to empowerment that had a deep impact in the societies and changed the traditional rules, like the Women's Movement or the Civil Rights Movement in the 1960s. In Italy too, many figures in the last century have worked for social empowerment of the poorest people. They looked for new tools raising the status of the poor relative to the mainstream system requesting the assistance of the state (often missing), and left today an important imprint on social movements. Notable among them were the founders of the Italian nonviolent-Gandhian movement Aldo Capitini and Danilo Dolci[12].

I personally think the development brought about by empowerment is more democratic, more complete and more sustainable development, as it starts from the idea that all the people involved in the society should be included in the process of decision making. Development should aim at achieving a consensus in the solution of the problems and the proposing of the future paths to follow by the society. So it is not important to think of it as an alternative or a parallel reality to the mainstream system, but as a resourceful force that can help communities improve and resolve even their apparent intractable conflicts or structural injustices.

But how is the social, political and economic empowerment, both in the south and the north of the world and fostering both an alternative or integrative power, related to the educational process? How can education influence the starting of empowerment processes at these different levels in our societies? First of all, education can be considered the principal tool of empowerment, as it allows individuals to become aware of their power and discover their talents, goals, interests, needs and so learn to build their own destiny. Secondly the educative process is something that can accompany the life of a person for a long time as we never stop learning, and the real educative process is a constant and continuous process, not just an experience that starts and ends inside the school system. The Commission of the European Community (2001) set *lifelong learning* , called the Lisbon Strategy, as the primary tool for the empowerment of citizens, aiming at transforming Europe into the world's most competitive and dynamic knowledge-based society. And even if the agenda is still far from being realized we can agree that the process of lifelong learning is the key for the constant empowerment of citizens and societies. Zygmut Bauman (2005), the famous Polish sociologist, in his recent book *Liquid life,* reminded us that in liquid modern settings, education and learning should be continuous, in an empowering process that would allow men and women to pursue their life goals with resourcefulness and self-confidence and in the "rebuilding of the now increasingly deserted public space where men and women may engage in a continuous translation between the individual and the common, the private and the communal interests, rights and duties" (p125).

Besides being continuous and constant, the educative process, in order to be really empowering, has to be also maieutic, and not just based on content and viewpoints to be poured into the minds of students. Without this empowerment, the only result of education is constraining the unfolding of brains and hearts of the students (even if unfortunately often our educational institutions do so). Empowerment needs to individualize learning according to one's capabilities and needs and Paulo Freire, the famous Brazilian educator, can help us to understand better how pedagogy can work efficiently and effectively in the empowerment process both individually and socially. In fact in his *Pedagogy of the Oppressed* Freire (1992) asserts "education either functions as an instrument that is used to facilitate integration of the younger generation into the logic of the present system, and bring about conformity to it, or it becomes the 'practice of freedom', the means by which men and women deal critically and creatively with reality, and discover how to participate in the transformation of their world" (p. 34). For Freire then, education can be a tool to transform society, not merely something to make young people conform to current norms, but to do so has to start from the "practice of freedom". According to him freedom will be the result of *praxis* — informed action — when a balance between theory and practice is achieved. And the teaching method has to follow the maieutic system, what he calls the "problem-posing" method, in which there is not a student-teacher dichotomy, as the educator constantly re-forms reflections based on the reflections of the student.

So if the educative process is to be the "leaven" of empowerment we can say it has to draw from *humanistic education*, the education that puts the human being and not the "knowledge" at the center (like the models of Steiner or Montessori or Tagore for example[13]) seeking to engage the whole person, in his/her intellect, emotions, social capacities, practical skills and artistic creativity, as all are important foci for personal and social growth and development. It is like "crafting" a polymath, a *Renaissance man*, a person who has abilities in different fields[14], leading to the notion that people should embrace all knowledge and develop their capacities as fully as possible. Martha Nussbaum, an American philosopher, reminds us in her beautiful last book (2010) how historically the humanities have been central to education even if today the profitable and technical skills – that are the only skills often taught in the universities – have eroded our ability to criticize authority, reduced our sympathy with the marginalized and different, and damaged our competence to deal with complex global problems. The loss of these basic capacities jeopardizes the empowering effect of education, as well as the health and effectiveness of our democratic societies, which need people able to think with their minds.

Today we have to revive the importance of humanities and the importance of humanism in the education process, but beside this we also have to understand how important the concept of diversity in the formation of a person is, in this globalized world. We could say the empowerment processes, and the educative ones that guide them today, are entering a new era, a new modernity, as we are all living in a multicultural global village and we cannot think anymore only with one interpretation of the problems or an ethnocentric vision of reality. That is why it is important to build networks and bridges and to understand different cultures, points of view and ideas represent enrichment to the empowerment processes and not limitations.

Different cultures and empowerment in a globalized world

As we know from natural sciences, the path of evolution is the passage from independence to interdependence, which is how we progressed from the first forms of life, which were unicellular organisms, to animals and human beings, who are able to build systems and structured societies. In the social sciences it is the same: individuals need to learn interdependence, go from individualities to networks and systems, if they want to grow as a whole, as a society. According to renowned historian Yuval Harari, our *homo sapiens* specie could evolve precisely because we were able to cooperate in great numbers (overcoming the collective action problem) and with flexibly (adapting to the changing environment). It was the innate cooperation attitude, balancing the competition of the "natural selection" that made humankind reach this level of growth. Therefore as the Austrian founder of human ethology, Irenaeus Eibl-Eibesfeldt, argued, cooperation, besides aggression, is the prime mover of evolution; and as cognitive scientist Steven Pinker showed, these "better angels of our nature" are more and more present today, reducing violence and aggression and increasing peace and cooperation in our current world.

So in a globalized world like the current one we have to learn how to use more fully these "better angels", to overcome discrimination based on differences, whether they are gender, class, age, religion, cultural origin or whatever other differences, if we want to evolve as humankind, creating a real interdependent and united social system and a universal growing community.

Empowerment in itself requires diversity and interdependence, because intercultural, interreligious, inter-gender, interclass and all the intergroup relations are what make societies richer and able to grow at all levels, politically, economically, materially and spiritually. History teaches us this but we as human beings still have to learn to cross boundaries, to go beyond the "fear" of someone different from us, beyond the mistrust that bring us to suspect the stereotype of the other. We need to reduce discrimination and avoid the risk of conflict and clash. We still have to fully realize what the Bulgarian philosopher Tzvetan Todorov (1999) defined as the cultural *recognition* of the others, throw away what Eibl-Eibesfeldt

(1996) called the "hate" innate side of humans and keep only what he called the "love", also innate, side, and try to build what the Italian intellectual Ernesto Balducci (1986, 2005) dreamt for the future man: a *"planetary human being"*. But in order to build such a global and cross cultural society, and empowerment to help such a society to born, we have to understand that every culture brings different points of view concerning reality, life and basic values, different epistemologies and ontologies, and so first of all we have to take into account these differences in order to be really constructive, creative and concrete in our future.

If we take into consideration the so called "dimensions of culture" for example, as defined by the Dutch scholar Geert Hofstede (2005), one of the most prominent and influential researchers in the field of "organizational culture", we see how there are similarities as well as differences across cultures and how we need to be open-minded and good observers to understand those differences. Hofstede utilizes six dimensions to compare cultures (Individualism/Collectivism, Feminine/Masculine, Power Distance, Uncertainty Avoidance, Long Term/ Short Term orientation and Indulgence/Restraint) in order to analyze societies and organizations and give leaders an understanding of how to adjust their leadership styles accordingly. Considering in particular the "power distance" dimension we understand, from what the scholar tells us, that a shorter distance between individuals and among groups implies greater equality and empowerment, but in a society where there is a greater "power distance", where people accept an unequal distribution of power, and accept "their place" in the system, it is more difficult to carry out empowering processes as there is a reluctance to speak up and ask for change. But this doesn't mean that in those societies which emphasize greater power distances it is impossible to realize empowerment; on the contrary, it is exactly in those kinds of societies where empowerment is more needed and can be carried out with more impact, as was previously stated in the examples of empowerment in the Global South.

However how can empowerment exist in societies that have a frayed social fabric or divisions at their interior, such as those experiencing conflicts in the Global South, or in Western societies that are still struggling to find a path of integration for all their citizens?

Robert Putnam (2000), an American political scientist, in his famous book *"Bowling Alone"*, could help us to answer this question. He makes an important analysis distinguishing between two kinds of social capital: bonding capital and bridging capital. "Bonding" processes occur when we are socializing with people who are like us: same age, same race, same religion and so on, and these are important steps to build relations and networks, and form the base of societies. But in order to create peaceful societies in diverse multiethnic countries like the ones in which we are living today, we need to also have a second kind of social capital says Putnam: the "bridging" one, that happen when we make friends with people who are not like us, like for example supporters of another football team. The scholar argued that these two kinds of social capital, bonding and bridging, are interrelated and able to strengthen each other, meaning that with the increase of one comes the increase of the other, but also that with the decline of one inevitably comes the decline of the other, leading to greater group tensions. For Hofstede this is exactly what happened in USA and Western societies since the 1960s. With a reduction of the bonding capital, in civic, social, associational and political life (going from "collectivism to individualism" in that author's words) came a reduction of the bridging capital, bringing us to new conflicts inside our societies. Hence today we have to build again the "bonding capital" in order to open space for the "bridging capital", and so for the empowerment of society as a whole and not only in some of its parts.

Going back to the cultural dimensions of the Hofstedes, and taking into account this time the "feminine/masculine" dimension, we see how societies stress competition/achievement or cooperation/nurture depending on which side of the dimension they traditionally follow and this is another important factor in the empowerment processes. In fact masculinity, in this model, is seen to be the trait which emphasizes ambition, assertiveness, acquisition of wealth, and differentiated gender roles, instead of femininity which stresses caring and nurturing behaviors, sexual equality, environmental awareness, and more fluid gender roles. So in societies that have a stronger masculinity dimension it seems more difficult to realize an empowerment that includes all genders, as the empowerment is more unidirectional, and so in those societies the best strategy for holistic development would be the emancipation of the discriminated gender, i.e. the feminine one, in order to create a more cooperative and global development. To learn from different gender perspectives in different cultures then is another important tool, together with the multicultural perspective, that has to be taken into account if we want to think about a real empowerment in our globalized world. On this issue it is enlightening to consider the contribution of Nicholas Kristof, an American journalist who wrote an interesting book with his wife Sheryll Wu Dunn (2009), on gender discrimination in different parts of the world. Drawing on many cases they show how a little help can transform the lives of women and girls around the world, helping us to see that the key to economic progress of a society lies often in unleashing women's potential, and they show us also how countries such as China for example have prospered more precisely when they started to emancipate women and bring them into the formal economy.

A final point to consider in this new globalized world, is the fact that different cultures and different epistemologies bring different approaches to environmental issues to the question on how we should relate with our planet, in particular in the future, when global warming and population growth will have consequences we cannot yet imagine. Jared Diamond (2005), an American scientist and author best known for his popular science books, reminds us that different cultures in the past had different attitudes towards environmental and survival challenges, and this determined whether they survived or disappeared. Today we have similar problems. As examples of different approaches China and Australia are trying to cope with environmental risks in innovative ways relative to our "old" approach, (as Diamond described in his book) and we cannot save ourselves if we don't save all together. So empowerment has an important role to play today, first of all because it teaches us to listen to all of society and not only to the elites or leaders From the "bottom" comes the popular wisdom that can become guiding wisdom for future leaderships, and this reminds us there is not a unique solution to the problems of the planet and the development of humankind: we have to learn from different ontologies and epistemologies in order to find the way for a real growth of the society and not risk our failure and collapse in the future.

But how do all of these reflections on a globalized world have consequences on the educative processes? How should we take into account these questions and integrate them in an educative path in order to make it more empowering for future generations? Personally, I think education cannot escape from the intercultural point of view, the multidisciplinary approach and the inclusiveness approach, all empowering elements that unfortunately are not always implemented in our schools. These elements should be our guides when developing the educative programs in our schools and in our governments. But many times this is not the case, as we saw with the examples brought by Nussbaum regarding the humanities. Occasionally this is the case, and what follows is an example of this type of educative process, based on international and experiential education, that I observed and in which I had the honor to participate.

In June 2012, I participated in a summer program in Vermont, USA, where 60 people from around the world gathered to study and practice peace building, in a course called "Conflict Transformation across Cultures"[15]. This is just one of the many international programs that use experiential learning as a tool for empowerment, not only for all the participants but for the communities to which participants return after the program. I was astonished by the amount of experience the participants brought to this course, and I have wonderful memories of the days passed together with these engaged people who brought their lessons learned to share in a process of common empowerment for the community that was built in those three weeks of program.

These kinds of courses that call people from all over the world are very important. International education is an extraordinary instrument in itself, as it helps to build networks, relations, connections, that strengthen and develop the knowledge of the diversity and so they grow and promote a culture of tolerance and peace. In addition, the way in which many of these international training courses are lead is very similar to the humanistic educational process discussed previously, based on developing the "positive view of socialization", as one of the following chapters of this book discusses when talking about humanistic education. This type of education empowers students in their holistic learning process in which they can choose, to some extent, the content and the goals of their training, and above all they can integrate it with their personal experiences. Their educators represented facilitators of learning more than source of knowledge. One important feature of this course for example was that the trained people became also trainers in their personal expertise, and there were planned activities in which participants had the opportunity to share their competences and experiences with their colleagues through short workshops or presentations. This not only allowed the new trainers to empower themselves as "first actors" on the scene but also allowed the colleagues to see how their peers were contributing ideas and knowledge, thus making the participants more aware of their own power and wishing to model the same next time.

Besides this the summer program in Vermont tried to approach conflicts from the broadest perspective, taking into account gender issues, environmental questions, migration elements, violence and nonviolence, reconciliation and so on. The method of experiential learning was put into practice with small learning groups that allowed everyone to feel secure in a safe environment and as such they could share openly in a respectful and cooperative way. This process of learning was accompanied by a process of "learning how to learn", as every participant had to reflect on the processes of teaching and training using both evaluations of the others and self-evaluation, with the effect that people wanted finally to learn more and more about different topics and different styles. Therefore, this program was a clear example of empowering training that could serve as a model for other international programs and study abroad courses also, not only for peace building studies.

I firmly believe studying abroad is more than just studying in a foreign country and building tolerant and intercultural relationships; it is a means of understanding and broadening one's identity. Feeling like "strangers in a new place" makes people develop more creative abilities and, at the same time, teaches them to be open to new ideas and to listen to other points of view that could represent important lessons learned to be applied when they return "home". The international and experiential education is an empowering process because it allows participants to integrate themselves in a globalized active world, a productive world community where each individual contributes with his/her own creative idea to the future development and progress of human society in its whole. Ultimately I believe international education can foster the building of a new globalized and professional society, spreading the diverse knowledge learned for the empowerment of all the citizens of a given society and not only of those who participated in the international experience.

Women mediation training as an example of empowerment

Citizens of every country in the world suffer from ethnocentrism, and perhaps those in western cultures suffer more. Europeans and Americans think the empowerment of women started in the Western world, in particular in the 1960s with the feminist movement, and perceive that had a big impact and many important repercussions on the whole of society. In reality in different parts of the world gender issues were already addressed and handled, often in ways consistent with the structure of their respective society. We can argue whether these different situations of gender relationships were really empowering or not for women, but there were already developed paths regarding how genders should have shared power. Women also discussed which aspects of life they wanted to keep and which ones they wanted to change, especially if living in a patriarchal, and sometimes, archaic society. So in a globalized world like the one in which we are living today, it is our moral obligation to look at other perspectives, other cultural and religious views, other epistemologies and ontologies, in order to understand better which kind of evolution and gender empowerment we want for our future generations.

An example of empowerment of women in which I have been personally involved is the issue of enhancing women's participation in peace processes. Women around the world, making use of the UN Resolution 1325 (October 2000) on "Women, Peace and Security", since the turn of the new century, started to create organizations, activities and networks aiming to influence mainstream political and economic power, in order to push for a "genderization" of peace processes in the current conflicts. Today many women from different countries have begun to exert an important impact in this area, and have created regional international networks of women working in peace issues (like for example the *N-Peace Network*[16]). Through trainings and workshops these women have been empowered to be peace mediators and negotiators). Still the role of women in this area needs to be improved today. According to UNIFEM[17] since 1992 women mediators have accounted for only 2.4 percent of signatures on peace agreements and the UN is yet to appoint a woman as a lead mediator in a major conflict.

Sanam Naraghi-Anderlini (2007), a scholar of gender issues in conflicts, enabled us to better understand the potential role of women in the area of conflict resolution and peace. Women, says Naraghi-Anderlini, have been discriminated against and excluded from formal peace processes until now. There had been a fundamental neglecting of the contribution of women participants in the process, at both the formal and informal level. In her book this scholar explained how women's associations played important roles in conflict or post-conflict areas, despite the lack of their inclusion in the formal peace processes[18] and she states how important it is to find ways to improve the expertise and preparation of the women, trough capacity building and empowering trainings, in order to make them able to fully participate in the formal negotiation and mediation processes in post-conflict areas.

Recently I had the honor of assisting in enhancing female empowerment processes in conflict areas, in particular in South East Asia which I had been visiting between 2012 and 2014. In this region, in particular in countries like Thailand, Burma, Philippines and Indonesia, I observed women playing a very important role in conflict resolution at a grassroots level, through engagement in informal diplomacy, local and international advocacy and also capacity building; in particular Muslim women engaged in solving the conflict between their state and the local Muslim minorities.

We often think the exclusion of Muslim women from political and civic participation is influenced by their patriarchal societies, which favor women's subordination to male authority. (Such an exclusion is correlated to poverty, according to the World Economic Forum's 2010 Gender Gap Index, 20 of the 25 lowest-ranking countries are Muslim-majority countries). Recently however, Muslim women have begun to have an important role in changing this situation, challenging from inside their societies the disempowerment of the women due to cultural hindrances, lack of knowledge and capacity building and sometimes a trend of radicalization of the Muslim faith, which pose greater obstacles to Muslim women's valuable participation to peace processes and to political and economic processes in general.

Shadia Marhaban, co-founder of LINA-Aceh Women's League and also a consultant for UN Women, has been training many women in Asian countries, from Afghanistan to Philippines, from parliament level politicians to grass roots level activists. In addition to training members of her own Muslim faith she also assists women who are members of the Buddhist and Christian faiths (including women living in conflict areas in South Thailand and in Papua-Indonesia). I had the opportunity to accompany Ms. Marhaban on several occasions and was amazed by her ability to inspire women and drive them to become an important and leading participants of their society. I want to share briefly her educative approach in order to explain how her work supporting women participation in peace processes represents a very good example of women empowerment.

Her trainings were based on various theories, the Hicks's (2001) "dignity approach"[19] as well as Burton's (1990) "human needs" and Kelman's (1996) "interactive problem solving" theories (that refers to the fact that all human beings have psychological needs that if threatened, can give rise to conflict). The Burton and Kelman approaches in particular focus on providing a forum for parties to discuss unmet needs, the insights from which can be fed into both psychological and also political processes. Burton's original list of "ontological" needs (needs that are fueled by the force of human development) included developing and maintaining identity, recognition, security and belonging. The strength of the trainer in this process is the ability to connect the principles of the theoretical explanation with the stories of the participants. This was done very well in the training programs in which I participated. The important element of those trainings was the application of theory to experience for a type of education that was quite empowering, following a process that started from a personal experiential learning going towards a more common and shared learning.

In particular, there were several elements in the trainings that are very much related to empowering education: practical elements (applying theories to concrete situations, either through case studies or through analyzing the processes within the group) interactive elements (involving the participants actively through personal and group reflections, role plays etc.), participatory elements (making the group itself a learning body and mobilizing its organizing capacities) and "elicitive" elements (drawing from the experience, knowledge and personal resources of participants through eliciting questions). Another important tool was the "public narrative: story of self, us and now"[20]. This emphasizes the importance of storytelling and messaging providing an overview of two crucial elements of mobilizing and empowering people: engaging them in why they should act to change their world (their values) and engaging them on how they should act to change it (their strategy).

The public narrative starts with the creation of a "story of self", in order to allow others to experience the values that move one to lead. The second step is the creation of a "story of us" which aims to expand on the ability of participants to communicate the purpose of the shared work and to create common cause through the exploration of shared values. And finally there is the crafting of another story of us, the "story of now", this time framing the current challenges in terms of concrete strategy, pushing participants to specify the actions they should take to address their shared future. This is a very good empowerment process as it creates initially strong relationships, trust and solidarity within a group, and then equips participants to engage with the others more effectively, creating a concrete, constructive and common plan for their future.

In conclusion, without drafting capacity building processes based on concrete empowering tools it will not be possible to end the discrimination of women and enable women to fully participate in our societies. If we want to create more equal and just societies, capacity building is the path, and not only women but men too should walk on that path for a real personal and social empowerment in our globalized world. These experiential learning experiences on peace building that I briefly presented represent not only an improvement of women's participation in peace processes but also a general process of empowerment for the society as a whole.

Notes

1   See the *Metric expansion of Universe* and the *Accelerating Universe* theories.

2   Henri Bergson, a French philosopher influential especially in the first half of the 20th century, developed the concept of *Elan Vital* as a kind of 'vital impetus' which explains evolution in a less mechanical and more lively manner, accounting for the creative impulse of mankind. He convinced many thinkers that immediate experience and intuition are more significant than rationalism and science for understanding reality.

3   During the fourteen and the fifteen century, together with Renaissance, in Florence and in Italy an activity of cultural and educational reforms born in order to oppose the medieval vision of life (with God at the center of the universe) with a new vision in which the man was at the center of the universe, as the maker and the owner of his own destiny. A great trust and confidence in the human intelligence started to spread, exalting the dignity of human being, their superiority over the other living beings and their countless creative capacities.

4   'Transformative learning' theory was firstly developed by Jack Mezirow, an American professor of adult and continuing education, at the end of the 1970s. It can be defined as a process of personal transformation with three dimensions: psychological (changes in understanding of the self), convictional (revision of belief systems), and behavioral (changes in lifestyle). It is an approach that tries to integrate rational processes and emotional ones.

5   Socrates, the ancient Greek philosopher credited as one of the founders of western philosophy, was using a pedagogic method (called since then *Socratic Method*) that is a type of pedagogy in which a series of questions are asked not only to have individual answers but also to encourage fundamental insight into the issue. This method is the origin of the concept of maieutics, the idea that the truth is latent in the mind of every human being due to innate reason but has to be "given birth" by answering intelligently proposed questions. As we can understand this method is empowering in itself as give the person the ability to express the truth from the personal perspective and experience.

6   One educational experience of this type for example was a summer program for peace building activists in Vermont, USA, on "Conflict Transformation across Cultures", in which I had the honor to participate and of which I relate at the end of this chapter.

7   *Ubuntu* is an African ethic and humanist philosophy focusing on people's allegiances and relations with each other (from a definition offered by Liberian peace activist Leymah Gbowee: "I am what I am because

of who we all are"). As South African Archbishop Desmond Tutu said: "Ubuntu speaks particularly about the fact that you can't exist as a human being in isolation. It speaks about our interconnectedness (…) We think of ourselves far too frequently as just individuals, separated from one another, whereas you are connected and what you do affects the whole World."

8   Welfare economics is a branch of economics that evaluate economic well-being, especially relative to economic efficiency and the resulting income distribution associated with it. It analyzes social welfare in terms of economic activities of the persons in the society.

9   Subsequently, and in collaboration with other political philosophers and economists, Sen helped to make the capabilities approach predominant as a paradigm for policy debate in human development, where it inspired the creation of the UN's Human Development Index .

10   The Grameen Bank is a microfinance organization and community development bank founded in 1983 in Bangladesh by Muhammad Yunus (Nobel Peace Prize winner together with the Bank). The Bank makes small loans to the impoverished without requiring collateral.

11   *General System Theory* is the interdisciplinary study of systems in general, with the goal of elucidating principles that can be applied to all types of systems in all fields of research.

12   Aldo Capitini was a famous philosopher, educator and political activist that started the idea of *omnicrazia*, 'power of all', and founded among other things the yearly "March of Peace" and the "Centers for Social Orientation-COS". Danilo Dolci was a famous sociologist, popular educator and social activist that fought against Mafia and social exclusion in south Italy and founded among other things the "Centers for Full Employment."

13   Rudolf Steiner was an Austrian philosopher that started the *Waldorf Education*, whose overarching goals are to provide young people the basis on which to develop into free, morally responsible and integrated individuals, and to help every child fulfill his or her unique destiny. Maria Montessori was an Italian educator founder of the *Montessori Education* that is characterized by an emphasis on independence, freedom within limits, and respect for a child's natural psychological development. Rabindranath Tagore was an Indian polymath that founded the *Visva-Barathi University* based on Socratic method, holistic teachings and on the believe that every person is a genius but all students may not bloom at the same time (so allowing students for example to continue their course till both the student and the teacher are satisfied).

14   The definition of *Renaissance man* comes from *Renaissance*, when *Humanism* considered man empowered and limitless in his capacities for development.

15   This is a course organized every year by the World Learning Institute at the School for International Training, which have among its alumni also a Nobel peace prize, Jody Williams.

16   This network consists of women activists from six Asian countries: Nepal, Indonesia, Sri Lanka, Timor Leste, Philippines and Afghanistan and the goal is to establish relations and collaboration in order to strengthen the role of women in peace building through trainings and workshops. See www.n-peace.net

17   "UN Development Fund for Women", since 2011 hast been substituted by UNW ("UN Women").

18   As an example we can mention the peace process of Aceh province in Indonesia, for which only one woman participated to the formal peace negotiation in Finland and in which there is no mentioning of what the UN resolution 1325 says about the adoption of a gender perspective in peace and security.

19   The ten elements of Hicks' dignity approach are: acceptance of identity, inclusion, safety, acknowledgment, recognition, fairness, benefit of the doubt, understanding, independence and accountability.

20   The "Public Narrative: self, us, now" is a Harvard University Kennedy School approach used by Marshall Ganz.

2

The Role of Language in Empowerment:
How Toxic Language Leads to Negativity and Erroneous Cognition, and Numbs Creativity

Fabrizio Guarducci

Why, at this particular moment, should there be a book on empowerment and education? The world is not getting on well, it needs to be renovated. In order to do this, the system of education needs to be reassessed. To bring about a serious change in schools, one must work on language.

Language is the life blood of the social system without which there would be no communication.

For example, let's look at economic language; considering the recent grave global economic situation, it is a good place to start. This language must be seen in the context of the new economy which has real effects and not just financial; the same applies to the online economy which is spreading spontaneously. In my opinion, we need to reflect on the creation of a participatory economy because up to now we have been victims of the economy. Let me explain myself better: jobs used to be created mainly by organizations and commercial companies, today it has become difficult to offer jobs that give economic stability to the worker because the large companies have become economically precarious themselves.

Being the head of a school, I give a graduation speech at the end of the year. I used to say that I hoped the students would find a good job, today I must change my words: I advise them to create their own jobs, to empower themselves and not to expect anything from a system which does not work. It is much wiser to invent one's own independent job opportunities.

The internet is the greatest form of empowerment. It gives everyone the chance to start a business without great expense. It is also easy to promote one's business on the internet. This is why it has become important that an appropriate language is available for these new economic interactions. It needs to be a new language that corresponds to this new way of working.

In this chapter the problems created by toxic language are discussed. The theoretical underpinnings for a more compassionate and expressive language are provided to remedy these concerns. The chapter ends with educational strategies and programs that effectively address the concerns and promote effective and affective communication.

As with changing the language of the economy, social language must be changed. Humankind's deterioration is mainly caused by the contamination of language. Toxic words create toxic thoughts and toxic actions and it is these words that have been preserved in social language (this argument is further explained in a following chapter). The social language of today is more structural than creative, in fact, the word has lost its function in communicating and has also lost its emotional impact. It has become only a means for classifying certain functions.

These considerations concern not only the daily use of language but also concern education, which unfortunately is no longer adequately thought through. It is no longer thought of on the part of the professors and the students as *magister vitae* (the idea of learning from the past). The academic university system of studying is the direct consequence of this lacking because the students are only asked to remember information and not to create. Some professors tend to 'train' students more than educate them. The professors would like to mold and shape the students to make them fit into the standards required by the system.

The aim of education is to help the students toward structuring ideas, and then they will be able to communicate them and fulfill them. Therefore, it is a good idea to get used to a spontaneous language and not a dogmatic one. This moment in history can give us the precious occasion to put into effect this change which could put us on track for ever more conscious actions.

The experience of self-empowerment on the part of citizens

throughout the world is quite recent and the goals of this philosophy are different from those of the current predominant economy. This leads to the necessity of suitable language so that there can be communication among those working in this new alternative economy.

We do not give serious thought to words, nor to their rhythm these days, we neglect their meaning which no longer makes a mark on our moral conscience. This is why communication has become mechanic and utilitarian, it can no longer affect our deepest self.

The language we use every day in our social life has been learned; at home, at school, at the café, with friends and on the street; it is the soundtrack of our existence and has important effects on each of us.

Between the language we hear daily (from the media and from others in general) and the language we choose to use, there exists an implicit relationship: we have been "contaminated" by this language; perhaps not always on a level of immediate reproduction of the same, but somehow in our intimate sphere, in our thinking, something has happened.

In fact, the reaction to an action is much more spontaneous than to a word which uses a code that must be understandable by both speaker and listener in order to be recognized. This is where neurolinguistics comes in and in particular the importance of mirror neurons which are true guards of the correctness in communication. The vibration the ear converts into sound is, to the subjective consciousness, what the ethereal vibration (that is, what the eye converts into vision) is to the objective or intellectual consciousness.

"But a word's interpretation depends on our experience. We see, hear and think and we feel every word through our personality. Our words evolve with us and because all men are different one from the other in their experiences, then it follows that the value they assign to words will be different" (Curtis, 1930, p. 78). "It is our speech that 'betrays' us; the audible expression of our thoughts and feelings reveals much more about us than our tangible appearance because it shows the order of our form-thought which we develop over time. These are intellectual expressions in their visible form, emotional expressions in audible form; and so the seen word has a relation to the thought, the sound of the visible word has a relation to the feeling; therefore, the tone of a word leads us to the heart of the subconscious self. Here lies the reason why the word we hear is more efficient than the word we see". (Curtis, 1930, p. 80)

By now we know that even from a physiological point of view we aren't immune to what others do or say. This is why social language needs our attention, and in an especially urgent way at this moment, due to the progressive impoverishment our language has been going through. Language has acquired ever more negative connotations in this counter-productive process. These connotations can be defined as 'toxic': a vocabulary of violence and aggression which calls up all kinds of violent thoughts and behaviors. These aspects, seemingly justified by the widespread diffusion of this negative use of language, are handed down to us by the superficiality of everyday routine. They have produced a language in great part automatic which is far from our sphere of emotions and is increasingly unable to express values. Not all the words locked up inside us are words of a negative connotation, although one will find that many are truly 'toxic' words that we carry around with us like a weight that pulls us down.

This type of language prospers in a society marked by materialism, most interested in creating needs to stimulate consumption. This type of language is of a level that makes the consciousness drowsy and limits creative activity. And what is more, conserving an interior dimension with language that characterizes its quality, not only no longer seems necessary but it is actually impeded by this numbing effect.

Linguistic *contaminatio* is a scientifically proven factor. Language is, in fact, developed by activating articulated dynamics which are interconnected. It is learned by imitation and in this phase, aspects of emotional sensitivity play an important role. It was neuroscience essentially that showed a separation between intellect and emotion does not exist, nor between thought and action (going beyond the theory of Descartes). Thus, we can affirm that toxic words generate toxic thoughts and violent actions. This being the case as Givone says, "words can be like poison, taken in small doses; that is, "if taken in very small doses at first they do not produce marked effects, but when they accumulate, they quickly take on a lethal characteristic"(Givone, 2012, p.55). This is a fact that concerns us and motivates us to react in order to work on making a change in values.

Specifically, the discovery of mirror neurons has been a determining factor in understanding how empathy could be a fundamental factor in the acquisition of language by triggering imitation mechanisms. Various experiments have shown the activation of the mirror neurons not only for transitive actions (directed at objects), but also for intransitive actions (not directed at objects). These mirror neurons have recently been discovered. While neuroscientists have known about sensory neurons which bring information to the briain, and motor ones that send messages to the muscles, these mirror neurons fire when *other individuals* act. This happens not only in humans but also in monkeys (Keysers, 2009, Heyes, 2010).

The hypothesis of work proposed here rests on the following: the observation that even on a neural basis the diffusion of a language of non-value, which is all too often aggressive, is quickly and easily becoming a rooted problem. Using this hypothesis however, one can propose a change beginning with a vocabulary using the strength of these same physiological procedures which will allow the perception of positive emotions and sentiments on a human scale once again.

Similarly, the UNESCO Charter notes, *Being that wars are born of the human mind, it is in the mind of men that we must raise the defense of peace.*

Thoughts are born in the mind. They manifest themselves in us and are contemporaneously present in words; therefore in pronouncing them one finds both the explanation of the experience and also the solution to adopt. From this, in fact, one understands how negative language promotes violence in the world and how, in the same way, expressions of value, words with a positive tone can regenerate people from the inside out and consequently this can be enacted in society and not only in lyric.

Words influence, transmit and evoke sensations which are then absorbed by the brain. These sensations, in turn, condition actions. But many sensations that generate values have become difficult to transmit because for those sensations in general, it has become challenging now even to find words. Unfortunately, the vocabulary that is stronger and imposes itself, that which endures over time, is an aggressive, violent one: a toxic vocabulary, strangely this is the one conserved by humankind.

In order to create new thoughts and words, one can use a type of guided maieutic process to educe the pursuit of knowledge. This stimulates reflection, a personal thought process through a narration which encourages sharing and the consolidation of one's own inner world.

Ancient people understood teaching as the possibility to learn and become educated in order to 'build' a person during one's lifetime: from an ethical-spiritual point of view, education, in fact, means build. Today, education is mainly only reproducing and remembering information. Unfortunately, more importance is given to scholastic knowledge while the first consideration should be to know one's own intimate self, one's own personal value. This is so important because then people could adapt a healthy attitude seen in their behavior toward themselves and toward others. With this in mind both Socrates' maieutics and Plato's dialogs are fundamental experiences in education. These are sources which all sciences up to now have continued to draw on, especially those interested in education and personal betterment. This has to do in a correct way with rediscovering and understanding one's own modus agendi e sentiendi (path of action and way of feeling). As a result empowerment will be possible, that is, everyone will be able to transform the separate self into a unified sense of 'we'.

The word is the fundamental building block in paving the way to raising the quality of life for individuals and collective groups which will, in turn, permit the manifestation of a democratic state structure. The word that can do this must be rediscovered in its creative force. The word triggers infinite mechanisms by its sound and by what it evokes in us. These mechanisms interact with our entire being, they call up our memories, all kinds of different experiences made by people, but also make us aware of the current moment through our very personal histories and preparations for life. This is why the word can be understood but also misunderstood and for the same reason, one must be truly aware of the word in order to, if necessary; cope with any misunderstandings that can occur. This is a general guideline. At our time in history though, the impoverishment of language is easily seen by all; words have become worn out, they have been 'tampered' with, as Gianrico Carofiglio says. Carofiglio says, "The number of words known and used is strictly proportional to the degree democracy is developed and also proportional to the equality of opportunity for people. Few words and few ideas, few opportunities and little democracy. The more words that are known, the richer political discussions can be and with this, the richer the democratic life" (Carofiglio, 2010, p. 21). Thinking of Zagrebelsky, Carofiglio notes how this proves to be a problem for democracy. This has been confirmed by scientific, medical and criminological research, that is, the most violent young people have poor and inefficient linguistic skills examining their vocabulary, grammar and syntax. Carofiglio states, "He who has no names for suffering, enacts it, expresses it, turning it into violence with often tragic consequences" (Carofiglio, 2010, p. 18). A problematic occurrence is created where not only families and teachers in general (also those involved in court cases of under-aged youths) but the entire society is called upon to take responsibility because by now this has become a matter pertinent to all of society.

To have a good language background, "to own" words, allows one to account for thoughts, give them form, organize them, share them; this permits an inner dialog and gives us the ability to manage ourselves and the world around us. If this dialog worked, a balance would exist and this is how empowerment takes place. This implies the willingness and the ability within the dialog to also improve the environment we live in: both at the individual, family, company, office level... our work environment, and also at the level of society in general where we experience our relationships. Empowerment is the force that people find within their inner selves that projects all their inner being out toward others. This gives stability and strength to confront others and creates a basis for life. Everything is born from that intimate dialog within the self, which if cultivated, builds a person in the positive sense and makes one capable of a future. Lacking this dialog, uncommunicativeness, depression and devastation are produced at a personal and social level.

Inner language has been called nonverbal language, the language of thought: "mentalese" which could have characteristics common to all people and to all languages; a basic language belonging to one who does not have a language of words, like small children and certain animals. Steven Pinker, a supporter of this thesis, by developing Noam Chomsky's theory, shows language as an inherited instinct in man, the consequence of a natural evolution. This academic proponent of cognitive science intended to demonstrate through his work that "language is not a cultural artifact that we learn the way we learn to tell time or learn how the federal government works. Instead, it is a distinct piece of the biological makeup of our brains. Language is a complex and specialized skill which develops spontaneously in the child, without conscious effort or formal instruction, it is deployed without awareness of its underlying logic, it is qualitatively the same in every individual, and is distinct from more general abilities to process information or behave intelligently. For these reasons some cognitive scientists have described language as a psychological faculty, a mental organ, a neural system and a computational module, but I prefer the admittedly quaint term "instinct." It conveys the idea that people know how to talk more or less the way spiders know how to spin webs" (Pinker, 2010, p. 10). It rests on the thesis that children must have an innate mental grammar which is common to all languages. It would be "a universal grammar that tells them how to distill syntactic forms starting with their parent's speech." Language, then, is not just a cultural invention but more the product of a special human instinct. "The idea that thought is the same thing as language is an example of what could be called a conventional absurdity: a statement which refuses common sense but that everyone believes because they can vaguely remember having heard it somewhere and because it is so full of implications." Pinker makes us consider how many times we find ourselves saying or believing that our words just don't do justice to our ideas because sometimes it isn't easy to find a term that exactly expresses a thought, as we all know. All this brought Pinker to hypothesize about a "language of thought": mentalese, this would be a language, or representation, of concepts and clauses in the brain where ideas are expressed including meanings of words and the sense of those enunciated (Pinker, 2010).

Words are not just treasure chests, they are also stones; as Carofiglio says, they are acts with precise consequences seeing as how *words make things*. He proposes reintroducing words with their proper value; in fact in the second part of his last essay, he presents a panorama of words to be rediscovered in their oldest and truest sense.

He also agrees with the idea that the narration of facts "isn't a neutral operation: communication often literally *creates* what we call reality;" here to emphasize his point he recounts examples from experiments that have shown how different language can markedly change the comprehension and the memory of an event. "The choice of words is then a crucial and founding act: they are endowed with strength which determines their efficiency and which can produce consequences" [....] "The *logos* – word, thought, the ability to recount – these distinguish man from all other living creatures" (Carofiglio, 2010, p. 29 and p. 60).

Word and thought are connected in an intimate way and are fundamentally a single process; of this the extraordinary philosopher Edith Stein is also convinced (she underlines this aspect also when she speaks of training work). In fact she states, "he who doesn't know how to express himself is almost a prisoner of his soul: he can't move freely nor reach others." In her opinion the essential function of language is "to express what is living in the soul and in this way communicate ourselves to others; this is then the path to reach a liberation of the soul and the spirit. Knowing how to express oneself in an appropriate way is something essential for all of humanity." All this has developed as a result of her studies on empathy in the field of phenomenology (compare to the processes of construction of intellective knowledge and of interaction as an exchange of experiences; Stein, 1997). And so she recognizes the essential role of language in the development of the spirit, the personality and social interaction. She even arrives at talking about the importance of *"etico-pratica* in the command of a language" (Stein, 2005, pp.254-256). One of her fundamental contributions to the field is the conviction that empathy cannot be reduced to a process of total identification with the life experiences of others, this because if the others were not here, a complete formation of the person would not be possible: "Thanks to the others, to the realization that they are there and to the possibility of experiencing them through empathy, our individuality is forged and prepared to encounter the world. Knowing the personality of the other person separate from me is an indispensable passage for my consciousness" (Pulina, 2008, p. 103). These concepts have also been explained in an essay on women in which Stern observes and outlines many peculiarities. Among these is language and its different use by women in comparison with men. This, in part, is due to the fact that women empathize much more easily. Based on these assumptions Yrigaray recognizes that a woman "uses language for communicating, *he* – a man – uses it as an instrument for conquering, for acquiring, for producing, for exchanging goods and information"(Yrigaray, 1997, p. 130).

The discovery of mirror neurons has confirmed the value of phenomenological thought regarding empathy and learning ability, knowing and knowing oneself. In fact, in this philosophical field, intersubjectivity plays a fundamental role in the construction of subjectivity (Praszkier, 2014).

To be synchronized to the frequencies of another person, sharing the other's emotional state is the principal form of empathy. Often this brings one to go beyond and take an active part in the other's life, trying to be helpful all the while feeling his suffering. After all, empathy springs from a special relationship: the mother-child symbiosis, it evolves from cognitive and emotional processes. The term comes from the Greek *empatheia* which is defined by Cortelazzo-Zolli (1992, p. 382): "(A) phenomenon in which a person creates with another a type of emotional communion as a result of a process of identification." It seems that this term was used the first time in Germany by Titchener. At the time, its meaning was "feel inside" and originally was intended, above all, as a sharing of esthetics. It later took on a psychological meaning.

In our world meeting others cannot be taken for granted; the technologies used today often help us make "virtual" relationships rather than real ones. In such cases a true empathy is difficult if not impossible to achieve. As a consequence, the reduction of an exchange of life experiences, even of an everyday type, determines a lack of training in the development of the cognitive processes of empathy. Language tends to weaken from a personal and private point of view. The channel that remains open is the one of social language: impoverished in its vocabulary, trivialized by the superficiality of relationships and crippled in the face of widespread aggressiveness.

The bombarding language of the media and of violent life on the streets, moves the axis of values from people to things, it dissolves the words of "feelings." But it is to these words that we must return, existential dissatisfaction tells us as much in a powerful way through often tragic manifestations in various social living experiences.

Significant negative effects of globalization have been noted for some time now; this worldwide phenomenon is taking over language by triggering systematic destructions of cultural diversity. Another worrying factor that is created is the one that regards or involves an expanding area of conflict: conflicts between groups that are between different populations, groups of people, ethnic groups. Conflicts between different cultural groups that are not equipped with adequate tools to recognize the problem and not prepared for a confrontation, the more or less conscious response they usually give is: refusal, fight, or at the very least the reaction is only to put up with diversity. This kind of a process which reduces specific identities to a homogenous level, compromises the opportunity to experience the values characteristically held by each group.

The awareness and the sharing of values seems, however, indispensable to the offering of cultural contents that are able to guide individual and collective life. We have been observing for some time a "progressive chipping away of truth and of values. This process ends up favoring necessities over ethics, "weak thought" over the truth, and the development of consumerism over the individual and his world" (Colzi, 1990, p.789). Emilio Butturini has noted that "the same magnitude of 'possibilities' with a contextual lack of solid and shared evaluation criteria, in the end, brings people to one single criteria that is of usefulness to the individual or usefulness to a small group. This moves the axis of values into the direction of an egocentric self-fulfillment. It forgets the duties of responsibility and social solidarity. [...] Actually in post-modern times there is no room for metaphysical and philosophical truths given the tendency to "settle" for a sort of 'surplus of means at the expense of goals' and given the predominance of reason" (Butturini, 1993, p.17).

Post-modern existence – intended here as a mentality due to fragmentation and deconstruction – has been called rhizomatic, that is, it lives on the surface, it loves the surface because it refuses grounding (Ghiani, 1995). In this sense some people have noted how one should reflect on our approach to consumption: "Consumption means consuming of energy, of resources, natural and human, it is the consumption of power that justifies the growth of yet more power. There is a perverse agitation in us as individuals at the moment we are called to consume for the perpetuation of the system. For this reason, consuming has become bulimic hyperconsumption, hysterical consumption, at times obsessive because it has also become the consumption of experiences, relationships, sensations and feelings that leave no traces" (Ghiani, 1995, p.20-21). "Post-modernity developed in a complacent acceptance of transience, of fragmentation and of chaotic discontinuity. [...] The truth is rigorously subjective truths, truths are nomads and therefore subject to thousands of linguistic games which have produced them. Even though this can make one think at first glance of a process of weakening in the capacity of influencing the world, it can lead one to believe there is a lesser degree of aggression exercised in the world by men, but paradoxically, all this allows men to look at the world as the place of infinite spaces where they can freely exercise their creative force without objective limits" (Ghiani, 1995, p.18).

When validity is given to this situation of fragmentation, to a subjective and linguistically manipulated truth, then one tends to believe that there must be a strength in it, what Ghiani calls "creative force" to use without objective limits. This creative force can be expressed in a positive way respecting others if we can return to an appropriate healthy language. It will allow us to consciously manage our lives. Actually it is through language which allows interaction between people that we strengthen our own identity to get to know others. A continual exchange of give and take is activated with others. All of this is important for life in a society like ours. We are always exposed to and immersed in every kind of diversity which is becoming ever more present and deeply rooted in our daily lives.

Even Giovanni Nencioni, president of the Academia della Crusca, noted we should maintain balance and sobriety from the start in exchanges with other languages; but in time such a practice has assumed the character of an emergency due to the exponential development of contacts and of contaminations. It has become imperative to be careful not to borrow words from other languages in order to better explain certain sensations, sensations standardized to meet material needs, at the expense of words that can communicate deeper sensations.

Galimberti says "Globalization is the decline if not the extinction of what the illuminists called universalization of human rights, of liberty, of culture, of democracy." Globalization, in fact, concerns only the economy, technology, the market, tourism, information. It suppresses every form of peculiarity, of identity and difference creating a false comfortable sense of certainty, namely that all cultures are alike.

The process of globalization can be opposed by the single thought, by specific identities, of which, writes Galimberti, terrorism is the most violent expression. After all, the greatest problem that triggers globalization, being implemented only on the basis of economic interests, is exactly that of terrorism. One cannot but be in agreement with him when he maintains that our century will be the century of terrorism if we do not introduce into the process of globalization the emancipation of peoples, their acculturation, food and water for all as well as the availability of medical treatment and the hope for a future."Because he who is without a future is capable of killing himself not due to depression like we Westerners, but as a plan however abominable and murderous that he will never see realized. This anthropological difference of such a radical nature must urgently be heeded because it tells us that men and cultures are not all alike, and anthropological uniformity toward which the process of globalization tends, if it can ever be a functional value in technology and in the economy of the West, cannot be brought about in a day" (Galimberti, 2009, p.301). [.....] Galimberti continues (2009, p.302): "The enemy is born as a result of the conditions of life that we are capable of guaranteeing only for ourselves."

Senghor was right when he affirmed the necessity to spread an authentic and conscious culture in order to create a "universal civilization." His historical presidency of Senegal and his poetic works always promoted this. The great proponent of Negritude said *True culture is putting down roots and pulling them up again; putting down roots in the depth of one's own native land, but also pulling them up means opening oneself to the sun and the rain to the fertile contributions of foreign civilizations.* Only in this dimension globalization will not be feared, but rather can become the occasion for mutual exchange; however, this presumes an important step: it would be necessary that not everything be played out in terms of market, in economic terms and that it is advisable to bring into these enterprises a superior dimension of ethics and spirituality.

An evident issue connected to globalization is the problem of security which expands into every environment, individual and social, however it is particularly urgent for everyday life in cities. For this reason, as mentioned before, if the city is only a place for the carrying out of economic interests then there is a loss a civil living, living together is the sharing of what is called involved citizenship.

Unfortunately forms of aggressive and violent language are spreading along with a language of fear, a fear of others and of the environment we live in; all of this at the expense of a language of human connection, of pacific communication between people.

Globalization is having a negative effect on social language as it has actually brought about the construction of a language which is more or less a code for exchange more than a true language. This is a change that has been carried out without much resistance because it has been put to use with consistency.

Language always expresses and conveys changes under way, even those of which we perhaps are not fully aware. Galimberti notes (2009, p.140), for example, how words have come into common use, words never before heard of, for psychopathologies taking on an accepted common meaning. This linguistic change is the warning light of something much more rooted. According to Frank Furedi, the pathologizing of the human experience (types of things considered normal up to yesterday) corresponds to the need to standardize individuals not only in their way of thinking but above all in their way of feeling. Even Nietzsche admitted "he who thinks differently commits himself to the madhouse."

After all, Pasolini foresaw and denounced the negativity of the "absolute economics" component also in the field of linguistics when he criticized the linguistic unification of the country by corporations. In his opinion linguistic unification should have begun from below and not from the corporate world. In his 1964 essay "Nine linguistic questions" he acknowledged that the creating, processing and unifying centers of language are not the universities, but companies. And he denounced the fact that the technocracy in the north of Italy at that time was representing the entire nation even from a cultural and linguistic point of view. He deplored the national linguistic standardization which failed to pay due respect to the characteristic values of dialectic microcosms while in his opinion the Italianizing of the nation should have started from below, giving appropriate importance to dialects and to values of each individual group of people. A constructed language Pasolini defined as "corporate" should not have been adopted (Pasolini, 1984).

He was convinced that people, even though poor in material goods, were free because they could express "the infinite complexity of existence" in their own language. In his opinion the world of particular cultures began to fall into crisis at the moment in which it faced the economic situation in the country's centers. This led to a feeling of uncertainty with regard to its own values and at times it led to denying its own life style.

In addition, Pasolini carries out another analysis which in some way contains a prediction of a decadent future which triggered globalization. The analysis is made in the moment when Pasolini faces the problem of linguistic changes provoked by standardized consumerism which leads to a single model of behavior, of anticipation, of dreams. These models were still diversified in 1968. In fact, the non-verbal language of the "hippies," the author notes and appreciates as more sincere, is criticized in two ways: in the beginning he recognizes the new ideas and stances of a breaking down but then later he considers it only standardization without freedom.

The world that subscribes to consumerism with the power that its advertising wields creates traps into which the young easily fall. In fact, according to Pasolini this happens when they choose clothes and exterior things, they are confusing exterior value with an interior one. He makes an example of the language of slogans, which in his opinion was so absorbed by people that it substituted a humanistic language. All of this brings him to predict a worrying future that is the expression of a world that does not take into account cultural diversities and the particularities of different territories (Pasolini, 2007).

All the issues this work is based on are present in his reflection: language impoverished by standardization given it through consumerism, together with the problems caused by a loss of values during this process. In a social-economic context, as at the heart of our own context, Pasolini warns of the concrete risk of the perversion of human beings manifested and in some respects caused and consolidated by the corrupt language of the negativism in our times. However, in his essays, he reflects on this serious situation and a ray of hope appears above all when he repeats his opinion that human beings really are different than these tendencies would have one think. So also here he affirms his own intuition: there is room for positive improvement which can be found in many people of good will and it is precisely those people who keep the world going.

Toxic language is implicated in and caused by all the societal problems discussed above. Educational systems are often produced by the culture in which they are located. Yet education can also be the pathway to solving these concerns. Education can confront culture rather than be its perpetuator. Schools can help students find their inner voice. Here are some strategies that have been successful.

Narration as an effective solution for change: Significant experiences

Narration at school

Three particularly inspired examples of this come from Federico Batini's workgroup of the Associazione Pratika in Arezzo, Italy, from the staff of Altra Citta' and from Agenzia Formativa dell' istituto Professionale di Stato L. Einaudi di Grosseto. They have made the object of their studies[1] and their experimentations the subject of narrative orienting. One should refer to their publications such as the projects of narrative orienting which have been carried out in many places.

This methodology has found a particularly appropriate area of application in the scholastic context so much so that the regional scholastic institute has called for specific courses for teachers in the above-mentioned associations. These courses are held so that the figure of the teacher beyond assuming the teaching function becomes a professional who is able to help students "bring out" and discover their own hidden capabilities. The success of these experiences has been shared with the students' families who were actively involved in the conscious growth process of their own children.

The proposed projects were structured by a direction of study that could stimulate the narrative production through a variety of stimuli and tools such as: the language of photos, oral transmission of stories, creative writing, film script writing and the use of audio-visual devices, the song and singing. Decisive in these experiences is the role of the facilitator. This educator is the one who helps people to express themselves without value judgment nor predefined ideas. This is why it is so important to adequately train the teachers and all those who find themselves in the position to carry out this delicate job.

The results obtained by these projects have been extremely positive, so much so that the Pratika association and the Nausika and Altra Citta' associations have been called to train not only teachers[2] but also consultants and orienting workers both through certification courses (post-graduate certification as Orienting Consultant) and through courses aimed at employment agency workers, workers in orienting centers, and volunteers and workers in the social services.

Autobiographical narration

Alberto L'Abate and Lorenzo Porta collected more than 300 autobiographies of young people in Florence and surrounding areas and they carried out research[3] using the Danilo Dolci maieutic method. These studies were commissioned by the city of Florence and were among the first of this type to be done in Tuscany.

Danilo Dolci was an important figure in the world of non-violence. He rediscovered maieutics and its effectiveness in words. He said: "In the first place maieutics must be practiced on ourselves, on our way of expressing ourselves – this is an opportunity for discovery- on our very words. The maieutics of the word is a continuing process which goes deeper and deeper and becomes ever more complex in its search for the truth"[4]. He emphasizes the importance of practicing this on a personal and collective level.

In reviewing his many personal stories, Dolci concluded: " ... to cleanse society of the supremacy virus it is necessary to treat the weak in a way that through organic communication, they become an alternative strength to that supremacy. Working together this way I believe helps free me of a dangerous tunnel vision"[5]. There was a lot of feedback on this and it was mostly positive, at times even moving to read.

Dolci reveals one of his areas of interest is schools. The reason for this is that schools suffocate a child's natural curiosity because they do not promote a direct experience of reality, preferring to "deposit" pre-fabricated notions in the minds of the young. Dolci was convinced that *our deepest self is the product of a communicative structure*[6] therefore it is this we should occupy ourselves with in order to create good communicative structures once again. These new structures could "contaminate" in a positive way.

Narration and the prison

The method of orienting narration is also used in prisons; I especially like to remember some drafts of fables and their illustrations by the convicts of the Istituto Penitenziario Mario Gossini (commonly called Sollliccianino) of Florence. These same convicts read their fables in school that have a parallel participation in the project where students had written and illustrated fables on the same themes. This initiative was the source of great human enrichment. The fables were such a great success that they were made into a book and a theater play. The play was staged by the convicts and children from the schools were called to help with the production. The organizers of this project (Fondazione Sistema Toscana)[7] noted a positive change in the convicts' behavior because it helped them (mostly the young ones from twenty to thirty years of age) reconnect with their childhood experiences and their parenting experiences. This took place thanks to the work on written and spoken language which gave the convicts the opportunity to reflect and also the opportunity to exchange things drawn out from within themselves with others.

Alberto L'Abate used the maieutic method of autobiographical narration in the Florentine prison Sollicciano on mafia convicts. The results were very encouraging.

These are without a doubt important experiences that one can read as the concrete and efficient role played by the rehabilitating prison sentence becoming an appropriate reintegration into society. In this way people within the prison learn constructive language, far from their origins which in the past led them to bad choices.

The theatrical laboratory of the "Associazione Cinema TeartroLux" produced another example of language for change in the "Casa Circondariale Don Bosco" in Pisa. This example was again made by convicts and came about because of the law "articolo 21." The goal was to encourage the capacity of communication, of introspection, dialog and interaction. In this way creative capacities were stimulated through writing, narration and acting in plays to recreate and discover innate qualities[8].

The word has proven to be a tool of 'liberation' and rebirth with these experiments done in elementary and middle schools within the Casa di reclusione at San Michele in Alessandria. Being that 90% of the participants were foreigners, to solve the language problem they decided to have each person choose a list of words to narrate a particular reflection, a memory or a wish for the future. "The use of an important key word made the convicts relax and bring to the surface something from their inner selves"[9]. The convicts then read their writings which became a video called "Piccolo dizionario cattivo" (naughty little dictionary).

The language of empowerment for rebuilding mankind

A new language for new perspectives: class experiments

To be able to express what one feels helps not only to create language that can generate life and values, but it also helps in not considering those negative effects of social language; therefore creative narration is an exercise that is important for the young to do constantly at school and in their private lives.

I carried out experiments at the Lorenzo de' Medici School in Florence. Their aim was creating awareness that could enable students to express themselves in an appropriate way. The following is a summary of the experiments.

Learning and talking about oneself through play

In this project the students were asked to divide up into teams, four in each team. They were invited to participate in what was called a special "Giro d'Italia" (famous cycling race in Italy). Start and finish was to be Florence. The teams earned one point for reaching each station.

This game created the right environment to stimulate important aspects of the learning process. Given that one learns through play, following the steps required by the game, they could internalize and also share actions with others. All of this brought them to access information held in the long term memory which is the fundamental reservoir for organizing and reorganizing one's existence.

The teams had to prepare and present a project at each stage of the "Giro d'Italia." Each project received an evaluation in points. The subject of these projects was conducive to helping the students express their thoughts, their opinion about the lesson which had taken place before. The subjects were posed in a way that encouraged the students to reflect and talk about themselves. The students were also encouraged in this self-searching by questions aimed at evaluating and developing their own ability to face the world outside.

During the course of the game, the students were asked the meaning of the words used in a context. This is a question which is usually followed by a greater awareness of lack of knowledge. It often provokes an uneasiness for lack of knowledge but at the same time it brings about the curiosity to know and to do a more thorough research on the matter. In this way one can begin to explain to the students that words have an origin, a meaning. When they have to admit they did not know, one can give them the feeling that they are missing something important. Then they are ready, motivated to know and to acquire information in an indelible manner.

Trying to get the students to talk about themselves tended to cause a great silence in about 80% of the class. Encouraging them to talk about themselves after the above described game reversed that percentage in willingness to speak. Actually the students felt they had a greater ability. With the stimulus of an award (metaphor for a goal) the students were interested in continuing 'to play.'

Introspection: a word that can bring back strength to a person

Another experiment that had exciting results could be defined as 'cabalistic.' Participants were asked to warm up by rubbing their hands together and placing them on their closed eyes and in that moment to try to describe what they see even if often it is not well defined.

This exercise has two outcomes, one is it requires some concentration and the other is it often detaches the participants from each other because it requires a greater concentration and reflection than normally required in daily life. Furthermore, describing what appears to their closed eyes involves a choice of words that cannot be automatic as is the case in common everyday expression. They find themselves describing colors, shapes, persons, and environment. The exchange of impressions between the participants showed the effort involved in using not the common social language but a personal language, more intimate with satisfaction for the people who experienced this.

Art as creation and as an opportunity for awareness

Another effective exercise uses art to bring to the surface people's interior world. The participants in this experiment are confronted with the observation of a painting and they are asked to spontaneously reproduce it in their own way. Some do not interpret the painting but only reproduce it in essence: the same light, the same colors.... Others, however, give it a personal interpretation that is clearly seen by all, and then the rest of the group begins to imitate a freer interpretation and to express themselves in an individual manner.

Generally one begins with changing colors, shapes and then goes on later in the experiment to arrive at an abstract expression. In this way self-esteem is increased and students also acquire a certain skill along with the self -confidence to believe they can do something, that they actually know how to resolve the task.

This experience was also proposed to people who had a passive way of expressing themselves in order to offer them some help with this. With these new skills, they were able to create a new language for themselves that reflected their autonomy: this had not only psychological consequences but also pragmatic ones.

For some, this represented a turning point in their lives; indeed, having a greater awareness of their inner world and a fair amount of confidence in their own capabilities, the same students who before could not imagine any kind of place for themselves in the working world, began to imagine the possibility of becoming the promoting manager of themselves.

These experiences have highlighted the importance of realizing these types of potential that sometimes we just are not able to recognize in ourselves without help. At the same time this type of experience offers us the possibility to reconnect with our inner feelings, strengthening our sense of personal security which is confirmed constructively by others. This actually changes what we call contaminated social language.

Language as a tool for security in cities

This way of working with language truly is valid. My experiences in this matter confirm it. Actually one can create a security project in a practical way giving autonomy and security to people, helping them to acquire the necessary perseverance to set up and carry through business objectives. The shared word is the necessary tool to activate joint community momentum which in turn helps bring about security that everyone can profit from.

It is a fact, someone who communicates with a sincere language that resists the toxic source is always listened to.

I have been experiencing for some years now social interaction with the inhabitants and the shopkeepers in the San Lorenzo area of Florence. This is where the school Lorenzo de' Medici is located. The use of appropriate language has brought about positive results which allows for a triggering of mirror neuron afferent mechanisms to spontaneously initiate constructive processes of integration.

San Lorenzo is a multi-ethnic neighborhood. This can be seen in the diversity of the merchandise offered in the shops including foodstuffs from all over the world. This has always been a historic market location, a place for people to meet. Today it is enhanced by the presence of immigrants from various parts of the world. The social tensions that run through the neighborhood in such a context are not always easy to manage, however, it has been seen that a dialog is possible if one approaches the others with a non-toxic language. This change is practicable. It is a different approach which helps people to express themselves and provides a more secure feeling in day to day life, so much so that urban spaces can be re-appropriated.

"Film spray": a language for creative business management

Another example of language empowerment as an effective tool is the 'Film spray' carried out in Florence but which reaches out to all the world online.

This festival helps make films known, not for sheer entertainment, but films of meaningful content that would otherwise not reach people. It is organized in various venues where the public can come, both scholastic venues and civil ones, where these full length films can be shown encouraging dialog among the viewers.

It is this same public who has enthusiastically participated from the beginning in 2009 to decide which films win. These films have subsequently come out in cinemas or been seen on television. This was because interest shown by the network of participants was interpreted for all intents and purposes as a market survey and as a consequence the film distribution companies who at first had refused the films had to change their minds and accept them.

In my opinion the most important aspect of the festival was not the promoting of "invisible" films. Instead, it was allowing the "non-winners" not to feel like victims of the system. In the past these creative individuals perceived the system was preventing them from expressing themselves because they did get the chance to show their films and recognize any errors in their work.

These experiences have highlighted the importance of realizing different types of potential that sometimes we just are not able to recognize by ourselves without help. At the same time this type of experience gives us the possibility to reconnect with our inner feelings, strengthening our sense of personal security which in part then becomes a constructive gift to others, in this way actually changing the contaminated social language.

The intention has always been to bring to light the power of existence, the power of planning, of relationships, of reciprocal exchange (Putton, 2010), to make education a tool of empowerment. In fact the objective of education is to make people aware of their own inner truth and of the goals they want to reach. People like this, aware and motivated, are able to produce creative work using the resources at hand, working hard to acquire new knowledge and build an efficient interchange of communication. Therefore, in the first place it is important to understand which objectives one intends to reach in order to, then, lay out strategies establishing a path which will lead to those objectives.

Education actually is empowerment, being that its goal is to create autonomy and independence. Education must establish a maieutic dialog of Socratic memory to show how there exists in us a heritage of implicit knowledge. It is important to note that, in doing this, you as an educator benefit the person, you make students feel more secure and motivated, more responsible for their own choices (Piccardo, 1995; Fabbri, 2005; Dallago, 2006).

Another experience of empowerment is that of the 'Film spray' in Florence where this festival makes films known that would otherwise go unacknowledged. This is done by showing these films at different venues, schools or public places and having the viewing public decide a winning film. Starting from the first edition of this festival in 2009, these films actually have had the possibility to be inserted into the traditional film market because of the favorable votes received from their audiences. The public's judgment was seen as a true market survey by the distribution companies that originally had refused these films and then were obliged to change their minds.

The word is also a fundamental tool in conflict resolution. These conflicts should not be fought out but should be transformed. This implies the decoding of the other's diverseness in a moment of listening attentively which can make space for a language of collaboration and not one of conflict.

Notes

1   Very significant are the related publications by the workers in these projects.

2   Compare also "A scuola di intercultura. Cittadinanza, partecipazione, interazione: risorse della societa' multiculturale" (the intercultural school. Citizenship, participation, interaction: resouces of the multicultural society) edited by A. Tosolini, S. Giusti, G. Papponi Morelli, Erickson, Trento, 2007.

3   This work has been detailed in a book edited by Lorenzo Porta: "Autobiografie a scuola: un approccio maieutico" (Auto biographies at school: a maieutic approach) edited by L. Porta, Angeli , Milan, 2004.

4   D. Dolci, quoted from "Atti del seminario: Giornata Maieutica. Il metodo nonviolento nell'esperienza di Danilo Dolci" (Seminar transcripts: Day of Maieutics. The non-violent method of experience by Danilo Dolci) (19 – 20 April 2002, Santa Maria dello Spasimo, Palermo) edited by Amico Dolci and Vito La Fata.

5   D. Dolci, *Gente semplici, (simple people)* La Nuova Italia, Scandicci, 1998, p. 144.

6   Compare www.danilodolci.toscana.it/scuolacitt.htm.

7   The manager of the FST audiovisual projects is Sveva Fedeli, compare activities in social work at www.mediatecatoscana.it.

8   Compare www.cultura.toscana.it

9   www.ristretti.org

3

The Power of Language to Make A Difference:

How Educators' Words Impact Students' Perception of Their Own Competence

Ronald R. Cromwell, Debra Baird, Tedi Gordon, and Branton B. Baird

> The word was spoken
> then pierced my heart
> never to be healed
> and all the remaining days
> it dripped blood on those
> who passed by me
> —Cromwell, 1993, p.20

As reflected in the poem, words have power to harm and destroy, but, at the same time, words can heal and build. Language is the first tangible interaction one has with the world of home, school and community. Language serves as the central construct in establishing how one learns to look at the world and find what is meaningful. According to the philosopher Martin Heidegger, "language houses the essence of being and the saying of the words puts that reality into existence" (Cromwell, 1993, p. 25). Language has power to shape reality and through changes in the use of language it is possible to change ones' own reality and the meaning of that reality. Education, both formal and informal, is a key that allows this shift in reality and empowers the individual. Failure in the education process, especially in using language to transform, contributes to failure of individuals to attain their full capacity and the intention of full, rewarding and contributing life.

In this chapter, it is proposed that language development and acquisition hold keys to the way we see the world and move within it. The relationship between language and the conceptualization of the world from a phenomenological perspective are explored. How are one's experiences affected by the language of peers, family, teachers, administrators, community, and media? Language is the medium by which human beings relate with the "other", and internalize pieces of that "otherness" as part of themselves because it shapes their world views and realities. Influenced by language, being, place and time result in the individual's sense of self and reality. Education and the intentional use of language allows us to make changes to place, time and one's personal reality, regardless of the past experiences or current conditions. Language is central and integral to the way in which one shapes reality, gains perspectives, forms dispositions, and communicates.

Language and Its Power

There is a Navajo saying that each morning the individual sings into existence our world. A Chinese proverb holds that it takes a thousand kind words to undo one unkind, harmful word. Many cultures agree with these proverbs and hold many of their own that request kindness and thought before speaking into reality what one is thinking. Recently, in an urban Alabama primary/middle school, a mother was overheard telling her 6-year-old child "Get your dumb A . . over here and give me an F...ing kiss!" The properly educated teacher was astounded, but began to better understand why the children in the middle school were constantly using this same type of language in everyday conversation. Since the entire school had been tirelessly working to correct the language and stop the use of "cursing" in the daily verbal exchange, the teacher became aware that foul language was a construct of reality for the students, and in this case, was used with the intention of endearment. With this insight, the staff of the school changed the way it dealt with cursing by explaining a more acceptable set of words for discourse and conversation in the time and place. By not dismissing the home language, but providing another set of "words" the teachers opened the door for middle school students to change their language and engage in words that have a different ability to shape their realities and world views.

According to Lantolf and Genung (2002), "Effective learning and motivation are always socially embedded" (p. 261). That being said, it is probably also true that ineffective learning and motivation are also socially embedded. Nardi (1996) contended that you are what you do and it is possible to understand that actions are driven by one's perception and world view. The interaction of language and language user is the origin of meaning and "reality" that result in action and doing. Learning or thought processes that pass through a preconceived accepted meaning, even at a neuronal level, will then be biased by language interaction. Negative thought and language will produce more negative thoughts and actions. School is one of the central places where language and intentional use of language to empower can influence the shaping of reality and the consequent actions of individuals. All cultures reflect on the interplay of language and sense of reality. If that is true, and Heidegger is correct, then language allows us to build reality. In accepting this premise, language can be seen as one of the most powerful tools a teacher or parent has to influence and help children grow. The language of teachers and parents must be carefully chosen and guarded in order to nurture the best possible outcomes. The challenge for teachers and educational institutions is how to ensure language is used in a beneficial way for every child.

The use of language shapes reality and can be seen in the following examples. First from a preeminent scholar, John Henry, Cardinal Newman, who stated in his treatise what a university, or an education, is designed to produce:

It is the education which gives a man a clear conscious view of his own opinions and judgments, a truth in developing them, an eloquence in expressing them, and a force in urging them. It teaches him to see things as they are, to go right to the point, to disentangle a skein of thought, to detect what is sophistical, and to discard what is irrelevant. It prepares him to fill any post with credit, and to master any subject with facility. It shows him how to accommodate himself to others, how to throw himself into their state of mind, how to bring before them his own, how to influence them, how to come to an understanding with them, how to bear with them.... He has the repose of a mind which lives in itself, while it lives in the world and which has resources for its happiness at home when it cannot go abroad. He has a gift which serves him in public, and supports him in retirement, without which good fortune is but vulgar, and with which failure and disappointment have a charm. The art which tends to make a man all this is in the object which it pursues as useful as the art of wealth or the art of health, though it is less susceptible of method, and less tangible, less certain, less complete in its result. (The Idea of a University, 1852, p.134).

And yes, even with this profoundly foundational idea of what education should be, the use of male-powered genderness in language was a part of Newman's basic conceptualization of the world and how it worked. In 1852, he would have never considered speaking of women in this light or even considering their presence in serious educational realms. The very issuance of this treatise reveals the place and time, as well as acceptable concepts that were agreed upon by educated people in that era; it places the boundaries of Cardinal Newman's reality in the language he uses. Newman's treatise, for all its truths and profound definitions of a true education, shows that for all the education one may have, the situation of time and place dictates the thinking and language of each individual. Escaping the time, space, and language bounds of one's own era is the most difficult of all accomplishments, but very possible, with the right tools.

In a more contemporary example, a local school district administrator reviews a file and indicates the student is from 'that' county understanding that folks from there really cannot "get" things in schools. The main reason they cannot "get" things in school, or at least the reason for that perception, is due to the way they use or misuse the language in the school. Usually, being from "that" county means the students are from rural areas, from the mountains, or from what is viewed as a culturally inferior geographical area considered being "less" than other areas from which children attend. Thus, the teacher interactions move to the use of language such as: "do not worry, you will not have to take that course; this is really over your head; your parents never took anything like this and will not be able to help." The consequence of this language is reinforcement of a reality that limits and harms, rather than teaches and helps.

From the onset of individual and collective being, language

shapes our reality. Initially, language patterns between home, school, and community are influenced by the student's place of residence (Heath, 1983). The residential place of children's homes can negatively or positively influence their success in school. Experiences in each particular place demand a particular linguistic proficiency. Heath conducted research on the language patterns at home and in the classroom. In *Ways with Words*, her intent was to explore the importance of linguistic capital. She did this by conducting an ethnographic study of schooling in the Piedmont Carolinas. The study compared two working class communities to a middle class community in a nearby town. Her findings revealed that the two rural communities of Trackton (African-American community) and Roadville (White community) had very different language patterns as compared to the town community. The influence of the lack of linguistic capital revealed that Black working-class children were not socialized to cope with the language patterns used in school and quickly fell behind. White working class children developed cognitive and linguistic patterns but did not gain interpretive skills to sustain academic success. The mismatch between language used at home and language used at school puts working class children at a disadvantage.

Language patterns of home influences the child's perception of reality and the place of school also clearly influences a child's world view. It follows that the place becomes an influencing factor in individual success as well. If the individual is successful at each step, opportunities and possibilities abound. However, if an individual is not successful at any step, or if the school/home/work does not provide opportunities for growth, then the possibilities and likelihood of success in society are stunted, slowed, or stopped. The power of language, its use by those around us, especially those with power and authority over us, causes the development of a reality that can "make or break" a child or an entire life.

Knowing Oneself and One's Reality

A phenomenological lens is used to reflect upon the ways of knowing one's reality through language. Phenomenology seeks to describe and interpret socially constructed realities by understanding how people experience certain phenomena. Language is one form of communication that provides the context necessary for construction. In philosophical terms, "knowing" involves an understanding of all that is around you. Knowing, shaped by language, is the essence of "being" in that it is the sum of all that one has been and will become, through all interactions and experiences around each individual. Each individual's reality is based on perceptions and understandings of the world and develops over time with growth and more interactions and experiences. Language is one of the most important components and is key in constructing that view of reality. Constructing a reality with accuracy is extremely important in building a personal reality that allows an individual to function well within the group while being happy within self.

Reality is really the mind's understanding of how outside input affects the person. In other words, the reality housed in language can also be described as that which gives meaning; however, it can be noted that language can mean more than words. Take for example a carpenter hammering away on a nail. When performed correctly, the nail almost sings a scale, and the pitch of the nail's singing gets higher and higher as the nail sinks and combines two pieces of wood. With each true strike of the nail the carpenter hears the nail's message, "I am performing as predicted." The carpenter knows this without producing words. On the other hand the carpenter can strike down with a glancing blow off the head of the nail; the audible "poing" tells the carpenter that the nail has flown off. The builder automatically begins searching in the supply of nails for a new one. This is communication in its purest form. This is the interpretation of meaning and the acceptance of reality through aural stimuli, functioning in the same way of language. In fact, it is a type of language.

Language in the very broadest sense can be found beyond the understanding of language as words. The goal here is to focus on all languages, but with an emphasis on language with the meaning of words. The language and the words of the home and then of learning environments allow for the transformation of self through the interactions at home and between curriculum, peers, teachers, and community. Regardless of initial experiences, language has the capacity to change one's life trajectory. The place of school is important because it is part of the social context of experience in which meaning is constructed (Kuntz & Berger, 2011; Massey, 1994; Tuan, 1977). Language is the mechanism by which students can be empowered to develop a state of being and reality that expands opportunities for life choices. Language of possibilities, as demonstrated in talking about a successful person, from the same socio-economic background who reached an important goal, may open doors and views differently than reminding a student of basic skills, requiring repetitive problems not based in something valued by the student, and insisting on quiet and compliance.

The important aspect is that somehow the person has to become empowered. That empowerment has largely seemed to have been through chance, at best, not by intentional planning by the schools. Planning for empowerment through language has not been identified as important enough to be the main objective of schooling, and yet, without it, there is a great loss of human potential. Educational institutions are positioned to make a positive impact on empowering students if that choice is made. A progressive or social reconstructionist approach to teaching provides experiences that empower students to make choices and decisions about their role in learning and the community. When language is used to encourage and open doors, it can facilitate a shift in the student's world and self-understanding. Asking what is your passion and how do you learn enables students in a much different way than telling them to obey the rules, do this learning so you can get a job, and do not be messy. Being is; one exists. But place, time and reality allow for changes to being that provide for more profound living and working, more profound understanding and enjoyment, and more flexibility to individual and group world conceptualization. All of this leads to higher levels of individual and overall human consciousness and the ability to achieve each individual's full potential.

The pivotal question is not just how much and in what ways is language used to suppress or oppress. Rather, more importantly, the pivotal question is in what ways is language used to put ideas and new views of reality into place to expand horizons and options and to increase the ability to move to take actions that reach higher goals? This question is especially important in schools and universities that prepare tomorrow's adults. How do educators work to allow empowerment through language, not imprisonment in a distorted reality? In what ways is thought and language encouraged to grow within and be expressed freely as ideas acknowledging the influence of language and words on meaning and the shape of reality and world views? The educator must be willing to engage in this dialogue and move to make a difference.

Understanding the Realities of Individuals and Groups

As previously stated, language allows us to build and shape reality. In accepting Heidegger's premise that language is the essence of being and that the use of words puts that reality into existence, then language has power to shape reality and through changes in the use of language it is possible to change ones' place in society, as well as one's own destiny. Language is one of the most powerful tools a teacher or parent uses to influence and help children evolve into what is possible. Language must be carefully chosen and guarded, to nurture only the best possible outcomes. Use of language that stifles and burdens is possibly the most damning early problem for children and the most difficult to undo.

Empowerment through language involves all aspects of life and living; consider the idea of being in the world or being-in-place, where place becomes being. The Buddhists have a teaching within the eightfold path to enlightenment (Lee, 1988). This is by no means a complete explanation of the eightfold path; however it is interesting that this ancient philosophy has devoted so much to developing "right speech." By having right speech, those on the eightfold path to enlightenment begin using the first principle of ethical behavior. The utilization of "right speech" is seen as a behavior which leads to further enlightenment. Language in this sense can enhance the mind's ability to expand the interpretation of meaning. Language is a behavior of the mind, but is it thought? Thought is guided by language, but it cannot be one and the same as language itself. Polyglots will often mix grammars and even phonetics when going back and forth between languages. This means they have thoughts, and the production of these thoughts into words sometimes becomes mixed up, a concept referred to as "interlanguage" in the work of Selinker (1972).

Language, in the sense of word, and thought are not the same. A person may have the language and the language ability with words but can at times be unable to give voice to the thought. There is a set of language that precedes language as words, exemplified in the special ability of deaf people. Their initial language is symbolic and later will take the shape of words. Language, in its many forms, especially in words, directs thinking to further creative development. This is why teachers should use caution in the language and words that are used in schooling. If not careful, students will have unhelpful thoughts, which will make it more difficult for each student to learn. Students must also be careful to understand why and to what extent the information they have been given will lead them to future creative discoveries. It is at this point that harm can be done to students by planting even the smallest distortion of reality. This is why the Buddhist's eightfold path insists that believers adhere to the "Right Speech."

It is the home of each individual that gives the first ideas and first words. The language of that home must always be respected as the originators of the seed of thought. Only through respect can children or adults move forward educationally. As discussed earlier in this chapter, the language of the primary care-giver is the language that is acceptable to the child, and unless respected and appreciated by the schooling institution, no further learning is likely to happen. Understanding student experience is key to instigating productive change in the language used in schools. Experience does not occur in a vacuum but must exist within a context. "The places we inhabit physically, emotionally, and cognitively help to form an essential aspect of our phenomenological selves" (Cannatella, 2007, p. 623). Language occurs through the cognitive process of being-in-place. Viewing "place" in terms of being illustrates the dynamic intersection between language and experience and the complex process of meaning making.

Place is a process constructed through the material and social world. Others have explored the phenomenological aspect of place by seeking to understand the continuous process of feelings, actions, and emotions that constitute being and experience. "Being-in-place" (Cannatella, 2007, p. 622) can be used as a theoretical framework to explore place as a process related to the language of students in school. Cannatella (2007) posited that the characteristics of place influence the development of self through an embodied sense of being-in-place. For example, cognitively, students know what language is acceptable in the principal's office. They make conscious and unconscious choices about what is said around the principal as compared to what is said around a friend's locker. Emotionally, they may express themselves differently in the principal's office than they would in the lunchroom. Physically, these emotions are expressed through the use of body language as nonverbal communication of discomfort or distress.

School places are important because they influence social experience largely through language. Cannatella (2007) explained that places do matter because of three characteristics that contribute to the process of being-in-place: (1) *Objective place* describes the material environment and organizational structures that are perceived through cognition; (2) Emotional connections are present when one *"dwells in place."* This refers to engaging, perceiving, and giving to the experiences of the place; (3) *Embodiment* of place is the physical movement and expression by the body. Place as a process is foundational to the on-going and ever-changing interaction of these dimensions. Interpretations of place shape experiences in the material and social environments of human beings. The place of school is influenced by the language used and beliefs. If it is a place of project based learning where projects are seen as important and valued, the place of school can touch a student in ways that will enable and change views. Instead of reading a science textbook and answering questions there are other options. Such an option is to ask a middle school class to assist in seeing what kinds of micro-organisms are living in the school bathrooms that might lead to illnesses and finding a solution for a healthier environment. This moves to respect the students and their ability to positively contribute. In Gordon's (2012) study examples can be found. A male student fulfils his expectations that math is difficult. He indicates he hates math, goes to class, and is asked to engage in taking exams. He states: "I am good in science and English. Ain't nothing against her, it just goes so slow. I hate math. It's dumb and gets harder; I am never going to use. I am going to have to take this math over." The frustration is evident in his physical reaction to the class. When he walks in the room he slumps in a chair and puts his head on the desk. In a different and more positive example, Gordon (2012) reports a student who loves the school because it has the most freedom of any school. The student states that "you can have your phone; you can talk, yell, and work on projects, even slide down the hall...But you know you can't do some things." Both students' school experiences were influenced by the interaction within the academic and social environment. World views were re-enforced; one with a negative consequence and the other with a more empowering outcome.

The above examples and illustration show the way in which "being-in-place" is constituted by the cognitive, emotional and embodied interpretations of place. Although distinct, the three characteristics of place cannot be separated because each relies on the other to form a sense of being. The environment is dynamic. Being-in-place involves a multidimensional process of adjusting and refining one's interpretations of place. It is the process by which cognition, emotion, and embodiment of an environment shape experience.

Gordon's (2012) study of student interpretations of the high school environment suggests that a reciprocal relationship exists between the cognitive, emotional, and embodied experiences of the students. For example, the language that the students used to describe teacher and student controlled spaces indicated positive and negative feelings. Relative to the findings concerning teacher-controlled and student-controlled places, patterns emerged based on the participants' feelings associated with such places. Teacher controlled places include academic places such as the classrooms, the library, and offices. Student controlled places might be the hallway, gym, lunchroom, and break areas. Negative feelings were associated with teacher-controlled places more than student controlled places. For example, a participant was a straight-A student and had negative feelings about his classes. Classes were described as irritating, miserable, upsetting, skeptical, and powerless. Another participant was a failing student who also had negative feelings about classes. These feelings were described as bored, unhappy, and nervous.

In comparison, more positive feelings were associated with student-controlled places than with teacher-controlled places. One participant was a very quiet and shy person who expressed feelings associated with student-dominated places as satisfied, calm, understanding, and courageous. Another participant was a straight-A student and associated feelings of daring, rebellion, freedom, and curiosity with student-dominated places. A solid-B student, said that student-dominated places were cheerful, and he felt content when in those places.

The previous examples illustrate how language, as part of place, can be used as a lens to analyze social environment. This means that place is a *thing* that is intimately connected to the individuals and informed by language. From classrooms to hallways to bathrooms, children are a part of the school and the language used in the school influence experiences. Casey (1998) explained that place has a virtual dimension because it is a place that one chooses to go and might incur possible action. Bodies and place are inseparable as well as distinct from each other. High school becomes a familiar place for the students because of the way they manage and negotiate the social environment.

Tuan (1977) emphasized that place is a special kind of object because it is where humans embody feelings, images, and thoughts in a tangible way. For example, the language used in an environment, such as a high school, can reveal the social roles of students and teachers, jocks and nerds, or loners. The expression through language is unique to each place: one speaks differently in the classroom than in the gymnasium. The choice of words used by the faculty, staff, and students in a school can articulate a social order or impact senses and feelings.

Educational Effectiveness of Teachers through Language

Bourdieu's (1989) notion of habitus is a framework to examine the educational effectiveness of teachers through language. He emphasized the importance of educational experiences as a key to the formation of self. Cannetella (2007) stressed the relevance of educational institutions because a school environment gives "a sense of place" that shapes experience. Does the language convey an open place of acceptance or a closed place of existence? If place is what happens locally through experience and expressed in language, then there are repercussions for educational practices. Bourdieu (1989) would add that educational practices influence the values and relations that are inculcated and reproduced within each child. Because habitus can be defined as the ways of acting, feeling, thinking, and being (Webb, Schirato, & Danaher, 2002) schools are instrumental in the construction of experiences that shape the individual's understanding of the self and the world.

Teachers must be aware of the learned language of children when they arrive in the classroom. No language is incorrect; it is just achieved through natural understanding of the space and time, with the home culture of the child introducing the first word concepts. Teachers cannot be effective if they do not accept the language a child brings to the classroom. Respect and appreciation of the richness of each child's heritage must be foremost in the minds of every teacher and school. When home language is acceptable to the school, then learning new places and realities is acceptable to the child. Spatial segregation influences the type of language accepted and used. People who are close together socially may use the same language. This spatial segregation is evident in the academic tracking of classrooms, encounters in the hallways, or participation in a particular sport.

Once the child begins to know that his/her reality has a place of respect in the school, then the reality will begin to change with learning about new and different ideas, concepts, and cultures. The work of Lawrence Kolhberg (1981) was extremely useful and influential in establishing this truth in the schools of the United States, and remains an embedded part of most school days, whether the teachers realize it or not. Kolhberg was responsible for the use of moral dilemmas to teach culture, language, and concepts, and revolutionized the consideration of other points of view in group settings, as a teaching method. His method allowed a consideration of time, space, and being, without religious overtones, which had not been done previously, and is still seldom done.

When people do not recognize the influence of social factors in shaping their thoughts and practices, then that is misrecognition. As people develop a comfort level related to their positioning within a social field and believe that this position is natural, then they have misrecognized the fact that they are shaped by society and produced to be particular kinds of people. Misrecognition occurs through the unconsciously inherited physical and relational predispositions shaped by a set of core values and discourses called doxa (Bourdieu & Passeron, 1977; Deer, 2008). These shared beliefs and values are reproduced through perception and practice. Ultimately, the doxa is viewed as true and necessary, thus creating misrecognition of the conditions in which individuals exist.

The impact of the educational field in the formation of habitus is evident in the study conducted by Chandler (2009). He examined the pedagogies of two white, male history teachers in North Alabama. An analysis of two qualitative case studies related to how the teaching of race and oppression within the context of their American History class revealed such conditions. The author concluded that their pedagogies misrecognized the power of natural and common sense explanations of America's race based history. The teachers presented an illusion that the progress of America was natural. This example illustrates the way in which human construction of beliefs can be reproduced within an educative field. The language used by the teachers in their lectures reflected a bias towards American individualism and was the medium through which the superiority of American expansionism was justified over the rights of other cultures.

Chandler (2009) illustrated the concept of symbolic violence that can occur through language. Symbolic violence uses a subtle form of violence that enables the dominant to dominate others (Bourdieu & Passeron, 1977; Bourdieu, 1990). This violence is not physical but symbolic in that schools exemplify a middle class culture through practice and language. Individuals are complicit in the exercise of this symbolic violence because it is not recognized as such. Social hierarchies within the school are produced and maintained by symbolic domination, not physical force. The system is perceived as legitimate, thus no "physical action" is needed to dominate the individuals. Pedagogic action is the subtle form of symbolic violence in educational institutions. The dominant plays out in the field of education through various practices and language to promote a particular doxa that legitimizes the positioning and life style within schooling. An example of this symbolic violence can be seen in the influence of media by the imposition of worldviews upon people (Giroux, 1999). Teachers should be cognizant of reproducing conditions of oppression through the language they use and the curriculum they choose.

Teachers and schools are the most important vessels through which children can find other realities that define their lives. The home gives the beginning, but the school can give the polish, if it is allowed. Unfortunately, most schools are sterile and impersonal places, where very little learning actually takes place, save that learned on the playground and other non-structured moments in the school day. Learning cannot take place unless trust and acceptance exists between each student and teacher, and language is the basis of that relationship.

Changing the Language of Schools

Educational stakeholders should be aware of the differences between language and its unconscious influence on practice. These forces oftentimes occur in subtle and discrete ways. How do students make meaning through language? How does language shape their actions? For example, groups of friends meet in the hallway between classes because they find it free of adult monitoring. The language they use with each in this situation will be different from the language they use when called to the principal's office. They may feel uncomfortable when called to the office so the language will differ. Yet, they may not be able to articulate differences between their perceptions, feelings of safety or anxiety, and the influence of that place, the hallway, the principal's office, have on their experiences. But how does language shape their behavior in such unconscious ways? Alternately, how does behavior shape use of language?

Empowerment and Language

Schools should be cognizant of the relationship between language and a student's success in life and school by promoting structures and methods to help those students who show signs of difficulties with language empowerment, and do so early in their academic careers. Without this help, students will continue to fall behind and lose all interest in formal education by early middle school. The high school drop-out rate in the United States will continue to be unacceptable, as it has been for several decades, because most drop-outs have no feeling of belonging, are not empowered through language and learning, and certainly are not encouraged to be empowered in any way. The fact that those who first speak a language other than English have the highest drop-out rate should be a bell-weather indicator for any who choose to acknowledge the challenge. According to the U.S. Department of Education, in a 2009 study of drop-out rates over time, the following findings were given:

Black and Hispanic students had higher event dropout rates than White students in 2009. The event dropout rate was 4.8 percent for Blacks and 5.8 percent for Hispanics, compared to 2.4 percent for Whites. The general downward trend in event dropout rates over the nearly four-decade period from 1972 through 2009 observed in the overall population was also found among Whites, Blacks, and Hispanics. However, the decreases happened at different times over this 37-year period for these racial/ethnic groups. The pattern found among Whites mirrored that in the overall population: a decrease in event rates from 1972 through 1990, an increase from 1990 through 1995, and another decrease from 1995 through 2009. Blacks also experienced a decline from 1972 through 1990 and an increase from 1990 through 1995, but their event dropout rates fluctuated and no measurable trend was found between 1995 and 2009. Hispanics, on the other hand, experienced no measurable change in their event dropout rates from 1972 through 1990 and no measurable change from 1990 through 1995, but did experience a decline from 1995 through 2009.

In stating the obvious, children who first speak languages other than standard English find it difficult to "become" in environments foreign to their language-based conceptualization of the world. It is the responsibility of the school to accept these differences in conceptualization and build bridges for those who are working through the disequilibrium of two or more competing world concepts.

In *Ain't' No Makin' It*, MacLeod (1987) highlighted the struggles and inequalities faced by inner city youth through the conversations and observations of the Hallway Hangers and Brothers of Clarendon Heights. The Hangers were mostly White, and the Brothers were Black, but both groups were from the same low-income neighborhood and attended the same high school. Conclusions drawn by MacLeod assert that structural inequality creates poverty, and that society is structured to create poverty and inequality, which is mirrored in schools. The work of MacLeod suggests the constructs developed with language influenced the end result.

Symbolic Violence and the Curriculum

Eisner's *Educational Imagination (2002)*, challenges traditional discourses surrounding curriculum. He views curriculum from a post-structuralist viewpoint, which means that the development and implementation of curriculum is influenced by the social, cultural, and political environment at any certain time. This historical bent to curriculum is manifested in the discourses of education, thus influencing the education of society's youth, which in turn, reflects the social structures. Educational institutions have the power and responsibility, through language, to change social structures that currently omit marginalized groups, engage in hegemonic practices, and perpetuate social inequities. Schools are responsible for engendering social and cultural behavior as well as values in young students. Who decides what is important within schooling? Whose values, beliefs and language are emphasized? How are these things decided? Understanding the effect of society and its dominant language on the discourse in curriculum and the ensuing effects on the individual challenges traditional approaches to curriculum.

Curriculum and society

The explicit curriculum and language in schools advertises what schools offer. These are public goals that encompass teaching children to read, write, to figure, and to learn content area material. This curriculum reflects the values that seem important to mainstream America and have not changed much over time. Implicit curriculum is that which is taught but not advertised by the school. It is the culture of the school and classroom and these can be most fully revealed in the language and its use. It socializes children to the values that are part of the structure of the place.

Behavioral objectives are another form of discourse that reflects society's influence. These objectives are based on student behavior, the behavior and content identified, and a specific criterion. Once again, the roots of these objectives reflect a historical influence. This discourse began in industry and the military where characteristics of performance are known in advance and there is a match between objectives and behavior. The assumption is that goals must be specific because it is a rational way to approach curriculum. The process of curriculum planning transforms ideas and puts into place that which is valued in society and thus shapes the schooling, influencing each child's development of reality.

Particular functions of evaluation emphasize the impact of society on schooling. Identifying educational needs and what counts in education is a function of evaluation. What matters is evaluated and reflected in the language used in evaluation and is based on one's philosophy and point of view. Ultimately, data are sought through evaluation that basically backs up one's point of view. That view and the associated language establish the purpose of education. If the goal is to empower, then the language and evaluations would reflect that; if the goal is to ensure norms, continued traditions, and affirm existing world views, then the evaluation and language will reflect this stance. Social, cultural, and political characteristics and beliefs often shape the educational goals, school culture and curriculum.

Curriculum and the individual

Many voices are silenced in school. The identity of one as being educated trumps the subjectivity one wrestles with as the recipient of this education. Eisner (2002) contends that schooling largely negates the needs of the individuals over the needs of a hegemonic society. The null curriculum is a good example. The null curriculum is the things that the schools do NOT teach such as law, anthropology, the arts, communication or economics to name a few. It is "…the options that students are not afforded, the perspectives they may never know about, much less able to use, the concepts and skills that are not part of their intellectual repertoire" (Eisner, p. 107).

Although Eisner thoroughly examines the many aspects of curriculum, he provides progressive approaches to curriculum, thus deconstructing traditional ideas about curriculum. This progressive approach results in a curriculum influenced by and touching the individual. Because identity is static, decisions concerning schooling are made within a historical context. Because Eisner views curriculum from a post-structuralist viewpoint, his possibilities consider the influence of social, cultural, and political influences that are housed in language. These influence the development and implementation of curriculum. The purpose of curriculum is to meet the needs of society, however, Eisner would have students be able to move effortlessly between society and school, recognizing the individual as well. This would emphasize the subjectivity of being, and would include the individualism and voice of all that participate in schooling. This may well result in educational institutions changing existing social structures to be equitable places of learning and where all voices are heard.

Voice: Listening to marginalized populations

Certain voices and words are heard and other voices are ignored. The meaning is gained from interaction and is constructed once it is received by another, thus becoming language. So, even though words of marginalized groups may be voiced, dominant groups within society may not really "hear" their voices. "Who" the voice emanates from affects the recipients' openness to really listening based on one's understanding of reality and position in the social, political, and economic arena.

It seems that in schools individual voices are not heard and those whose language might change a perception of reality are often left out. This is especially true for individuals with different abilities. Erevelles (2002) states that a surplus population exists which includes disabled people, permanently infirm, the aged, the illiterate, and the racialized underclass. This surplus population exists on the margins of society and their voices have little impact on the way they are able to live their lives within the social, political, and economic atmosphere of a capitalist society. Others speak for them and about them, but not with them. Bilken (2000) makes a similar argument that discussions about disability and inclusion do not reflect disability voices. Students with learning disabilities are treated as units of analysis. The voices that are heard concerning their lives are medical and legislative discourses (Reid & Valle, 2004). The emphasis here is that disabled voices are marginalized in society; and while serious, there are other voices and languages not heard in the system of schooling. Hearing all the voices is the key and this requires opening doors, listening to those not always heard, and changing the languages that has limited options and narrowed the shaping of one's reality.

Opportunities for All

This chapter explored the relationship between language and the conceptualization of the world through a phenomenological perspective. Language influences one's reality, which is socially constructed through experience and interactions with others. The student experience of school, very much informed by the language used, is a critical place. It can shape reality and construct a process of cognition, emotion, and embodiment that is related to the language used by educative stakeholders. School is where each individual's shaped reality is lived on a daily basis. But the doom of a narrow and limited reality is not absolute as educators have the capacity to transform each student's life through intentional use of language and well developed opportunities and choices. The reality of each student is formed initially through home and community; however, school plays an increasingly vital role in the evolution of one's formation of self, dispositions, agency, and aspirations. Educational institutions should change the language of schooling to encourage all parts of the system to establish aspirations for the future, to avoid symbolic violence through the curriculum, and to listen to all voices, including the marginalized voices of the communities.

Language in schools had been subsumed by the emphasis on such issues as curriculum, school reform, or accountability. Adding the importance of the language used by each school in daily practice can better inform the decision-making in the educational institutions. Educational stakeholders can benefit from a general understanding of student's conceptions and use of language in shaping a reality and understanding their experiences in school. Applying this understanding to the school experience can promote action to create schools as positive learning environments.

How might schools achieve the status of a place where all can bring their world view and learn about others while learning about their own? Only through empowered language of teachers and administrators may a school become a place of acceptance and growth. The empowerment of students seems foreign to current public school administration practices. Students are not allowed any power to determine their growth and learning; all is predetermined for them by immobile structures and policies. Empowering students through language may be a channel through which real growth and movement forward is possible. It may contain the hope that all children can learn. And if they develop a noble sense of reality shaped by the language around them; perhaps, steps will be taken to seriously enable all to reach the highest potentials.

> She walked into a classroom
> Heard an unbelievable dream
> And danced into her future.

4

Literacy Education:

The Antidote to Oppression

Maureen Fitzgerald-Riker

Literacy is a powerful catalyst that sustains personal, economic, and political change. This is one reason why global advocacy agencies such as UNESCO carefully monitor literacy rates of societies throughout the world. But how literacy is defined and measured is not a uniform process. In Niger and Panama, literacy rates are self-reported through household surveys in response to the question, "Can you read and write?"(UNESCO, 2013). In the United States, literacy is defined and monitored by age through annual standardized tests which are designed to evaluate specific reading components such as comprehension, writing, and vocabulary. Before we can proceed to the analysis of how literacy empowers us – the focus of this chapter – we must first create a working definition of literacy. Once we forge this definition, we can then discuss personal empowerment, social empowerment, and global empowerment in the ensuing sections. Each of these sections concludes with relevant classroom practices, followed by a summary of the various levels of literacy empowerment, and the future directions for literacy education.

What is Literacy and When Does Empowerment through Literacy Emerge?

Literacy extends well beyond deciphering letters into sounds, sounds into words, and words into sentences. It is a vehicle for accessing and sharing complex thoughts. Literacy, meaning reading, writing, and the ability to discuss complex concepts, expands our perception of ourselves, others, and the world. It is by no means a passive process but rather a dynamic social practice which helps us to reflect on and make sense of our world. We question and evaluate our world as we interact within diverse communities on a local and global level to initiate change.

Literacy development begins at birth. Almost immediately newborns realize crying elicits attention from caretakers. By their first birthday, babies associate specific sounds such as "mom" and "bottle" with specific people, responses, or objects. Infants realize they can affect their world through sound, and that specific sounds, such as "cooing" prompt an affectionate smile, while crying, is effective for immediately getting needs met. This awareness and association of meaning with sound is the very start of language acquisition (Byrnes & Wasik, 2009). It is a universal process independent of what language is assimilated. Correspondingly, deaf infants acquire sign language by mapping meaning onto gestures and developing syntactical, morphological, and phonological structure during preschool years (Goldin-Meadow, 1999; Gutierrez, Williams, Grosvald, & Corina, 2012; Thompson, Vinson, Woll, & Gabriella, 2013).

Literacy development is based on language acquisition. Children first develop familiarity with the sounds, inflections, and words of their native language within a socially interactive environment before they associate sounds with letters and letters with words. Young children need to listen to mature sentence structures in order to arrange words within sentences and comprehend written text. The more caretakers read to and speak with pre-school children impacts how quickly they acquire literacy. Children raised in language rich environments acquire substantially more vocabulary at a quicker rate than children with minimal language exposure. This advantage has a sustained impact on literacy development. Reading and conversing with pre-kindergarten children over a sustained time period impacts how quickly they acquire literacy. Once literacy is acquired, vocabulary and conceptual understanding expands beyond the immediate environment. Literacy empowerment begins before children attend school with the acquisition and development of language.

Personal Empowerment through Literacy Confidence and Efficacy

Children raised in language rich environments are more likely to come from middle and upper class families (Hart & Risley, 1995). This immediate advantage creates status within educational environments based on class. Students who have been read to and conversed with extensively during their preschool years acquire vocabulary more quickly and can read independently at an earlier age. Students who read well are more academically successful; this allows them to spend more time engaged in reading which has a significant impact on furthering reading proficiency (Allington, 2013). Vocabulary knowledge directly and positively affects reading comprehension and it is an indicator of overall academic success (Hirsch, 2003; NICHD, 2006). Proficient readers learn up to five times more words than struggling readers (Kuhn & Stahl, 1998). Their ability to read grows exponentially. Studies have demonstrated that on average, high achieving third graders often have the same degree of vocabulary knowledge as low achieving high school seniors (Beck, McKeown, & Kucan, 2013; Smith, 1941). Continual growth in vocabulary and comprehension empowers proficient readers with a sense of efficacy.

Conversely, struggling readers are conscious of their lower status in the classroom. These students formulate an inferior self-image which is often reinforced by participation in remedial reading interventions and limited academic success. Competing school initiatives can contribute to the lethargic growth of struggling readers by using independent reading time for remedial interventions that address isolated reading skills (Allington, 2013). Consequently, struggling readers continue to fall behind their peers in spite of the intervention services provided. The ongoing remediation reinforces the assumption that the difficulty in learning to read lies solely within the student rather than the educational system. It also erodes self-esteem. The dropout rate for struggling readers is substantially higher than for students who are academically successful (Hoff, 2012). Struggling readers lack self-esteem and a sense of efficacy due to the ongoing failure to reach proficiency in reading.

Access to Complex Concepts and Critical Thinking

How well students read impacts their access to complex text and the opportunity to think critically. This is not to say that students who fall behind in reading are not capable of complex thought but rather, they have less opportunity to wrestle independently with comprehension of complex, multifaceted concepts. They spend more time learning to read rather than reading to learn. Listening to complex sentence structure prior to attending school positively impacts students' abilities to analyze complex text. When struggling readers or non-readers are presented with complex topics, they're engrossed in decoding and deciphering text rather than analyzing text meaning and implications (Byrnes & Wasik, 2009). This lack of reading fluency creates a dependency on the adequacy and availability of auditory conceptual explanations of teachers and peers. Perceptions expand by clarifying, analyzing, and questioning concepts. Non-readers depend on shared discussion in order to expand topics. This contextual support for struggling readers is not always available or timely. Additionally, the public nature of analyzing complex topics through questions and discussion is risky for non-readers because it exposes their illiteracy.

Literacy as a Shared Reflection

Literacy is a reflection of human values and shared experience. Social values are introduced and reinforced through the books and stories children read. The folktale of *The Boy Who Cried Wolf*, reminds us of the importance of being truthful. *Number the Stars* warns us of the horrific consequences of intolerance and genocide. History books inspire and remind us that like our ancestors, we are capable of leadership, efficacy, and innovation.

Many students see themselves reflected in the books read in classrooms and are empowered. Many do not. Children of color have only recently seen themselves reflected in trade books read in school. History books provide limited accounts of the rich history of African Americans, Latinos, Native Americans, and women. These accounts are narrow and therefore inherently viewed as narratives of exceptional individuals. For example, black history is a celebration that focuses on the accomplishments of Dr. Martin Luther King Jr.; but what is omitted from the African American struggle for equality is the story of how effective the African community was in successfully implementing organized and unified marches. Likewise, history textbooks ignore the astounding risks African slaves went through to learn to read in midnight schools. By the time the civil war came to an end, former slaves insisted on building and running black schools in the post-war south. It was because of these schools that the illiteracy rate of African Americans dropped from 95 percent in 1860 to 70 percent in 1880; by 1910, this rate declined further to 30 percent (Anderson, 1988). These ignored accounts of African American history attest to the value placed on education by former slaves and are personally empowering when included in the curriculum. Who is empowered in the classroom depends on what is taught as well as what is not taught. The absence of historic accounts, folktales, and trade books reflecting non-traditional students creates an empowered dominant culture that becomes normative as well as a standard for comparison. Unlike the dominant culture represented in elementary school curriculum, students from non-dominant cultures can be disempowered by the limited number of trade books, historic accounts, and folktales they see themselves reflected in. Is their culture, race, or gender not as prolific as other cultures? Less capable? This curricular imbalance also undermines the ability of *all* students to appreciate and value diversity.

Implications within the Classroom
　　Teaching is a political act. What is taught and how it is taught can empower all students or reinforce a dominant group standard. An inclusive curriculum that intentionally incorporates non-traditional, historic, community values and accomplishments rather than exceptionalities is empowering to non-dominant races, ethnicities and genders, and encourages cultural respect from all students. This entails thoughtful consideration of whose history is taught and what books are read. Teachers who research and intentionally choose historic narratives empower all students and encourage cultural respect.
　　Additionally, struggling readers need time to read books at their appropriate reading level in order to develop vocabulary, fluency, and comprehension skills essential for understanding and

critical analysis of complex concepts. This reading time must be considered sacred and essential for success. Progress is motivating and foundational to a sense of efficacy. This is not to say that targeted interventions should be abandoned. Rather, they should be implemented without diminishing independent reading time.

Closing the gap in vocabulary between students from diverse socio-economic statuses cannot be achieved solely through direct instruction. However, creating a word rich environment within the classroom encourages children to become wordsmiths who celebrate and ponder word meanings and have the tools to independently acquire a rich vocabulary. A classroom that is a word rich environment creates a word consciousness; it is a place where words are analyzed and celebrated and opportunities abound for students to try out new vocabulary in a safe and edifying environment. Students are taught Greek and Latin roots of words and read-alouds celebrate unusual, exceptional, and unfamiliar phrases and word choice. Classroom walls are plastered with these words. Students become word sleuths and share discoveries with classmates in reading groups as well as throughout the day. The daily time allotted for literacy always includes word exploration. Vocabulary is continually growing, not through memorization, rather through student initiated discovery.

Social Empowerment through Literacy

Participation in Community and Political Decision-making

The relationship of literacy to political decision-making goes beyond the ability to read ballots and initiatives. Through the analysis of opposing arguments and complex issues we participate in community decision-making at a local and national level. Articulated discussion allows us to evaluate multifaceted issues, voice our opinion, and influence others verbally. The inability to access and consequently analyze multifarious text and arguments presented online, in newspapers, and in journals divorces the struggling reader from the public decision-making process. There is limited passion in proposing and resolving issues that we have difficulty discerning and discussing with others. Informed dialog as a form of literacy empowers students to participate in community and political decision making.

Poverty and Education

Literacy also plays a critical role in alleviating poverty. Generally, the completion of formal education beyond high school prepares students for gainful employment. Dropping out of high school limits employment options to jobs that barely pay sustenance wages. Inappropriately, the greatest drop-out rate in the U.S. is among minority students from families with low socio-economic status (United States Department of Education, 2011). Additionally, students who drop-out of high school are academically unsuccessful particularly in English and mathematics (United States Department of Education, 2011). School success is dependent on the ability to read well and as students' progress through the grades, the focus on learning to read shifts to reading to learn. Failure to learn to read well takes a toll on students in the upper grades because so much of schoolwork, from science textbooks to literature assignments, is tied to literacy proficiency. Struggling readers fall further behind their peers and require greater support to succeed in high school.

Struggling readers are also confronted with a universal ideological belief that through education, particularly literacy, you can overcome poverty if you are bright and work hard enough. This belief implies that those living in poverty are intellectually limited and/or unmotivated (Freire, 2000). Rather than evaluate the effectiveness of educational policy, culpability is placed on contrived inadequacies of students. Curriculum is often "dummied down" and expectations lowered for these students when the perception is they do not have the intellectual capacity or motivation to succeed. This has a disempowering effect on struggling readers, particularly those from lower socio-economic backgrounds. Conversely, this fallacy attributes academic success to confirmed intelligence and a positive work ethic. However, this ideology conflicts with research on academically successful students who are primarily from middle and upper class families. They generally come to school with more sophisticated vocabularies and extensive experience with books. Through conversations with siblings and adults, these students were exposed to complex text structures and given opportunities to develop productive vocabulary. This advantage, which is prevalent in students with higher socio-economic status, impacts how well students read as early as first grade (Hart & Risley, 1995).

Early success in literacy is an empowering and decisive factor in academic success.

Leadership Skills

The purpose of education is the theme of ongoing debates. Likewise, access to education is historically granted, denied, and justified by popular beliefs about the purpose of education. Our history is riddled with examples of the varying educational objectives that disempowered and empowered targeted segments of the population. The following lists a few of these examples:

Instruction was legally denied to African Americans because slave owners recognized that it is harder to repress a literate society and educating slaves would negatively impact the existing economic structure (Anderson, 1988).

Before women received the right to vote, they were denied access to universities; their education was limited to normal schools where they prepared for what was considered socially appropriate employment as teachers (McClelland, 1992).

Schools became centers for social welfare by offering adult education classes in English and civics as well as kindergartens to care for preschool children during the industrial revolution when it was deemed necessary to *Americanize* the large influx of immigrants from Europe who brought with them diverse cultural practices (Spring, 2011).

Boarding schools were employed to acculturate Native Americans. Students were removed from reservations, forced to cut their hair and forbidden to use their native language while placed in Indian boarding schools where they were isolated from their families (Adams, 1995; Spring, 2011).

During the Cold War era, science and math education were funded and augmented to ensure that the U.S. remained competitive in the developing space program (Spring, 2011).

Currently national educational focus is on science, technology, engineering, and math (STEM) expertise as the U.S. economy expands its leadership in computer and software technology. Large amounts of funding are granted to universities through the National Science Foundation for projects that focus on improving STEM education and recruiting students into STEM fields. As students are recruited into high tech jobs, they are certainly empowered economically. However, there are unseen costs to these focused STEM programs where developing expertise takes place within context-independent domains. There is also limited exposure to liberal arts and social sciences within these programs. This confined educational focus ignores the interconnected and complementary nature of knowledge essential for developing the skills needed to work in a global and culturally diverse world. In opposition to the national focus on science and technology, education is the current cry for humanistic education which prepares students to reflect and discuss multifaceted issues, participate in local and global decision making, and creatively interact and transform their world. Humanistic education is grounded in a liberal arts curriculum that empowers future generations through the development of critical analysis, cultural competency, communication proficiency, and leadership skills.

Hidden Curriculum

What is influential but not transparent in schools is a persistent, hidden curriculum based on class as well as ideological beliefs about the purpose of education. Schools may teach to national standards and core requirements but teaching pedagogy differs from school to school. Past research uncovered diverse teaching methodology that is tied to the prevailing social class of the school's population (Anyon, 1980; Ladson-Billings, 2009). For example, students in elite, upper class schools are given greater autonomy in selecting and self-directing their assignments. Their work is project based and mimics tasks performed by executive directors of corporations.

Teaching methodology in schools with populations from a lower socio-economic class includes more prescriptive assignments that incorporate less analysis and decision-making. Are students from lower socio-economic neighborhood schools expected to perform more regulated work that is less lucrative, less creative and void of the need for critical analysis? Although most schools are a composite of teaching methodologies, there is a definitive difference between low income, public, urban schools and private, elite elementary schools. The latter focus on critical analysis, autonomy, and self-direction. These are essential leadership skills that can empower students to initiate change.

Implications within the Classroom

All students can acquire the leadership and communication skills afforded through literacy instruction within the classroom. Teachers who are aware of competing pedagogies purposely structure inquiry projects that allow students to self-direct their work regardless of class. These teachers are grounded in their own educational ideology and articulated purpose of education and create opportunities such as literature circles, for critical analysis and autonomous discussion while presenting diverse perspectives through a variety of thoughtfully selected books. They consciously develop leadership skills including critical analysis, autonomy, and self-direction as an integral part of the curriculum. However, this form of inquiry learning is only successful when students are taught rules for respectful discourse beforehand (Cohen, 1994). These include facilitating dialogs by inviting participants to share diverse perspectives and effectively addressing peers who dominate discussions. These are lifelong skills which will empower students beyond the elementary school years.

Integrating themes across the curriculum emphasizes the interconnected and complementary nature of knowledge across disciplines. An example of integrating disciplines would be to discuss economic and social implications of illegal immigration in current events while comparing and contrasting components of cultural, political and geographical regions. Likewise, reading, critically analyzing, and discussing historic fiction such as *Esperanza Rising*, (a novel about Mexican-American immigration in 1920s) in light of the current impact of immigration reform provides significant depth to an ongoing social and political concern. Integrating themes across disciplines empowers students by adding relevance to curriculum; it prepares students to think critically as well as lead and act in a global and culturally diverse environment.

Equally as important to student empowerment as integrating themes across disciplines is recognition of the Algeresque fallacy that poverty can be overcome solely with hard work and intelligence. This sweeping generalization ignores the complexity of factors contributing to poverty and implies that poverty is the result of limited intellectual ability and/or indolence. Teachers and administrators, who unconsciously subscribe to this misconception, often hold students with low socio-economic status to a lesser academic standard than students from middle and upper class families (Ladson-Billings, 2009). Families of students living in poverty are assumed to be apathetic to the student's academic success (Delpit, 2006); an alternative perspective is that the classroom may be an intimidating or even hostile environment for many families. Furthermore, restricted parental involvement is a norm in some cultures that mandate leaving school matters solely in the hands of professional teachers. Empowering students living in poverty includes maintaining high standards for learning and implementing effective interventions when needed, which develop literacy skills critical for continued academic success. Reflective teachers recognize the damage that misconceptions wield. They know the importance of reaching out to families through phone calls and emails to provide substantive ways for families to support academic success as well as celebrate student achievements.

Global Empowerment

Literacy is recognized internationally as a basic human right (UNESCO, 2006). It is requisite in order to address global human welfare and sustainability. Social and electronic media, international travel, and trade have brought worldwide poverty, hunger, conflict, and environmental sustainability to the forefront of our awareness. These concerns are interdependent and transcend national borders and policies. Through literacy education global citizens develop the capacity to reflect and work collaboratively on these social and economic concerns that impact the world at large. Education precedes rather than follows political and economic change. Critical thinking, cultural competency, communication skills, the ability to creatively apply knowledge to goals, and to evaluate the global impact of policies are indispensable for collectively confronting common issues and transforming the world into a more just habitat.

The expertise of technologically advanced nations or a well-funded initiative does too little to transform the world into a place where conflict is peacefully resolved, environmental degradation is halted, and poverty is eradicated. Transformation requires empowered citizens capable of analyzing historical causes of their anemic economies, deteriorated infrastructures, widespread poverty and disease. Sustainable change cannot be imposed but rather initiated by those impacted by these social and economic issues. These issues must be addressed creatively and collaboratively while the global long-term impact of solutions is assessed. Literacy education is the foundation of this empowerment.

Implications in the Classroom

Currently, content standards do not integrate global literacy across subjects nor is it systematically incorporated into a single discipline. This is unfortunate since all students benefit when given opportunities to critically analyze the interdependence of nations from a socio-economic, environmental, and political perspective. Awareness of diverse distributions of resources and opportunities among nations provides depth to social studies analysis particularly when examining the causes and resolution of historic conflicts and immigration among nations as well as current events. Global literacy must be integrated within content standards and assessed or competing curricular goals will undermine this opportunity.

Additionally, cooperative inquiry learning within the classroom is integral to developing global literacy and emphasizes the importance of considering various perspectives. It encourages students to develop lifelong skills essential for collaborating across cultures.

Genuine application of global literacy skills can be implemented through service learning projects that focus on empowering global citizens rather than donating finite resources. Organizations such as Heifer International provide opportunities for students to fund and give livestock to families in less affluent regions of the world. Along with the donated livestock, the organization provides education and resources on the care and breeding of the animal thus encouraging financial independence. Habitat for Humanity is another organization that brings global citizens from diverse regions of the world together in solidarity by working side by side on common goals.

Conclusion

Literacy is a powerful catalyst of change that empowers citizens living in the U.S. as well as citizens living under oppressive political and socio-economic conditions. It is foundational to critical analysis, autonomy, collaborative cross-cultural discussion and interaction. Language acquisition and development play a significant role in literacy development. Students who are raised in a language rich environment are positioned and personally empowered to successfully develop the literacy skills needed to critically analyze and articulate complex concepts. Literacy develops leadership skills and empowers us socially to participate in local and national decision-making. Finally, literacy empowers us globally by developing the capacity to work collaboratively on social and economic issues that transcend cultures as well as national borders and policies.

This places tremendous responsibility on teachers who must ensure children continue to develop as proficient readers, writers, and speakers. Classrooms must be word rich environments that offer multiple opportunities to access complex text and exercise critical thinking skills. Teachers can choose to empower students by purposely structuring inquiry projects which encourage learners to work collaboratively, scrutinize and respect various perspectives, and self-direct their work. Standards are held high for *all* students and books are thoughtfully chosen to reflect a variety of cultures as opposed to one dominant culture.

Additionally, global literacy must be integrated within curriculum standards and assessed. This includes developing awareness of socio-economical, environmental, and political interdependence of nations in order to understanding the impact of diverse resource distributions and conflicts. The integration of service learning within curriculum standards provides the opportunity to authentically apply and assess literacy skills used to impact the global environment through collaborative, negotiated projects with well-defined objectives. Literacy extends well beyond deciphering letters into sounds, sounds into words, and words into sentences. It is the impetus for personal, social, and global empowerment.

5

Humanistic Education:

How Teachers Empower Students to Collaborate in Their Own Learning Process

John Scileppi

There are many images of education in contemporary society. Many adults look back on the schooling they and their friends experienced and recall examples of physical, verbal and emotional abuse committed by teachers who tried to force them to conform to social norms and taboos. Current students wonder whether schooling has any relevance to their lives. While they are less likely to experience physical abuse from teachers, they are still fearful of being bullied or ostracized because of their perceived sexual orientation, body shape or ethnic or religious backgrounds. These youth are disappointed that educators did not intervene to create an environment in which they and their classmates felt safe and secure. With perceptions similar to the above, it is no wonder schools often fail to meet their objective of facilitating student learning. The above beliefs about school also can explain high drop-out rates and absenteeism. Taxpayers who support public education are not getting their money's worth, and the philosophy of the school system could be at fault. Of course others have very different perceptions of schooling. Some adults have fond memories of a kindly teacher who showed compassion when they encountered some personal tragedy or obstacle. Perhaps they recall a teacher who believed in their potential and encouraged them to do their personal best. Or perhaps a teacher invited students to make choices relevant to their career goals about what they were to learn. Current young people might express satisfaction when an educator showed the connection between what is being learned and "real life", and a teacher who developed a classroom management style that emphasizes cooperation and respect for others in the classroom that generalized beyond the school and influenced peer group interactions for the better.

Humanistic education is consistent with the more favorable view of learning in schools. Humanistic education can enhance the empowerment of students and of communities. In this chapter, the two views of socialization are presented. As each view generates a different model of the ideal school, humanistic education is seen as developing out of the positive view of socialization. Then the various aspects that comprise humanistic education are described and how John Dewey's progressive education influenced the development of this philosophy. The chapter ends with descriptions of how this approach can be applied at the primary, secondary and higher levels of education.

Humanistic Education and Two Views of Socialization

Before describing what humanistic education entails and its many attributes, it is worthwhile to first address the above attitudes toward schooling and conceptualize the context in which they developed. Zigler and Child (1969) identified two views of socialization focusing on how children participate in the socialization process. As education is among the most important agents a community utilizes to socialize youth, the view of socialization adopted by a society affects the goals, objectives and activities within the schools (Dunn, Scileppi, Averna, Zerillo and Skelding, 2007). Zigler and Child differentiated the two views as positive and negative. These views refer to the perceived degree to which the child either helps or hinders the socialization process. That is, does the child behave in an active way to foster socialization or does the child resist attempts to become a law-abiding and productive member of society. Proponents of the negative view hold that human nature is essentially evil and the person is motivated by purely selfish concerns. The only innate drive is hedonism – and possibly aggression – and adults must break the children's spirit in order to curb their natural instincts. Those in authority must show the child is powerless and that to gain any success in life, the youth must conform unquestionably to the rules and norms of the adults. While this might be an extremely polarized description of this view of socialization, one can see elements of it in the writings of Freud, Calvin, and even Golding's (1978) *Lord of the Flies*. In Golding's novel, a group of preteen boys marooned on an island after a plane crash fight among themselves and develop into selfish, aggressive and 'savage' subhumans. The positive view of socialization, on the other hand, is that the basic nature of children is good, and they are essentially sympathetic and motivated by social interest. Their compassion for others is at least as strong as the desire for selfish gain, and children are active agents in their own socialization. They want to self-actualize within the context of society and find and achieve their existential life goals. This positive view is supported by Rousseau, Rogers, Adler and Dewey. While it is likely that many teachers develop a philosophy of education incorporating elements of both views of socialization, describing the two positions can lead to new strategies to help children learn in schools.

Each view of socialization affects the process of schooling. The negative view results in schools in which students must comply with many regulations. Philip Jackson (1968) for example described classrooms in the typical public school as requiring 25 or so students to sit in specific seats for long periods of time. They are not allowed to talk to each other except under very limited conditions. They are expected to comply with every rule the teacher establishes. Note that few adults work under these repressive conditions. Government legislation and union regulations would prohibit employers from imposing such oppressive conditions. This classroom environment is not a good preparation for life as responsible, decision-making adult citizens in a democratic society. While Jackson's description of this type of school was written nearly fifty years ago, there are many examples of similar classrooms today. The positive view of socialization encourages schools to respect the individual dignity and uniqueness of each student. Educators serve as guides and facilitators rather than law enforcers. Learning environments are set up – as much as possible – to enable students to learn content of their own choosing in ways that meet their diverse student learning styles. Open classrooms with various "learning stations" set up in different locations throughout the room enable learning to take place in a more individualized and less regimented fashion. Schooling is seen as a preparation for the responsibilities of living in a democracy, and freedom and responsibility are built into the learning curriculum. In short, through the positive approach to socialization, the student is empowered to learn, and is viewed as being motivated to contribute productively in one's community. Humanistic education was developed out of this positive or active socialization perspective.

Humanistic education is an approach to the teaching-learning process that fosters self-respect and a sense of achievement in students at all levels of schooling. It is based largely on the theories of humanistic psychologists such as Abraham Maslow and Carl Rogers and it attempts to counter the passivity and alienation of students. Humanistic education emphasizes the uniqueness and dignity of each learner. Proponents of a humanistic approach to learning believe the student is an active agent in the socialization process; that is the child wants to be a productive member of the community. Educators do not need to force the child to learn, the student is an eager participant in the process (Scileppi, 1988).

According to Rowan (nd), there are five themes in contemporary humanistic education. These include a) educational systems should enable students to choose the content and goals of their education, b) educators and the curriculum should respond to the felt and expressed concerns of the students, c) schools should address the whole student, attending to feelings, choices, behaviors and communication, d) evaluation in the classroom should emphasize self-assessment in which students reflect on their own learning process and seek out feedback and data on their goal attainment, and e) the teacher should be more a facilitator of learning, encouraging and supporting growth rather than serving merely as a source of knowledge. Each of these themes is elaborated upon below in order to understand more fully what humanistic education involves.

Students should be in control of the content of their learning. They should be able to choose –within limits – which subjects they wish to learn and when they will learn them. This could take different forms. For example, a school system might appropriately require students to learn to read. One student may be interested in how to raise rabbits, and another in finding out more about the lost continent of Atlantis. Humanistic educators should attempt to find relevant and age-appropriate materials on either topic. The children learn how to read by researching a content of interest to them. An alternative but still humanistic approach would be to start with the child's interest, and then design the entire curriculum for this student around this interest. Thus a student interested in how a motorcycle engine works can learn reading, mathematics, physics – and if the educator is especially creative – social studies, economics, public speaking, writing, engineering and other disciplines. Students can use their own interests as motivation to learn, and they will experience a sense of empowerment or control over their own lives.

Similar to the above, educators should respond to the perceived needs of the students. Students are much more motivated to learn if they perceive a connection between problems and concerns they experience and what is to be learned. The first activity of teachers should involve good, active listening when interacting with students. They should encourage students to express their hopes, goals, aspirations and dreams. After clarifying these intentions, humanistic educators should design the curriculum around these goals. Teachers should show the connection between students attaining these objectives and reading, writing and arithmetic. Students may become aware of problems existing in their communities. They might learn from electronic or print media or from overhearing parents and other adults talking about environmental resources being wasted, and that we will be in great need of clean water or air or saving trees. They may discover that unemployment is hurting the families of classmates or that crime is endangering their safety. The children might take these concerns into the classroom, and develop teams of cooperative learning groups to read what can be done about these natural and social problems. Through this approach, the student is motivated by felt needs to learn and is making the connection that schools are places where real life issues are discussed. The students will be encouraged to seek out solutions and implement those that are within their power. Creating or participating in recycling programs, writing letters to legislators, volunteering in community-based programs are only a few possible activities groups of students can do at almost any level. This reinforces the idea that schools are great places to be since such important topics are addressed. Notice how a creative educator can teach many disciplines – and show how the different disciplines have real-life applications. The issues discussed can also relate to the local baseball or football team, the desire to attract a movie theater or more recreational facilities to come into the community... or whatever is the felt and expressed needs of the students. Thus the curriculum becomes relevant to the everyday life of citizens living in the community (Kanna, 2010).

The third component of humanistic education is to treat each student holistically. While cognitive aspects might still take precedence in the schools, the physical, affective, social and moral spheres should also be considered. Students hopefully will grow into capable contributing members of the community. Educators should have a role in this holistic process, or else students will begin to separate the intellectual life from the rest of their existence. As educators, we don't merely teach history or mathematics; instead, we teach *students* history or mathematics or other subjects. Establishing discipline in the classroom can either be accomplished by imposing rules on students or by expressing the need for order and then asking students to participate in setting up rules for classroom conduct and the consequences that will happen when these democratically chosen rules are violated. Common moral principles such as the "golden rule", respect for one another, altruism and cooperation, personal responsibility for choices and completing work on time, all aspects of character education are as important as learning appropriate grammar and computing. Similarly, good health is a topic that can be addressed. Schools are places where nearly all youth of a given age in a community attend on a regular basis and helping to promote good health and prevent illness can have a meaningful impact on the future well-being of the entire community. Teaching the value of exercise and providing opportunities for exercise and describing what behaviors are high-risk for disease and how to avoid them are activities that most schools accommodate. Humanistic educators might also attempt to offer alternative ways to accomplish these objectives, again consistent with the interests of the students. Good nutrition can also be addressed in ways in which humanistic themes are implemented. Finally, educators should be aware of the emotional and psychological developmental crises, stages and needs of the students and creatively and cooperatively address these in the classroom. Incorporating these holistic strategies creates a setting for the student to move forward in the process of self-discovery, and with this the ability to symbolize and make meaningful what is learned.

One method of implementing this holistic approach to learning is to utilize cooperative learning groups. Students gather in small groups of three to seven students and attempt to work on a learning project or solve a problem. In the process students learn academic content and skills from one another, and they also learn to interact socially and productively. Many students are motivated to learn more fully when they do so in these cooperative groups. Emphasizing the value of holistic learning, two researchers, Sullivan and King (1999) investigated the effectiveness of using cooperative groups to help fifth graders solve personal and social problems together. These researchers found such groups facilitated student empowerment and provided support for the youth as they progressed through this transitional period.

A fourth element of humanistic education is to emphasize self-assessment in how the student's performance is evaluated. As an eventual responsible adult in the community, students need to participate in assessing their own behavior and in seeking appropriate feedback on the extent to which the goals they have agreed to undertake have been attained. Traditionally, schools have relied exclusively on the teacher and test-based assessments. Students then suspend their own ability to judge the quality of their work and over time lose this intrinsic ability. In this sense, the education process is actually teaching students not to think independently, rather to rely on the judgment of others. As a result, these individuals later on as adults must rely on others for this function, and advertisers and politicians are only too happy to fill this void. These outside opinion leaders will inform us that buying a particular product will make us good persons, and if we vote for their favored candidate we will contribute to the well-being of the community.

Schools can and should encourage students to assess their own performance. Teachers might for example help students develop "learning contracts" in which the students identify what will be learned, by what deadline and how they will demonstrate that the objective has been met. Both the student and teacher sign the contract and on the deadline (or a short period before the deadline), together discuss whether the contract has been fulfilled. The student is also encouraged to use the feedback from the prior contract in establishing the next one. If the recently completed agreement was too easy, the next one should be more challenging; if the objectives of the previous one were not met, the next contract should be less demanding. In this way the student learns to assess his or her own performance and to set appropriate and realistic objectives and goals for the future. Notice also that humanistic assessment focuses on what the student has accomplished, not what the educator has done. This process also enables students to set appropriate and attainable goals for themselves.

The final component of humanistic education according to Rowan (n.d.) is that educators should facilitate learning and not merely convey knowledge. Students with access to the Internet and other electronic and print media have an almost infinite amount of readily available information. If all teachers do is impart information, their activity is redundant and their method of conveyance of the information – perhaps by lecture – is less effective than the multi-media and electronic presentations available to the students. Instead, educators can be model learners: exciting students about the process of learning to learn and encouraging students to want to learn. While a certain amount of lecturing is probably necessary, the rest of the learning might involve activities whereby the student solves problems using the information learned, or creatively synthesizes various aspects of what is learned or even critiques the quality and accuracy of the information available. In this way, educators become motivational guides for learning rather than sources of information. Teachers should be supportive rather than critical, and understanding rather than judgmental. The teacher and students engage in cooperative interactions; the relationship should not be adversarial.

Some have criticized humanistic education on the basis that its effectiveness in enhancing student achievement has not been empirically measured. Gary (n.d.) has noted that while some programs developed out of this approach have been evaluated, humanistic education is more a philosophy of education, an approach to how teachers and students interact, rather than a set of specific techniques or interventions. As an approach, the intentions of educators are noble, but their goals are not easily defined. This becomes problematic when researchers attempt to measure specific learning outcomes of using this orientation to the teaching – learning process.

To clarify this issue regarding evaluating effectiveness, it is important to distinguish between the philosophy of humanistic education and programs that may be generated through the approach. For example, non-graded schools could be developed out of the humanistic educational principle of respecting each student as a unique individual. In a non-graded school, students are grouped according to performance level and not by their age or grade level. The students in such programs do not receive graded report cards. Instead, non-graded programs allow students to be presented with instruction appropriate to their ability and performance, and those students who learn material more swiftly can advance into a different grouping sooner than other students who might require more time to master the information. Such non-graded programs can be evaluated for effectiveness, and Gutierrez (1992) has reviewed the empirical literature that assessed student achievement in these programs. He found that in elementary schools, non-grading enhanced student achievement if this type of program allowed teachers to provide more direct instruction at the appropriate level, but the achievement results were not as clear if the non-graded component was used to construct a framework for individualized learning. Note that there may be many other interventions generated to meet the humanistic goal of respecting each child as an individual, but this goal is not measured. Instead humanistic educators with this goal produce a specific program and then the academic achievement of students participating in the program can be measured.

Before concluding this section on the activities that comprise humanistic education, it is important to point out that learning in the classroom occurs in the context of the school and community. As each element of a social system must be consistent with the rest of the system, planning to create a more humanistic atmosphere in the classroom needs to be done in conjunction with other decision-makers and stake-holders in the local school system (Scileppi, 1988).

John Dewey's Progressive Education as the Root of Humanistic Psychology

Many of the ideas and activities Rowan described as comprising humanistic education have their roots in the approach of John Dewey. The American philosopher of education and functionalist psychologist John Dewey developed his idea of progressive education in the early part of the twentieth century. He emphasized students as growing and becoming productive citizens, and that education assisted in the process of their becoming immersed in larger social spheres (Dewey, 1916). The role of education in the United States according to Dewey was to mediate between the individual student and society; it should help to form bridges between the newly arrived immigrant children and those who were native-born Americans (Bredo, 2003). As society changes, the school curriculum must also change, enhancing students' ability to adapt to the evolving culture. Processes rather than content should be emphasized, and students should be taught how to think for themselves and how to use information to solve real, contemporary problems. The curriculum should present these social issues and concerns in a manner appropriate to the students' developmental stage. The curriculum should include practical subjects that in Dewey's time included typing, home economics and civics (Asher, 2003). Schools should also strive to build character and encourage democratic values to be learned and applied (Pajares, 2003). Education should emphasize active learning. What matters is what the student – not the teacher – does. The teacher's purpose and role is to encourage the student to actively attempt to understand the problem and then to work to find an effective solution. If the teacher merely lectures to the students and they passively receive information, Dewey would contend that the school was failing the children.

In order to test and demonstrate these principles of pragmatic, progressive education, Dewey established the innovative "lab school" at the University of Chicago. Educators from across the nation came to observe these socially responsible processes in action, and schools changed from an exclusively cognitively based place for the teaching of writing, reading and arithmetic to an institution which socialized students, preparing them to become productive citizens in a democratic society. Dewey continued this experiment in education when he resigned from Chicago and assumed a parallel position at Columbia University in New York City. Schools helped to empower students to become happy, well-adjusted adults who could function well in their communities. Dewey inspired many educators and psychologists to continue the experiment in learning that he began, and gradually progressive education became more commonly known as humanistic education. What follows are some applications of this orientation to education which hopefully will assist the reader in understanding the scope and range of possibilities that can occur in schools when a humanistic approach is implemented.

Some Applications of Humanistic Education

The following discussion highlights some examples of learning programs based on a humanistic approach to education. They are presented to stimulate the imagination about what could be done to implement this perspective more fully. Some of the programs described below deal with elementary and secondary education while others target higher education. None of these programs is presented as a 'perfect' example of humanism, but it is hoped that readers might choose some aspects to implement in their own educational situations or to use the components as jumping off points in developing new programs. The specific applications presented below certainly do not exhaust the possibilities available. They are described here only because the author had "first hand" experience with each of them.

The School of the New Community of Chicago.
 I have been actively involved in the teaching–learning process for over four decades. While most of my teaching has involved the college level, I began by working cooperatively with a group of local residents, parents and educators from the border communities around the Kenwood-Hyde Park section of Chicago, adjacent

neighborhoods with very different demographic backgrounds. Some 18 community members from North Kenwood, Grand Boulevard and Kenwood-Hyde Park began to meet weekly in 1969, a time of great social and political unrest on Chicago's Southside to discuss issues and problems that adversely affected the community. Concerns differed in the three adjacent neighborhoods – the first two had high unemployment and substandard housing and health conditions while the third was a more affluent community, with ethnically diverse populations – that did not interact with each other – yet all the participants at these meetings agreed that the local public schools were in trouble. Classrooms were overcrowded, schools oversized, de facto segregation existed, drop-out rates reached 70%, and the curriculum was very rigid and did not utilize a problem-solving approach. Of the 46 neighborhood problems identified, the group decided to address the issues relevant to education. By 1971, the School of the New Community of Chicago had been founded, and the intent was to create a humanistic learning center that could serve as a model school. The goals of the new learning center were to enhance individual growth and social responsibility through addressing local problems, utilizing the diverse cultural backgrounds, ages, skills and interests of the students, staff, parents and community residents. Everyone involved would be encouraged to participate in the planning and operation of the school and the educating of the students. Learning was to focus on the students' experience and curiosity; and in the curriculum, reason and memory were to be balanced by imagination and creativity. The curriculum was intended to be open-ended without goals pre-determined by adults. Teachers were to be responsive to the students' needs and interests. Goals of student self-awareness, and growth in personal and communal pride, power, success and hope were to be fostered in a non-competitive setting. Finally, the community was to serve as a learning resource for the students (Pitman & Scileppi, 1971).

In order to accomplish these goals, the following humanistic educational methods were utilized.

Learning contracts. Students and teachers met to develop learning contracts. Students proposed issues to investigate and with the teacher decided what learning activities would help them to learn about the issue. Deadlines or at least progress markers were explicitly stated so students could evaluate their success in understanding and perhaps even solving the problem. The contracts were developed jointly by the student and teacher, and the report of how the activities specified in the contracts were completed became an important component of the student's portfolio.

Five areas of learning. Although there was no pre-determined curriculum, students were encouraged to include in their learning contracts as many of the following five learning areas as possible. These included problem solving, creative skills, social skills, communication skills such as reading, speaking, listening, and writing, and heritage or culture skills. It is relatively easy to relate these five areas to the traditional disciplines taught in most schools. Yet it is important to note that these traditional disciplines were addressed without the need to identify a 40 minute period as the time to cover reading or mathematics or some other subject.

Open classroom. To assist in addressing these areas of learning, rooms were set up with activity centers positioned at different locations within the space. The activity centers were rich learning environments with books arranged with their attractive covers displayed as in a bookstore rather than as on a library shelf. Staff-prepared exhibits and other materials were arranged to stimulate curiosity. Some locations were quiet zones for reading while elsewhere there were tables for group activities and projects. Teaching staff, called "enablers" responded to the interests of individual students and demonstrated how the resources in a specific activity center might be helpful in achieving portions of the students' learning contracts.

Humanistic ways of learning reading and creative writing. Many staff and volunteers at the New Community School utilized innovative methods to teach reading and writing that evolved out of an empowering humanistic framework. For example, one volunteer tutor met with the youngest students individually. These children had not yet learned how to read. The volunteer asked the child to tell a story which was audiotaped and then transcribed onto a sheet of paper using large block type. The volunteer then showed the typed paper to the student and identified it as the story the student previously told. The children, amazed to find their stories were "published", became highly motivated to learn to sound out the letters and read the story. The students were then encouraged to take their stories home and read them to their parents. The parents were very pleasantly surprised by how much their young children learned in such a short time, and through their praise of the students learning, the parents helped to create attitudes of self-efficacy (Bandura, 1997) and empowerment in their children. These young students became hooked on reading, and as a result, they learned an important skill that enabled them to explore many new vistas.

A staff member attended a creative writing workshop and then returned to the school to teach both other staff and the students. When students expressed an interest in writing creatively, the teacher recreated the writing workshop she attended. The teacher responded by asking the learners to visualize a picture in their imagination. One student described an athletic young man swinging a scythe cutting down the grass and brush in a field, preparing it to become farmland. Another described a young girl in a ballet costume preparing for her first performance as a dancer. The students then were asked to present their story in writing. They were asked to give all the details: colors, sounds, smells and tastes. If there were individuals in the "picture", what were they thinking and feeling, what were their hopes and fears? What happened before the picture, and what happened afterwards? The students were then asked to develop a plot and in a short time, they were preparing the framework for a short story. Notice that the story evolved completely out of the student's own imagination. The students were empowered to write about themes that interested them. They were encouraged not to feel others were judging them; the stories were their own creations, and no one knew their stories better than themselves. The students eagerly looked forward to developing more and more creative stories.

Age diversity. Students ranged from three year olds to those preparing for high school equivalency exams. While in most schools, students are divided into age groups, in New Community, they all met together. Teenagers act far more responsibly when they are 'taking care' of younger children than when they are only with their age peers. The older youth realize their role as models for the younger children, and they also wanted to serve as surrogate teachers for them. Additionally, the motivation to learn of the younger children was enhanced when they observed the 'big kids' engaged in learning activities. The same experiences that occur in large families among siblings of different ages occurred in this learning center as well. The staff understood the teaching potential present in this age-diverse student grouping and they fostered its realization.

School without walls. Community volunteers and staff identified resources available in the neighborhood and the surrounding city that could be great learning aids for students working on diverse projects. Museums, art galleries, various university institutes, businesses, civic and political organizations, houses of worship and agencies became 'classrooms' for the New Community students. Rather than teaching mechanical drawing at the school, interested students were sent to observe professionals in local businesses designing homes and offices. None of the students complained when they were told their drawings must be precise and perfect at the drafting concern though many students in traditional schools express this complaint to their teachers when mechanical drawing is taught in a regular classroom. Also relatively young students can learn through internship and apprenticeship programs. There were many fine libraries in the neighborhoods surrounding the New Community School, and frequently our students utilized some of the library facilities of the University of Chicago as they investigated the topics of interest to them. A few university professors were on our advisory board, and they helped facilitate the young students connecting with the world-class resources available through the university.

Utilize local community human resources. Neighbors who are artists or business leaders or professionals in diverse fields were invited to volunteer and discuss their work with the students. Even a single mother who was able to budget funds so as to live on food stamps presented an informative and beneficial talk to the students. Parents and other community members offered to share their skills – both professional and survival – with the students, and the youth perceived these volunteers as true community leaders. Students gained the skills that these adults shared, but perhaps more importantly, the students learned about many career paths open to them. The boundary between the school and neighborhood was an open one, and anyone who had an idea or plan as to how to enhance learning was encouraged to visit the school.

The school as a community gathering place. The school staff scheduled activities to celebrate the various cultures, or public forums to discuss relevant local issues, or opportunities for groups to air differences and resolve conflicts. Students attended these meetings and reflected on the significance of these issues in their own lives. In some cases, students sat in on meetings of tenant unions or they volunteered in food buying cooperatives or day care programs. One suggestion to increase parental participation and at the same time prepare students to run a business was to establish in the New Community School a laundromat. It was proposed that students would staff the business and parents would drop off their laundry. While the clothes were being cleaned, parents could observe what was happening in the open classrooms and perhaps volunteer to tutor or enhance learning in some way. Lack of funding and some governmental regulations prevented this suggestion from being implemented. Some criticized the concept by calling New Community the "Laundromat School". The school board and staff wanted the school to be a resource in the community and to create as symbiotic relationship between the 'town and gown'. In a sense, the New Community School helped to empower the community by providing a meeting place and a focal point for public forums that was not allied to a particular religious or political group. During the tenure of its existence, many residents in the neighborhoods around the school saw New Community as an important local resource and a friendly non-governmental institution.

The school's 'border' location. The New Community School was located on 47th Street and Ellis Avenue to enhance easy access and integration of students, parents and residents from each of the three neighborhoods. Initially the school met in the basement of St. Ambrose Catholic Church, and then added 'branch' locations in the meeting room of the First Baptist Church of Chicago, and on the first floor of a religious community residence and in a board member's living room. Recruiting students from the three areas was made less challenging by choosing a border location as students felt comfortable meeting on the border rather than in the "turf" of another group. Students from different cultures learned how to interact productively with each other.

The Board of the New Community School. In most schools, the school board holds the school's charter and is the ultimate authority in the school, and this was true also in the New Community School. The by-laws of the school stated that three groups were to be represented on the board in equal numbers. The first two groups were students and staff and the third group was comprised of parents and community members. A community member, the chapter author, was elected as the first Chair of the Board, and the Vice Chair was a nine year old student. All hiring decisions were made by the Board, and the student members' input was always given significant consideration. For example, the students wanted to hire an intelligent young adult man in the community who had an interest in motorcycle repair and racing. Board members interviewed the prospective teacher, and described the humanistic philosophy of education to him. The candidate was asked how he would implement this approach and he described how he would teach physics, mathematics, reading, library research, civics and other disciplines and skills through his interest in motorcycles. The Board unanimously chose to hire him as he "understood" the teaching approach of the school and many of the teenaged students were interested in motorcycles. The new teacher explained to the students for example that the motorcycle engine could be made more powerful by increasing its compression ratio, that is, the ratio of the volume of the air-gas mixture when the piston is fully extended to when the piston is fully compressed within the cylinder. The educator continued that since the top of the piston is curved, the best way to calculate the volumes for the compression ratio of the bored out cylinder was to use calculus, and so the students learned this mathematical tool. The students walked to the teacher's machine shop, and they first observed and then participated in milling the cylinder head to achieve the greater compression ratio. The instructor then discussed the physics of gasoline octane ratios, and how their 'souped up' motorcycle would require gas with a higher octane number to get the most out of their engine modification. The students were happy to learn math and science as these disciplines were seen as related to real world applications in which they were interested. The instructor cleverly generalized from their interest to discuss other concepts within these disciplines, and then to use motorcycle racing to teach lessons in civics and economics. All the students who participated in this project felt a tremendous sense of accomplishment when the modified engine was reassembled and reinstalled on the motorcycle. Excitement and satisfaction was great when the engine started and the instructor demonstrated the increased performance that was the result of the students' work.

Unfortunately, the funding goals for the New Community never were sufficiently realized. Small grants were received, some tuition was collected, paid teachers were assisted by unpaid volunteers, neighbors contributed space rent free and donated materials, but after 18 months, the operation ended. Still, the innovative applications of the humanistic approach were tested and found to be workable. Other alternative schools developed during the 1970s and many of these learning components continue in learning centers throughout the nation.

As a final example of what can be done at the pre-college level, a college student recently told me of a program she had initiated to help and empower at-risk high school students. As part of her honors' project, Lauren Hall (personal communication, September 2011) chose to integrate her participation in the Marist College Debate and Advocacy Society with her work in the Poughkeepsie Liberty Partnership Program (LPP), a mentoring and tutoring program for at-risk high school students. Lauren, with the help of Marist faculty and LPP staff, developed a speech/argumentative skills curriculum designed to enhance student self-efficacy (Bandura, 1997), a strong predictor of academic success. Developing self-efficacy is essential for empowering youth as self-efficacy enables the individuals to believe that they can be successful if they put effort into achieving their goals, that is, they have the power within themselves to achieve. The youth learned how to debate through the program. The debates were held in the main theater at Marist College with their parents, other relatives, peers and program staff in attendance. Ms. Hall reported the effects on the students and their families were dramatic. The youth enhanced their critical thinking skills and the ability to articulate their positions and rejoinders. They developed the ability to prepare persuasive, well-reasoned and logical arguments supported by appropriate evidence. Perhaps more significantly, they changed their self-perception. Instead of being at-risk youths, they saw themselves as college-bound. Their parents also raised their expectancy of success for their children. The high school students, through participating in this program made less salient the ascribed status of being at risk and replaced it with a favorable achieved status, that of an intelligent, successful debater (cf. Sarbin, 1970, and Teed, Scileppi, Boeckmann et al, 2007). The more educators can transcend the stigma of labeling learners as being of low socioeconomic status or coming from impoverished neighborhoods or other categories associated with failure, and emphasize instead the accomplishments of the learners and their successes in any of the various spheres of their lives, the more likely they will become productive, effective contributing citizens in the community, proud of their achievements. Lauren Hall has been accepted into Teach for America, a program in which she continues to utilize her creativity to empower other youth in a school with special needs students.

The XL Program at Saint Xavier College in Chicago.

After having researched a number of learning strategies that became part of the typical activities of the New Community School and elsewhere, I wanted to explore whether some of these ideas developed out of the positive view of socialization and John Dewey's educational philosophy could be implemented at the college level. During the Spring 1972 semester, a group of faculty at St. Xavier College (now University) in Chicago, Illinois met together and proposed such a program that utilized a number of components of the humanistic approach. Once approved by the plenary faculty, the proposal became the XL Program, a semester-long program for interested and capable incoming first year students (Scileppi, 1973). In this student-oriented, multidisciplinary program, college freshmen chose problems or issues that they desired to study, and then contract with faculty members to learn how various academic disciplines would investigate their area of interest. XL Program faculty assisted the students in clarifying their problem or focus, and they suggested resources and disciplines that might be helpful in pursuing their interests.

Upon entry into the program, XL students met as a group to discuss their individual interests. To facilitate sharing, staff and students participated in an interpersonal communication workshop for the first two weeks. They then broke into small groups to clarify and draw out each other's ideas and proposals for projects. XL staff served as guides, learning facilitators, and co-evaluators of learning and growth. These educators reviewed proposals for appropriateness, feasibility and consistency, and suggested college faculty members with whom the students might contract. Once projects were clarified, students then met with college faculty to contract to learn how the faculty members' disciplines could shed light on their interest. The methodology of the discipline was always a component of the contract. The contract also contained the student's learning goals, activities to meet these goals, methods of demonstrating that the goals have been met, and the deadline for completion. Students in the XL Program met together weekly to discuss their progress and what they had learned about their topic. Staff encouraged students to keep up with their projects. Each student could take between 6 and 15 credits during the semester to pursue their problem oriented research. During the 1972-73 academic year, the first year of the program, 36 students enrolled in 300 credits, contracting with faculty in art, biology, economics, education, English, humanities, philosophy, political science, psychology, sociology and theology (Scileppi, 1973).

Among the problems investigated were:

How does a child view the world?
What is the political machine in Chicago?
What are the effects of sensitivity groups?
What is the effect of the mass media on voter behavior?
How has religious education changed since 1960?
What is the effect of divorce on children?
(St. Xavier College, 1973 p. 2)

Thus in this program, students chose their own content of learning, and they had major input in selecting the style in which they were to learn this content. Consistent with both progressive and humanistic education, the learning was problem-oriented, and of relevance to the learner. In addition, an important objective of the XL Program was to demonstrate that students could integrate multiple academic disciplines around their interest, making education more relevant to their lives (Meyer, 1972). A final objective was that students would be responsible for their own learning. This objective was perceived as both a preparation and an opportunity for the students to experience empowerment in their lives.

In evaluating this program, the XL staff found it to be appropriate to those students who wanted to direct their own learning for a semester around a theme of their choosing. This requires both self-discipline of the student and an appropriate level of guidance from the staff. Students increased their critical thinking ability as measured by the Watson-Glaser test of Critical Thinking, their motivation to learn was enhanced, and they developed self-directed goal attainment skills.

Those students who chose to register for the full 15 credits in the XL Program tended to do better than those who registered for fewer credits. The staff believed the most likely reason for this finding was that the students who took regular or traditionally taught college courses along with the XL Program had difficulty integrating both the more structured and less structured learning experiences. For many, the deadlines for papers and exams stated in course syllabi and frequently mentioned by teachers in the traditional courses produced a level of urgency greater than that found in the clauses of the XL Program learning contracts. As a result, progress on fulfilling the learning contracts suffered somewhat. From a systems perspective, greater synergy or smooth functioning within a system exists when all learning activities have a similar level of structure (Scileppi, 1988)

The final conclusion from the XL Program evaluation concerned faculty time. Due to the need for students to contract with multiple faculty members, the program consumed a greater amount of faculty time than is usually spent with individual students. On the other hand, many of the teachers involved in the contracting found the experience enjoyable and productive as they liked the opportunity to interact more closely with students who expressed a great interest in learning. As students agreed to learn on their own, teachers were free of the need to prepare lectures for those in the program. A suggestion was made to deal with helping faculty make the time spent with XL students more efficient. Faculty members must maintain active research interests for tenure and promotion. Teachers might be encouraged to present on their own research interests to interested XL students prior to the beginning of the semester, and students might decide to meld their own interests with those of the faculty thus benefitting both student and contracting teachers. The chapter author resigned as director of the program after the first year in order to take a different position elsewhere and is uncertain whether this suggestion was implemented. Regardless, the XL Program was an evolving organic program that demonstrated the value of developing a program based on humanistic educational principles at the college level. Through publicizing this learning option for incoming students, the Admissions Office reported a rise in applications and enrollment during the following academic year. St. Xavier College in 1972 was in danger of closing due to low enrollment, and now this institution is succeeding so well it has become a university.

Oglala Sioux Community College in Pine Ridge, South Dakota: Empowering the Reservation Community.

The Pine Ridge Native American Reservation in the southwestern corner of South Dakota is among the poorest communities in the nation. In the 1970s, according to the Industrial Development Department (1975), the unemployment rate in Pine Ridge was 34% at a time when the national unemployment average was 4.5%. A majority of the population on the reservation lived below the poverty level (Maynard & Twiss, 1970). The reservation, bordered by the Badlands to the north and the Black Hills to the west is a very large area (50 X 100 miles), and is sparsely populated with 15000 living there. Of these, 75% were Native Americans, who were fairly evenly split between the more traditional "Full Bloods" and the "Mixed Bloods" who are more acculturated to the larger society. Tribal politics often found these two groups in conflict and frequently in the 1970s this conflict had erupted into violence. There were few credible institutions on the reservation, and many residents perceived the federal and state governments as implicitly conspiring to curtail or eliminate tribal customs and perhaps the tribe itself. While there were many federal agencies operating on the reservation, few members of the Oglala tribe were able to obtain work in these agencies as a college degree was needed for nearly all the positions. On the reservation, residents could only complete their secondary school education as there was no college located there. The nearest college in South Dakota was over 100 miles away in Rapid City, and once youth left the reservation to attend college, they rarely returned. Thus the simple rule that required positions to be filled by college graduates caused a "brain drain" on the reservation. The jobs went typically to non-Native Americans living in communities that bordered the reservation. Because of another regulation that no alcohol was allowed on the reservation, residents traveled to these border communities to drink. Residents more than occasionally drank too much and their behavior became overtly inappropriate. Those living in the border communities (which of course profited financially from the sale of alcohol) developed unfavorable perceptions of the Native Americans, and when these Caucasians went to work in the governmental agencies on the reservation, they brought with them their prejudices. These forces worked together to produce a terrible situation at Pine Ridge, and in 1973, residents on the reservation fed up with the conditions present there staged the 'Second Wounded Knee Uprising'. For the next few years, there were many violent encounters among the Full Bloods, Mixed Bloods, Bureau of Indian Affairs (BIA) police and the FBI (Dewing, 1985, Coleman, 2000, Laird & Chapman, 2010). Something needed to be done to improve the conditions and establish trustworthy institutions and beneficial policies on the reservation. For a more complete presentation of the conditions leading up to the events of the 1970s, the book, *That these people may live* (Maynard & Twiss, 1970), is an excellent resource.

To address some of these concerns, the Oglala Tribal Council 1n 1971 voted to establish a community college on the Pine Ridge Reservation. Initially called the Lakota Higher Education Center, the Oglala Sioux Community College (OSCC) was formed. This institution of higher learning was chartered by the Oglala Sioux Tribe and accredited through Black Hills State College and the University of South Dakota (Oglala Sioux Community College, 1976). The mission of OSCC was, "….to educate our people to live successfully by assisting each person to a goal that is both desirable and attainable" and supports "the right of each person to determine his own future and to take pride in his Lakota heritage…" (OSCC, 1976, p. 1). Due to the large size of the reservation, college centers were established in nine villages on the reservation. By 1975, OSCC was offering associate degrees in eight disciplines including education, social services, business, nursing, Lakota studies and general studies.

While OSCC was seen as a tribally created institution with the potential to benefit reservation residents, most of the local people did not become involved in the community college. Because of the brain drain described above, and the effects of poverty and unemployment, relatively few tribal members living on the reservation had high school diplomas or GED certificates. Among those who did, few wanted an associate level college degree. As a result, OSCC staff decided to conduct a continuing education needs assessment (Scileppi, 1976). Nearly all the OSCC staff participated in conducting this survey. The district college center staff administered the survey to 320 randomly selected adults living in the various reservation communities. A relatively high completion rate (64%) reflected the determination of the district staff in reaching out to residents in their communities. As a means of empowering the community, survey respondents were asked not only what topics they would like to study in these non-credit programs, but also what topics they would like to *teach*. OSCC became truly an institution for and of the reservation residents. Based on the survey, the college offered workshops in creative arts, land usage, carpentry, and health care/first aid. The community responded very favorably to this initiative and enrollment in both credit and non-credit offerings increased dramatically in the very next semester. To reflect the aim of the college to restore pride in Lakota heritage, the third annual graduation ceremony was held on June 25, 1976, the centennial anniversary of the Battle of Little-Big Horn (OSCC, 1976).

The college increased in both numbers and credibility on the reservation and in the region and by 1979 it was given candidate accreditation status by the North Central Association of Colleges and Universities (NCACU) (OSCC, 1980). In 1983, the college began to offer a bachelor level program in elementary education and it received full accreditation from the NCACU. To reflect the college's new status as a four year college, its name was changed to Oglala Lakota College (OLC). Today, OLC offers a Master's Degree in Lakota Leadership and Management, 11 bachelor and 20 associate level degree programs and enrollment has reached 1400 (Oglala Lakota College, 2010).

Although at least initially when the academic courses had to be approved by the supervising state colleges, the policies and procedures utilized in the academic program were fairly traditional and structured, OSCC and later OLC became an institution which empowered the community. Many initiatives were begun to advocate for reservation water rights and to overturn treaty violations involving land ownership in the Black Hills. Many tribal members developed enhanced pride in their reservation community, and the college is a sign of hope for the future of the tribe.

Developing Empowering Course Syllabi and College Teaching Strategies

While some readers who teach in colleges and schools that are in more mainstream communities than the Pine Ridge Reservation might not find the above applications generalizable to their work, the next few strategies can be tried in traditional secondary and higher education settings. Each of these strategies developed from a humanistic perspective attempts to enable students to have input into what is learned, to encourage student reflection, insight and participation and to assist in designing the structure and process of the courses in which they are enrolled.

Multiple options for assignments. Since students have diverse individual learning styles, it is beneficial to consider multiple ways for them to demonstrate they have learned required material. Giving such options acknowledges that there are many ways in which students can demonstrate competence in a discipline. While the options vary in different content or subject areas, the following is given as an example of what is possible. In a course on personality theories in psychology, in addition to the exams that all must take, students are provided with a list of optional learning projects. Some of these projects involve reading either lectures or entire books written by the theorists whom we are covering. Through this option, students get an in-depth insight into a specific aspect of the theory in which they are interested. Another project is to analyze a hypothetical case study from the perspective of one of the theorists. This provides students with the opportunity to demonstrate they can apply a theory to an individual with psychological issues. A third option is for students to conduct a survey to test empirically the accuracy of a specific principle of a theorist covered. For example, Alfred Adler described personality characteristics of individuals in each birth order (oldest, middle, youngest or only child in a family), and students could construct a personality assessment to see if these traits are correlated to the person's birth order. A final option is for two students to work together on a "shared learning" project. In this assignment, students are given a thought provoking question related to the course. The student first answers the question independently, and then seeks out another student in the class who is doing the same project. The two discuss their answers, and then write a paragraph indicating what each learned from the other. Each of these assignments is given a point value which reflects the teacher's estimate of the amount of learning possible in each option, and the students' grade in the course is a combination of their scores on examinations and the total number of points for the projects submitted. For the same letter grade one student can choose to get very high exam scores and submit fewer optional assignments, while another could get lower exam scores but submit more projects. In this way, all students learn the same core aspects of the course as assessed on the exams, but each can individualize the course learning by choosing his or her own types and number of projects.

In generating the various optional assignments, there are a number of theories that can assist in the process. Gardner (1999) provides seven frames of intelligence for example, and an educator can develop projects that will interest students with each learning style. Jerome Bruner (1966) has a simpler approach. He indicated that students can learn material by enactive, iconic or symbolic representation. Those who learn enactively want to engage the subject by sensing and doing. These students like to observe principles being applied and they want to manipulate conditions in some way to understand how they work. Internships and research projects are assignments of choice for these students. Those who are more iconic learn through pictures and diagrams. These students can learn through graphs and flow charts. Seeing photographs of some aspect of the material or watching a video or constructing a map or diagram of a process are good learning activities for these individuals and tend to pique their visual imagination. Finally, some students prefer symbolic representation of information. These students learn best when listening to a lecture or reading a book. Bruner's point is that students can learn by any of these styles, and providing students with options allows them to find an assignment that maximizes their learning. Also, when students get "stuck" in one mode, they have the opportunity to switch to a different learning activity which will help them overcome the obstacle. If individuals gain success experiences in learning because they could choose projects consistent with their learning style, they will perceive themselves as more capable students, and they will be more motivated to study harder and aim for higher academic goals.

Brief five-minute essays at the beginning of each class. To encourage students to read the assigned materials in the textbook and to urge them to reflect on the topic, I develop a thought provoking question I give to students at the end of a class session to be answered at the beginning of the next class. The question reflects the central theme of the next class, and typically can only be answered by reading the assigned material. The question is one that requires much thought, and frequently does not have a definite answer. The students then answer the question in writing during the first five minutes or so of the next class session. The answers are collected (as they also serve as a way of recording who is present) and then the class members discuss their answers. I have found many creative reflections are expressed during this discussion, and it allows each student to participate and contribute. I usually limit the time the students have to write the essay as this further motivates them to participate in the discussion to demonstrate their understanding orally even if they have not completed the thought in writing. This process helps also to make certain the students are thinking of this central theme as the class session begins. Students receive either an 'acceptable' or 'not-acceptable' grade for the essay. For this grade, I assess whether the student has read the material and is prepared for class. The grade does not necessarily reflect whether their answer is accurate as the class lecture and discussion which occur after the essay is written clarify the information.

Mid-course correction. In most colleges, students complete course evaluation forms at the end of a term. Teachers frequently use the feedback from these student evaluations when they plan future course offerings. Whatever insights appear on these forms are helpful to future students but as the current course is finished by the time the faculty member reviews the information, these evaluations have little value in affecting the learning of the students who completed the forms. In addition, the preferred classroom climate for one group of students might not be the hoped for learning setting for a different group of students. For example, one class might like to discuss information, and another might want more lectures. To enable students to provide feedback in a timely manner that could affect the teaching and learning style within a semester, teachers can ask the students to engage in a 'mid-course correction'. Originally, this term was used by the National Aeronautical and Space Agency (NASA). When a moon rocket was fired, for example, NASA engineers would calculate where the projectile should be half-way through the trip, and then observe where the rocket actually was at that point. If there was any variance between the two locations, the engineers could then take corrective action to ensure the space shot arrives at its intended destination. In the same way, a teacher might also utilize a mid-course correction. After students have taken the midterm exam and completed half the term, the teacher might ask how the semester is going, and how might the teaching/learning strategies employed in the first half of the course be modified for the second half to enhance learning. When I have used this technique, I find many good suggestions. Some groups ask for more exams to break down the material into smaller segments. Others ask that study guides be available earlier. Still others ask for additional media resources. In case any student is fearful of recrimination for making critical suggestions, I usually provide an anonymous method of giving me feedback in addition to the class discussion. By expressing willingness to receive suggestions, and then to implement some of them can enhance rapport between the students and teacher, and this in itself can increase the students' motivation to learn.

This mid-course correction is consistent with a number of humanistic principles. Students have an opportunity to give meaningful input regarding their learning. They can suggest teaching strategies consistent with their preferred learning style. In addition, there is a greater equality in the classroom roles of teacher and students. The teacher demonstrates both responsibility and flexibility; responsibility in that the course has been well planned, and yet flexibility in being willing to make reasonable modifications to enhance student learning. Modeling these behaviors is beneficial for students as they grow into adulthood and assume positions in society that require these abilities.

Equivalent learning requirement for absences. In every term, some students are going to experience illness, emergencies, and tragedies which require them to be absent from class. Occasionally, students may choose to miss class for reasons that are not as serious. If teachers are placed in the role of deciding when the reason for the absence is valid or not, their role becomes more similar to law enforcement officers and less similar to being compassionate educators concerned for the learning and holistic development of the student. Yet, teachers cannot let students skip class based on feelings or other whimsical reasons. Another approach to this situation is to emphasize learning. When absent, a student loses the information value of listening to and participating in class discussion. The insights and helpful ideas that emerge from the class discussion or that the teacher may convey to the class are not available to the absent student. The teacher is unable to certify that the absent student has learned the same or similar material or skills that the other students have learned. To remedy this loss, teachers can require students to demonstrate equivalent learning when they are absent for *any* reason. In my courses, I construct assignments that students are to complete that compensate for the learning that occurred in the class they missed. In personality theories, I require students to read an additional primary source work written by the theorist covered during the missed class. In community psychology, a course where applications are emphasized, students are to read an additional paper describing an application of relevant principles in a local agency. In a course on the history of psychology, students must find a paper written by one of the pioneers in the field covered when they were absent. In each case, students read the paper and write a summary and reaction. While they were not present to hear interesting and relevant concepts discussed in that class, they will learn different but relevant and equivalent material through this compensatory assignment. Students can also suggest alternative relevant activities to demonstrate learning when a class is missed. If students are ill, I often offer them the option of taking a grade of Incomplete which allows more time to finish these assignments and the rest of the course.

A final note regarding humanistic education should be mentioned. As with any approach to learning, the specific classroom intervention program must be consistent with the rest of the school system. If a school is established under a negative view of socialization, educators advocating for humanistic learning applications will be perceived as opponents of quality education. Administrators and other teachers will be highly critical of the approach and will take action to prevent its implementation. In addition, students moving from a more traditional classroom to a more progressive one during a typical school day will experience problems in the transition. The students might need adjustment time to feel comfortable and think creatively in the more open environment of a humanistic inspired learning setting. These same students will encounter opposite challenges when returning to a more passive, teacher-centered classroom. When attempting to implement a new humanistic intervention, determine first whether the stake holders in the school district or system are open to this change. These administrators, board members, teachers and parents may need to be persuaded that a humanistic approach is of value to the students. Frequently it is beneficial to begin an innovative intervention by getting approval to establish a demonstration project with a small group of students than by trying to insert a humanistic class period into many students' typical school day. Other educators might be invited to see the new learning program in operation, and they may be more favorably inclined when they observe happy and empowered students learning together productively.

Humanistic education is grounded in progressive education and the positive view of socialization in which students are active agents desiring to learn and to be productive members of their community. Humanistic education can be very empowering as the students can choose the content of their learning and the style in which to learn this content. Yet by enhancing student awareness of current problems confronting society, they will include in their goals the desire to address them and to be contributors to society. Both the needs of the individual student and the community are met in this process. There are many worthwhile applications of this approach at each level of schooling. Creative educators will certainly develop new effective programs which can evolve out of this philosophy.

6

Value Clarification:
The Basis for Informed Life Choices

John Scileppi

Upon reflecting on my own experience of growing up as a student, and also on having taught for over 40 years, I am amazed at how poorly students make decisions about some of the most important aspects of life. When asked about what I wanted to be when I grew up, throughout most of my own schooling I said I was going to be a medical doctor. My father was a physician, and I received medical toys and chemistry sets as a child. My relatives and friends thought this was a good idea for me; it seemed to fit in so well with my family's values. It wasn't until I actually applied to medical schools and went on admissions interviews that I found I had no interest in medicine as a career. I found the idea of dissecting cadavers caused me to become nauseous. I wanted to help others; but not if it involved a lot of "blood and guts". When I speak with my college students and advisees, I find many have the same uncertainty about their futures. I ask seniors to write a major term paper on their intended career; six months later, they ask me for reference letters and the fields to which they are applying have little to do with what they wrote about in their term papers. Vocational concerns are not the only areas in which they are confused. Years ago, my advising was more personal than academic. College students would describe their confusion about whether to marry their current boyfriend. Often the conversation would start with, "He wants to marry me," or "My Mom really likes him," or "My roommate thinks he is cute or funny." I would then acknowledge the feelings of these other people, but I would ask, "Do you want to marry him?" Students often found this question impossible to answer. A big problem that is present in contemporary society is that young people are so bombarded with persuasive messages from the media, peers, family members and others they have lost the ability to be in touch with their own feelings and values. That is, they are unable to make decisions based on their own needs and passions, and they are at the mercy of the social forces around them.

Education can be empowering if students can learn to "pull their own strings" rather than to be the marionette puppet of others. Those around the student may not intend to manipulate or exploit, but the effect is the same: the student has lost the ability to place value on experience. These youths are no longer in touch with their true feelings and are likely to trust the judgment of others over their own. In this chapter, values and value clarification are discussed. After introducing these concepts, empirical studies of the effect of clarifying values on the lives of students are presented. Then the technique of value clarification and how this can be taught in the schools are described. Finally, the debate regarding whether value clarification should be covered in American public schools is discussed.

Perhaps the best way to introduce the study of values is to define what values are. Milton Rokeach (1971) differentiates two forms of values in his definition, terminal and instrumental. Terminal values are beliefs regarding preferable end states of existence. When growing old and looking back on our lives would we be more pleased to state we lived an exciting life or that we accomplished something major? While nearly all terminal values are perceived to be "good", each of us will emphasize some and ignore others. On the other hand instrumental values deal with preferable modes of conduct. As we live our lives each day, do we strive to be helpful or courageous or loving, for example? Rokeach and his fellow researchers performed content analyses of samples of published writing of many literate societies and they found that there are only 18 terminal and 18 instrumental values. These listings are presented below.

Rokeach's List of Values
(Each list presented alphabetically)

TERMINAL VALUES	INSTRUMENTAL VALUES
A Comfortable Life	Ambitious
An Exciting Life	Broadminded
A Sense of Accomplishment	Capable
A World at Peace	Cheerful
A World of Beauty	Clean
Equality	Courageous
Family Security	Forgiving
Freedom	Helpful
Happiness	Honest
Inner Harmony	Imaginative
Mature Love	Independent
National Security	Intellectual
Pleasure	Logical
Salvation	Loving
Self-Respect	Obedient
Social Recognition	Polite
True Friendship	Responsible
Wisdom	Self-Controlled

While cultures may differ in how these values are expressed, Rokeach believes these value listings are comprehensive. It would be difficult to find a value that is not somehow related to one or more of those listed.

Values can also be viewed as guides for living. When an individual has clarified that a value is truly held, this value impacts the life of the individual.

From another perspective, Frondizi (1971) noted that there is a hierarchy of values beginning with the more subjective matters of taste and ending with universally held objective values. Subjectively, I may like casual clothes and you might prefer formal clothes, I like green and someone else likes red, I like jazz and he likes classical music. These tastes and preference are important to the person but they are subjective values and are not to be argued, but the differences merely accepted. Universal values such as the "Golden

Rule" become the basis of philosophies of life. They become ethical codes and ultimate concerns. Nearly every person understands the value of "Do unto others as you would have them to do unto you.", even if he or she doesn't always live by this belief. In between these two extremes in the value hierarchy, Frondizi includes aesthetics. While I might like jazz music, musical critics can describe the qualities that make some jazz pieces better than others. Similarly there are ways of judging the goodness of plays or of paintings or foods or clothes.

A final perspective in understanding values is to consider that values are central, abstract or comprehensive attitudes. While typical adults hold countless thousands of attitudes, they adhere to only a small number of values. Changing the priority a value has for the individual will affect many attitudes. Raising the value of family security will affect an individual's attitude toward financially saving for retirement or taking out insurance policies or purchasing home alarm systems. All these attitudes and behaviors are subordinate to the value of family security.

Milton Rokeach (1971, 1979) demonstrated empirically that values are central and comprehensive attitudes, and when a value is changed, a significant effect on attitudes occurs. In a study of Michigan State University first year students, Rokeach randomly divided the students into a treatment and control group. Both groups received the list of terminal values described above, and were told to rank the values in terms of importance from "1" (most important to them) to "18" (least important). The list was printed on two-copy carbon paper. The control group was then administered a brief survey on attitudes toward civil rights. When this survey was completed, the students in the control group were thanked, asked to hand in one copy of their ranked value list and civil rights survey and were dismissed. The treatment group completed the same value ranking; however when they completed this assignment, they were asked to hand in one copy of the ranked values and were then exposed to a brief three-minute manipulation. The experimenter stated to the group that he had done previous research with college students using the value listing, and found college students typically rank "freedom" as among the top three values, and "equality" in the middle (eighth, ninth or tenth). Rokeach went on to explain there may be many interpretations of this result but one meaning is that college students are selfish. They want freedom for themselves, but are less concerned about freedom for others. The experimenter then asked students to review their own list. The civil rights survey was administered at this time to these students; they completed it, were thanked and were dismissed.

The results of this brief value manipulation were dramatic. The students in the treatment group expressed significantly more favorable attitudes toward civil rights. Rokeach interpreted this effect as resulting from his pointing out a value inconsistency. Few students view themselves as selfish, yet the explanation regarding how they ranked the values seemed plausible, and rationally supported the view they were selfish. The students already handed in one copy of the value ranking, so they couldn't change their answers. The only way they could prove to themselves they were not selfish was to adopt a more favorable attitude toward civil rights. This then reduced the value inconsistency and resulted in the significant attitudinal difference described above. Rokeach wanted to observe whether the change in attitude was temporary or permanent. As he had the names and contact information of the students in the study, both 3-5 and 15-17 months later, he sent this information to the NAACP, a noted civil rights group, and asked this organization to mail solicitations to students in both groups as part of the NAACP annual membership drive. The dependent variable in this part of the study was the number of students who applied to join this civil rights organization. As in the first part of the study, a significant difference was found between the two groups. A much greater number of students in the treatment group joined the NAACP. To join, an individual needed to complete the application, enclose the membership fee, put the application in an envelope, stamp it and place it in the mail, a rather involved process. The students did not know they were invited to join as the result of their participation in the study months earlier. The difference in outcomes between the two groups was not just significantly different but dramatically so. Some 25% of the experimental group joined the civil rights group compared to only 10% in the control group. As a final measurement, Rokeach obtained permission to add a few civil rights questions to a health survey all graduating seniors complete. This measurement – taken three years after the brief three minute value inconsistency confrontation manipulation – again resulted in a significantly more favorable attitude toward civil rights in the treatment group relative to the control. Thus Rokeach demonstrated that altering a value priority has lasting and meaningful effects on attitudes.

Since this chapter focuses on values, it is worthwhile to discuss the ethics of the above research study. It is important to note the study was developed in the 1960s and ethical codes for social scientific research have changed greatly during the past 50 years. Currently our standards for informed voluntary consent and for the anonymity of research participants have tightened considerably, so it is not fair to judge a study by modern standards that were not in effect when the research was conducted. However, it is still worth noting the students who chose to participate in this study had the expectation they would not be permanently affected by the study. Those in the treatment group who received this brief manipulation in fact were quite different afterwards. As a result of the manipulation, these students reflected on their approach to life and decided to become more involved in civil rights and in advocating for equality for all. This author – and I expect most readers – see this particular change as favorable; however the participants were at the mercy of researchers who could just as easily have created a change that many would not like. Today, researchers need to have their proposed studies reviewed by an ethics committee (in the US these are called Institutional Review Boards or IRBs). The IRB would require that all participants are informed regarding the possible consequences the study may cause. Of course the researchers could have responded the outcome of this study was far more life-changing than most would have expected. While it is unlikely this study can be replicated today due to the tightened ethical standards, the study continues to be important in demonstrating that confronting inconsistencies in a person's values can have dramatic persuasive effects on the individual's attitudes and behaviors.

The Study of Values in Academic Disciplines

The study of values is important in philosophy, psychology and education, as well as in other disciplines; yet it is not emphasized sufficiently in many public schools. As alluded to above, philosophy courses in ethics and aesthetics must include the concept of value. A discussion of ethical models or systems would be incomplete without focusing on the values underlying each model. For example, determining the proper relationship between the individual and the community must involve a weighing of values for example.

Psychologists of the humanistic school of thought consider self-awareness as a necessary precursor to mental health as without such insight persons do not know who they are or how to decide what is important. Self-awareness requires that an individual has reflected on values. According to Carl Rogers (1951), students can either take others' values thinking they are their own, or they can reflect on their very being and discover what their inner being is disclosing to them. If they accept external sources of valuing, the students will never become aware of their own feelings and motivations. A child is in touch with genuine feelings, but over time, we lose this self-awareness. This process of losing touch begins when parents express their evaluation of the child's behavior and gradually the son or daughter accepts the parent's view and de-emphasizes his or her own "gut" feeling. The child accepts the other's value and loses the intrinsic ability to place value on things or behaviors. As the child progresses through school, there are many forces in society trying to persuade students to accept these introjected values: marketing and advertising firms urge us to buy specific products, peers encourage students to engage in high-risk behaviors likely to lead to substance abuse, teachers and parents try to map out career/professional futures for the students. The list of external influences is long. Each time students accept these values, they tend to lose touch with their inner voice. While the messages from the outside may be beneficial, they deprive the student of the self-awareness needed in order to make authentic choices. The long term effect is alienation from self, and eventually, the individual becomes a robot and an empty shell with no ability to discern the true spirit within. In mid-life, according to Carl Jung (1960), this can lead to despair, depression and aimlessness as the person finds little-meaning in the activities and goals others have held as being important. Another psychologist, Sidney Jourard, (1971), considered that in a loving relationship, individuals need to give of themselves for the relationship to develop. To give of oneself, a person must be willing and able to self-disclose feelings and beliefs. In order to self-disclose, a person must be in touch with true values and priorities. Thus humanistically-oriented therapists urge clients to clarify their own values both to achieve self-awareness and to develop deep and fulfilling human relationships.

Finally, the study of values is important to educators. As was discussed in the previous chapter, education is moving away from merely learning academic content but instead is emphasizing the more affective, feeling-oriented aspect of learning. It is less important to memorize when the European Union was formed than to reflect on and perhaps debate how the forming of this international union has affected the lives of those living in Europe and elsewhere. The entomology of the word education implies "to draw out from". This includes helping students become aware of their own positions. Humanistically-oriented educators note that merely teaching engineering students how to build a highway through a populated urban area is less important than weighing the effect the highway will have on displacing large numbers of residents and disrupting their lives. As was pointed out in a previous chapter, John Dewey (1916) advocated that if students will eventually vote in democratic societies, they must learn the ability to evaluate the quality and likely consequences of various proposals so they can make informed decisions. In addition, humanistic educators include character education as a goal of the school since encouraging students to develop as moral persons is also required for becoming a good citizen in the community.

Some movements in education are working against the goal of teaching students to become better citizens able to critically evaluate ideas and proposals. In many nations including the United States there are laws and regulations which require schools to teach content in key disciplines, sometimes referred to as the STEM subjects (science, technology, engineering and mathematics). As a result of laws like No Child Left Behind Act (U.S. Department of Education, 2002), school success is measured by how many students pass academic content criteria. These national educational systems are restricting students from learning how to think critically and to understand the value issues involved in the content they are learning. Greater and greater proportions of the school day are taken up with preparing students to pass exams in these STEM areas, and there is little time left over to address affective learning. Students are losing the ability to assign meaning and value in their lives as a result. Instead, as educators, we can help students draw out their true inner voice. One way to accomplish this is to teach value clarification in the schools, and have students make their own decisions based on their awareness of the promptings of their inner being. The methods for doing this are discussed later in the chapter.

The Influence of Values and Value Clarification in Our Lives.

As has been discussed, values as guides to living help us to become more aware of our true priorities and this leads to self-direction. In addition understanding our values and sharing them with others leads to enriching interpersonal relationships. Regarding this latter point, values are at the core of nearly all of our communication. If an individual were to reflect on recent dyadic or two-person communications, it is likely both individuals shared their preferences for food types or cars or clothes, they probably discussed and debated their political concerns and hopes or their religious and ideological perspectives, perhaps they expressed their educational and work aspirations along with their fears and anxieties about achieving these objectives, and maybe they also described what they liked or disliked in the other. All of these interchanges focused on values. Our relationships will be more fulfilling to the extent we share – and encourage the other to share – values. Thus expressing values is central to our significant interpersonal communication.

There have also been many empirical studies which have assessed the effect of value clarification on the lives of students. Kirschenbaum (1977) reviewed the early research literature on what was then the new and developing field of value clarification. He found many studies showing the impact of value clarification on the lives of students and adults. After participating in value clarification exercises, students at many levels of education were less apathetic, more purposive, less conforming to peers, more energetic and better critical thinkers. They followed through on decisions and had higher self-esteem. Finally, these students had lower rates of absenteeism, more certitude regarding choice of major and career, and had higher grades. Regarding the latter point, I directed a graduate program for over ten years. In this role, one of my responsibilities was to evaluate whether candidates would be successful students in the graduate program. To do so, among other sources of information, I would review the applicant's academic transcript. A common pattern of grades was that potential students did relatively poorly in their first and second years of college, and then performed better in their final two years. When reflecting on the possible reasons for this pattern, it is difficult to believe courses at the upper level are easier than introductory ones. Also the pattern could not be the result of some selection bias such as weaker students drop out of school. Recall that I observed transcripts of the same students over the four years of higher education. Indeed, the most plausible explanation was that students clarified their vocational values and goals as they advanced through college. When I observed this pattern, I frequently asked students what happened that caused their grades to rise over the four years. A frequent answer was consistent with this hypothesis: "I volunteered in a program relevant to this major and I realized I really liked it.", or "I shadowed a professional in the field and liked the activities this individual performed." Thus students' academic performance increased when they decided what they wanted to do with their lives, that is, when they clarified their values.

Mosconi and Emmett (2003) empirically assessed the effect of a school value clarification curriculum on high school students' definition of career success. The curriculum, consisting of four 90-minute sessions, focused on defining values, prioritizing the values, reflecting on the forces influencing value formation and relating values to future choices and one's career. The researchers found students were able to identify more of their own values and had a better grasp of their values as a result of being exposed to this curriculum. This finding is consistent with Kirschenbaum's earlier literature review.

Value clarification can also help to reduce drug and alcohol abuse among students. Simon and deSherebenin (1977) described a study they conducted with high risk teens. The value clarification strategy was very simple. The researchers instructed the classroom teachers to ask their students to identify and write down 20 goals they would like to accomplish when they reached adulthood. The teacher indicated the lists would not be collected and were solely for the students' benefit. The youth were given 20 minutes to develop their lists. It is likely that most indicated they wanted to be doctors or lawyers or teachers, they wanted to go to college, they wanted to marry and raise a family, they wanted a good-paying job and a nice house and other, similar goals. The teacher then asked, "If doing drugs is one of your goals, how many of the other 19 will you not be able to accomplish?" Most of the youth in the treatment group realized not many professionals abuse drugs, and most addicts are unable to maintain good jobs or stable family relationships. This exercise enabled them to weigh the value of doing drugs against the other 19 goals they wanted to achieve. Compared to other drug prevention methods, this value clarification strategy resulted in less drug use among these high risk teens.

Researchers have also demonstrated that value clarification is an effective method of reducing other negative behaviors such as unhappiness and maladaptive behaviors. Thompson and Hudson (1982) randomly divided ninth grade boys (approximately 15 years old) in a residential school into two treatment conditions, counseling and value clarification. The value clarification intervention was integrated into the regular academic curriculum. Houseparents assessed the frequency of violations of the school's behavior code and actions indicative of the individuals' level of happiness or unhappiness with life using a pre and posttest design. Compared to a no-treatment control, both value clarification and counseling were effective treatments, but value clarification was less costly and resulted in no stigma.

Value clarification has also been found to enhance prosocial orientation and behaviors. Zuo and Wei (2008) presented junior and middle high school students in China a series of classes which emphasized modeling, empathy training and value clarification. Compared to a typical class control group, the students in the experimental class had significantly more favorable altruistic and pro-social value orientation and behaviors. Thus the addition of value clarification to the curriculum has many desirable effects on the lives of adolescents.

Value clarification has also been applied to specific groups of students. Easterbrooks and Scheetz (2004) summarized the literature on the effectiveness of value clarification curricula on teaching students who are deaf or hearing-impaired. They found such programs can contribute to character education and critical thinking, and they presented lesson plans and strategies for developing such programs.

Thus value clarification has been found to be an effective tool in the classroom for helping students become more aware of their true values. Such educational programs have many added benefits such as helping students develop into productive members of society who are happy and goal directed. Educators knowledgeable about this process can design worthwhile programs to enhance the affective and cognitive growth of their students.

Differentiating a Set of Values versus a Valuing Set

Before describing the process of value clarification, it is important to make an important distinction. Father Aquinas Thomas, (personal communication, 1980) the former Director of New Hope Manor, an addiction recovery program for young adult women in New York State, differentiated between a "set of values" and a "valuing set". While this appears at first glance to be a play on words, Father Aquinas was attempting to convey that the values we often say we hold are not the same as the ones that truly influence our lives. These superficial values, what Father Aquinas called the set of values, are merely characteristics we want others to believe we possess. A student might want a teacher to form the impression that the student is very responsible and an eager learner, and this might be merely a strategy to hide not having completed the assigned readings. Similarly, a man correctly accused of stealing might want to convey the impression he is really very honest and would never take someone else's property. His honesty does not guide his life; instead it is only a deception to convince others he did not commit the crime. In a sense, these sets of values are only for export; they are intended to influence other's perceptions, and they do not affect how the individual lives on a daily basis. On the other hand, a valuing set is truly a personal guide to living. A valuing set reflects the person's true motives. For example, an athlete may practice a sport for hours a day. Others looking on who do not have this valuing set would think this seemingly endless behavior was a foolish waste of time. Yet for the athlete, the time spent practicing is of utmost importance. Similarly, a valuing set helps us to identify strengths and weaknesses. A salesperson interested in making a commission might reflect on why a potential customer did not ultimately buy the service or product. The staff person might try changing the sales strategy or the way of interacting with the next possible customer as attempts to improve the selling process. A salesperson without this valuing set will more likely be watching the clock, waiting for the work shift to end. Dedicated musicians practice the same piece over and over to get it just right, another example of a true valuing set. Finally, a valuing set makes a person's behavior meaningful and worthwhile. Choosing the right gift for a loved one could take hours of thought and shopping. Buying a gift for a distant relative as a method of meeting a required social expectation might be seen as a rote chore, best completed swiftly. Thus there is a difference between the internal motives that drive our behavior and external values which are more for show as they represent our "pretend selves" – the persons we want others to think we are.

When discussing value clarification, the intent is to help individuals discern their true valuing sets and not the superficial set of values. At New Hope Manor, Father Aquinas used value clarification to help the young women overcome their drug addictions. The residents came to the program as a result of being arrested for crimes (drug selling, stealing, violent behavior) related to their addiction. The judge allowed these women the option of residing at New Hope instead of going to jail. The program consisted of many interventions, but the main theme was to encourage the women to clarify and confront their true valuing set. A typical program component – similar to many programs – included a point system. When a resident performed desirable behaviors, she would receive "points" and after amassing a specific number, she could apply to move to the next level and have more privileges. At New Hope however, the point system or token economy was modified in important ways to teach value clarification and confrontation. A major difference was that the resident seeking advancement had to make her case to a group of other residents. Group members could ask about the motives of the candidate wanting to advance. For example, a resident could get points for making her bed in the morning. When asked why, a candidate who responded she did so because she wanted to advance to the next level would be denied. The behavior was performed only for extrinsic reasons. A candidate who said a bed made well reflects how she was getting her life in order and demonstrates her becoming a responsible person would be granted the promotion. Also, by using a group to decide, members could challenge the accuracy of a statement. A candidate who said she was trying to get along with her peers might be reminded of a fight she had provoked the day before, for example. The young women had to demonstrate that their valuing set had changed. What was once desired (drugs, an unregulated life) was not seen as good anymore, and instead these were replaced by the desire for personal responsibility, self-development, contributing to her community

The program was very successful. The young women who graduated (completed) New Hope were not only drug-free but became model citizens. Some as part of the re-entry component of the program came to the college where this author teaches. Although their secondary school grades were at best mediocre and often less than that, these re-entry students in college were among the best students academically as they used their time productively in terms of their priorities. One New Hope graduate was chosen as the Valedictorian of her class. Socially, they were contributing members to the campus and encouraged other students who were drug abusers to participate in a New Hope outreach program. These New Hope students discovered meaning in their lives through clarifying their valuing set and they went on to attain graduate degrees and to assume significant roles in the community. Had it not been for New Hope Manor and its value oriented program, these women would probably have lived a life of crime, incarceration, and institutionalization.

Other researchers have found value clarification works well with populations similar to the women at New Hope. Edwards and Allen (2008) for example, evaluated the effectiveness of value clarification program for urban, delinquent pregnant adolescents and teen mothers in an alternative school developed for this population. Using a pre and posttest design, an eight month program altered attitudes toward alcohol and drugs, and the participants had a greater appreciation of work and of family. They also valued more highly planning for the future, honesty, and a structured living situation. They were less likely to waste time or to engage in violent behaviors.

The Value Clarification Process

The Method of Simon and His Associates
Now that the case for how values can affect the lives of students and be empowering has been made, it is worthwhile to consider how value clarification can be accomplished in the schools. There are two effective strategies described in the educational psychology literature; these are the methods of Simon and his associates (Raths, Harmin & Simon, 1966, Simon, Howe & Kirschenbaum, 1972) and Casteel and Stahl's (1975, 1997) method.

Simon and his associates viewed the value clarification process as the application of critical thinking to the affective valuing process. That is, the individual applies a set of criteria to determine if a desired goal is truly a personally held value. If done correctly, value clarification is not indoctrination; students should be striving to discern what are their true valuing sets and not just adopting the values of the teacher. Additionally, after students clarify values, they can judge the appropriateness of their values and then decide whether to retain or to change them. Without clarifying values and realizing that they chose these values subjectively, students would not be in a position to evaluate them and perhaps choose to change some of them.

These authors considered that there are seven criteria that need to be met before a person can demonstrate to oneself or others that a value is truly held. These criteria are that the value has been a) chosen from among alternatives, b) chosen freely and c) with reflection on the consequences, d) that the individual prizes the value, being glad with the choice and is e) publicly willing to affirm it, and that the individual has f) acted on the value and g) in a repeated and consistent fashion. These seven criteria can be reduced to three main categories, choosing, prizing and acting. Each of these criteria is elaborated below.

A youth cannot choose a value if everyone in the individual's social setting holds the same value. One of the empowering processes of higher education is that students come from many backgrounds. Students are exposed to different views of reality sometimes for the first time in college. Previously, students may have uncritically accepted the parents' view of the world, believing that "good" or "smart" people all believed in the same religious orientation or political position of their parents. The parents' view may have been supported by like-minded people in the same community. When students go to a college in a different community, they find intelligent peers hold diverse values. Merely accepting the view of the dominant peer group at the college is not enough as this can be as imposing as the parents' influence. The student must perceive all the various value orientations, evaluating their strengths and weaknesses and then make an informed choice. In addition, the student must consider and project the possible consequences of the decision. "What will I do if my parents don't like my choice?" "How will this choice affect my life and my future, socially and occupationally?" "How will this choice affect humankind?" This process is not a once-in-a-lifetime decision; it is likely, especially during the school and college years, that a student will "try on" numerous value orientations before settling on one viewpoint. Once this decision is made, students can begin to define themselves in terms of their own personal conviction.

Once chosen, students can now prize their value. They will become associated with groups of like-minded individuals and attend gatherings of that association. They may wear articles of clothes that signify or witness to this value. According to Simon, students are willing to "shout from the mountaintop" that they support this value. Wearing the insignia of a political party, displaying a religious medal, putting on special clothes or cutting one's hair or growing a beard or showing that one is engaged or married are examples of publicly affirming a truly held value. Their self-concepts change as they begin to see themselves as members of a religious group or a political party or as engaged to be married.

Finally, and perhaps most important, the third criteria demonstrating a value has been clarified is behavior. Frequently, I ask advisees who state they want to be psychologists or educators or engineers or doctors how they have acted on their choices. If the students can describe courses taken, books read, lectures attended, volunteer or work activities performed consistent with the value, then there is a strong likelihood that the value is truly held. If none of these – or similar behaviors – have been practiced, I encourage the students to gain this experience. If months later, there still is no relevant action, I ask the students to consider whether this value is their own idea or the dream of someone else in their lives. The perspective could become a truly held value once the person acts on the value and likes it, but otherwise currently it is not. Kirschenbaum (1985) questioned whether these steps are sufficiently quantifiable to justify the category criteria, but if not criteria, they can be seen at least as processes. Encouraging students to reflect on whether they have chosen, prized and acted on a value can help them understand their true priorities.

There are many ways Simon's value clarification process might be included in the curricula of schools at any level of education. Teachers can convey the method by first giving instruction regarding the three above-mentioned criteria and then having students read a biography or even a novel (if the main character is well-developed), or see a play or movie. The students might discuss first what likely value the main character might hold and then see if there is enough information to demonstrate the individual chose, prized and acted on this value. If the criteria have not been met, what other value(s) might the character hold? It is likely this active and creative application of critical thinking and the effect of the entire class debating the issue of value clarification, will result in the students remembering the biography or novel or movie or play more completely. Once students have completed this exercise the teacher may encourage them to reflect on their own values and see if the criteria have been met. This process is empowering as once the students learn the process, they can apply it in life-defining non-academic areas of their lives. Thus learning this skill can be helpful to students throughout their lives.

Another typical way in which Simon's method has been taught involves students performing the Fallout Shelter Problem (National Curriculum & Training Institute, 1994 as an example). While there are many variations of this exercise, typically students are asked to play the role of the main decision maker supervising fallout shelters, safe places to go in case of a global nuclear disaster . Ten people appear at a particular shelter that is designed to hold six for the length of time needed before it is safe to leave the shelter. The ten individuals are each described briefly. The exercise is set up so the student decision maker is not one of the ten, and those who are chosen may be the last inhabitants of the world. Thus the student is to choose six and eliminate four. In my teaching I use this exercise in a course on interpersonal communication in which students learn skills such as assertiveness, active listening and conflict resolution as well as value clarification. I have the students work on the problem separately, and then they are asked to come together in small groups to choose one group list. I usually give a 20-minute time limit for the group to develop a consensus decision. The groups then report their choices and the reasons for them. Each individual in each of the groups has performed the three steps of the method: they *chose* the individuals who would enter the shelter, they *prized* their choices by publicly defending them and they *acted* on the choices. While this would be a complete exercise in helping the students reflect on their choices, I usually go a step further. I ask the students how they communicated their choices to the other group members, and how they acted toward each other in coming to a group decision. Did they take the stance, "My choices must be the ones the group accepts, and I will force this to happen," or did they decide, "I want to get this exercise completed in as brief a time as possible, so I will go along with whatever others choose." I ask them whether they attempted to listen to each other with understanding, and whether they treated each other with respect. Did they use the conflict resolution strategies discussed in a previous class session? While it is probable the choices the student made regarding whom to allow into the shelter represented a set of values to please the instructor or other classmates, the method of interacting in the group is likely to be indicative of their valuing set.

Ohlde and Vinitsky (1976) found using the Simon method does actually affect value awareness. These researchers designed a seven-hour value clarification workshop based on this approach and randomly assigned students to either this activity or an interpersonal communication workshop. As measured by an occupational value survey, students in the value clarification workshop had a significantly greater awareness of personal values than those in the interpersonal communication workshop group. Thus the effects of Simon's approach can be empirically demonstrated.

The Method of Casteel and Stahl.
   Casteel and Stahl (1975, 1997) have developed a value clarification technique specifically designed for use in the schools and integrated into the curriculum. Similar to Simon's approach, using this method is likely to lead not only to enhanced value clarification but also increased learning of academic content as well. Casteel and Stahl's method involves four stages, comprehension, relational phase, valuation and reflection. The technique can be used in any subject or discipline in which a teacher assigns readings for students to review. In a history class, the topic of the readings might involve a world event with many consequences such as the assassination of a national leader or a declaration of war or initiating a social movement. In a science course, the topic might involve the effect of creating new chemical compounds or whether energy needs should be met through the building of nuclear reactors or is global climate change the result of human activity. A literature class might discuss whether the actions of a protagonist led to the most desirable outcome. This latter example can be modified by having students read only the first part of a short story or novel until the main character is facing a significant dilemma and have the students project various courses of action this character might take based on different valuing sets. An ethics class could discuss issues such as end of life choices and the morality of euthanasia. The list of possible topics is limited only by the level of creativity of the educator. Whenever possible, the assigned readings should reflect varying positions on the issue so that students have knowledge of the positions of experts who differ on the issue.
   Once the topic and readings have been selected, the value clarification process can begin. The first phase according to Casteel and Stahl is called comprehension. It is important that all students in the class have completed the assigned readings. The teacher asks

a series of questions which determine if students are prepared to discuss the material. Some teachers might not allow the student to participate in the discussion if they cannot achieve an acceptable score on this test. This frequently serves as an added incentive for the students to be prepared since many want to become involved in the group activity. Passing the test and then orally discussing the answers comprises the comprehension phase. That is, the students have demonstrated they are knowledgeable about the "facts" of the material.

The second or relational phase begins with the teacher (or the students) suggesting a value issue that emerged in the reading. Using the previous examples, "Was it good that the social movement was begun?", or "Should the nuclear reactor be built?", or "Should the main character perform a certain action?", or "Is euthanasia a moral activity?". Then students are to take the facts of the readings and line them up as supportive of one or the other side of the issue. In effect the students – without judging the quality of the argument – are lining up the pro and con information and the associated conflicting values. Some educators allow students to suggest arguments or facts not mentioned in the readings, while others limit the discussion to the arguments presented.

The third phase is for each student to take a stand and make a valuation statement. The statement can be any of four types: preferential, consequential, imperative or emotive. Each of these is described below.

Students can make a preferential statement. They can indicate liking or disliking a particular position for example. Depending on their developmental levels, students should be able to give arguments or reasons supporting their preferences.

Students can make a consequential statement. Taking this position will have a list of benefits or drawback for oneself or for one's family or for society or for the environment.

The statement can be imperative, that is leading to an action. "I will write my legislator, asking her to support (or oppose) the proposed nuclear reactor." Or "I will join the movement." Or I will write my own novel if the main character doesn't behave this way."

The fourth type of statement in this valuational stage can be emotive. The students are asked to express how they feel as a result of making this decision. "I am relieved by this choice.", or "I am fearful of the consequences, but I must take this stand.", or "I am sad there are no better options."

The final stage in this value clarification process according to Casteel and Stahl is called the reflection stage. In this stage, students are asked to reflect or think about how they made their choices. What was important to them? Was it their preferences, their likes or dislikes? Did the students choose to focus on the consequences, and if so, what type of consequence was most important? For example was the most salient outcome financial or social? Were the greatest concerns legal or ethical or based on religious convictions? Did the effect on my family or social or ethnic group outweigh the effect on the nation or world? The student might also reflect that the imperative is most important: the value is more strongly held if he or she is moved to act on it in some way. This reflection can help them as they make future decisions since now they know what aspects are most important to them. Students can also conclude that their decision making was based on shallow concerns, and this could lead them to rethink how they come to choose their values. As with the Simon method, this technique can be generalized to other issues the student may encounter when reading a newspaper or listening to the speech of a political candidate. The student gains the tool of being able to clarify one's own values. This last consequence is perhaps the most significant benefit. Consistent with the proverb, "If a man is hungry and you give him a fish, you have fed him for a day, but if you teach him how to fish, you have fed him for the rest of his life." The student now knows what is subjectively most important and can apply this learning in all future decisions to be encountered.

The Controversy of Teaching Value Clarification in American Public Schools

Previously in this chapter, many of the empirically demonstrated benefits of teaching value clarification to students of various ages were described. Research has shown students are more motivated to learn as they become more involved in the topic and are more interested in critically evaluating and debating arguments and cognitive information. In addition value clarification enhanced character development as shown through reducing drug abuse and in increasing pro-social behavior, appreciation of family and a greater effort in planning one's future. Given all these favorable outcomes, one would expect school boards and state educational departments would be eager to encourage the inclusion of value clarification in the curricula of American public schools. Unfortunately, this is often not the case. Many teachers who have taught the value clarification process have come under attack by school board members and parents who believe the approach is an indoctrination attempt of some sort (Scileppi, 1988). In some cases, state educational department staff members consider that value clarification is a form of secular humanism, a quasi-religion which promotes value relativity. As such they see the teaching of value clarification as a violation of the principle of the separation of church and state as specified in the first amendment to the United States Constitution, and thus they believe this technique should have no place in public schools. Judge W. Brevard Hand of Alabama has ruled value clarification cannot be taught in public schools. However, many of his legal opinions have been overturned by higher courts, and the issue is still an "open question" (Goldberg, 1987, Hartman, 2011). It is unfortunate and ironic that those who would like to see moral and character education programs in the schools are frustrated by strongly religious neighbors who fear that morality is declining among youth in contemporary society. While a strong point can be made that the moral development of children should be the responsibility of their parents, having the issue of values and value clarification supported by teachers in the schools will only enhance the students' appreciation of the need to establish a personal moral compass. The issue is still a current one and many state education departments and school boards continue to explore and debate the implications of this prohibition. Private and religiously affiliated schools in the United States do frequently include value clarification in their curricula, and find it effective in enhancing the moral and character development of their students.

As can be seen, value clarification while controversial can influence the lives of students. Through this process, learners can go beyond mere rote memorization of content and gain a greater understanding of the topics covered. Furthermore, they learn about themselves and become empowered as active participants in charting their futures. Students become more aware and are able to listen to their own inner voice when confronting decisions that must be made. The techniques of value clarification can be applied at nearly every level of schooling. It is limited only by the willingness and creativity of the educators to incorporate this process in their classrooms.

Specific Applications of Empowerment through Education

# 7

Self-Management of Behavior:
When We Know Better, We Do Better

Elizabeth Quinn

As discussed in the previous chapter entitled *Values Clarification*, values are the underpinnings or foundation for one's inner voice and are generally reflected in one's behavior. While the definition of each value can be subjective, the following are universally accepted as basic human values: freedom, pleasure, achievement, truth, self-direction, fairness, equality, loyalty, respect, and care or benevolence. Students' ideas about these values and how each is most appropriately implemented in their lives are often shaped by parental and environmental influences. Through the process of values clarification, educators can help the student define and more purposefully "live" the values one espouses, thereby being directed by one's inner voice – or pulling one's own strings.

To live purposefully such that one's experience is satisfying and one has integrity, self- management is important. Historically, self-management was considered "character education" and often taught from a theoretical point of view without the practical, skills building strategies students could practice to develop such character or learn to manage themselves effectively. The ability to manage oneself is more than a philosophical orientation regarding being one's own master; it requires self-awareness and possessing the skills to do so.

In this chapter, the techniques for managing behavior toward general life goal attainment are introduced, followed by the specific application of these techniques relative to empowerment. Included are methods for managing cognition, or thoughts, and feelings (affect) as they directly influence behavior. The relationship between these three elements of basic human functioning and motivation are then described. Finally, the chapter ends with a discussion about the role self-management plays in leadership.

Introduction to Self-Management

The Value of Being Self-Directed

To be self-directed means one is responsible and accountable for his or her feelings, thoughts, and behaviors. At first pass, such responsibility would seem obvious, and yet we live in a world where many are inclined to abdicate this responsibility to others. We buy products we don't need because advertisers tell us we do; we accept the self-serving claims of politicians who want our vote without checking the evidence supporting (or not) those claims; and we go into debt for things we cannot afford and do not need because we think having more "stuff" will gain us favor among those we wish to impress.

The need for approval often stems from early childhood when conformity is more rewarded than independent thinking. Suval (2012) discussed the motivational power of our need to be validated by those who are important to us. Therefore, if our perceptions about the world, ourselves, or others, our dreams and life goals, and our behaviors are different from those whose opinions matter, we may be less inclined to honor our own values, ideas and wishes, particularly when we fear we may lose the approval of others if we do. Horney (1942) theorized about how our anxiety regarding the loss of approval and subsequent affection results in the development of neurosis which drives our behavior toward pleasing others at the expense of being true to ourselves. According to Horney (1942), and many other psychologists, such abandonment of our "true selves," is often unconscious and yet it results in abdicating responsibility for and control over our lives.

When we allow others to control our lives, when we allow others to "think" for us, the result is often significant unhappiness and the sense that our lives are not our own. Managing one's own life makes one less vulnerable to outside negative influences. The value then, of becoming self-directed is increased autonomy, maximized potential for self-actualization (Maslow, 1970), and overall improved quality of life. Myers, Sweeney, Popick, Wesley, Bordfeld, and Fingerhut (2012) stressed the importance of educating students about how to manage themselves in an effort to better prepare them for careers, particularly in the areas of clinical practice. These researchers found graduate students' perceptions of stress were minimized by better sleep, hygiene practices, strong social support, and cognitive restructuring.

Goleman (1995), in his book entitled *Emotional Intelligence,* discussed the practical ability to manage oneself socially and emotionally, which he called emotional intelligence (EQ), as being the most critical factor in personal and professional success. He believed the appreciation of one's own, as well as others' emotions, demonstrated well developed self-awareness and such knowledge should be used to inform one's thinking and behavior. He advocated for developing EQ through self-management to generate mutually beneficial social relationships and promote intellectual growth (Labby, Lunenburg, & Slate, 2012). Goleman (2005) identified the following skills as indicators of EQ: a) self-awareness or having a realistic understanding of one's own feelings; b) self-regulation or management of one's emotions such that one is able to control anger or other impulsive responses to emotions; c) motivation or internal inspiration which is the ability to motivate oneself without external reward for behavior; d) empathy or vicariously experiencing the feelings and thoughts of others; and e) social skills or the ability to understand and communicate with others in ways that foster healthy, positive, pro-social relationships. Challenging the traditionally held believe that IQ was the most significant factor in success, Goleman (2005) argued these skills comprising emotional intelligence are far more important and encouraged providing students with opportunities to develop these competencies.

Stephen Covey (1989) in his book *7 Habits of Highly Effective People: Powerful Lessons in Personal Change,* also advocated for the development of emotional skills as one endeavors to master his or her own destiny and create the life one desires. He proposed the practice of these habits, or living by these rules, is the key to success. The habits include:

1) Be proactive – have a personal vision for your life and take responsibility for the decisions you make as well as their consequences; don't make excuses;

2) Begin with the end in mind – live according to your values as you accomplish your life's goals; live every day as a reflection of the strength of character you most wish to possess;

3) Prioritize – practice time management and focus activities on goal attainment (including strengthening interpersonal relationships); spend your time actualizing the goals identified in Habit #2;

4) Think win-win – establish a pro-social attitude that drives decision making such that solutions involve a 'win" for both parties; treating others with dignity and respect fosters interpersonal relationships and strengthens one's own character (another win-win);

5) Seek first to understand, then to be understood – is another habit that reflects Covey's value of empathy and interpersonal relationships; this habit suggests problem solving is enhanced through open mindedness, effective communication, and mutual respect.

6) Synergize and manage attitude – appreciate the importance of teamwork and the contribution of others to make goals/dreams a reality; no one accomplishes great things on his or her own; managing one's attitude means recognizing positive cognition is key to personal effectiveness; and

7) Sharpen the saw – continually reassess your resources (including energy and health) to ensure balance in an effort to maintain a sustainable, long-term, effective lifestyle; Covey encouraged exercise for physical renewal, prayer (meditation, yoga, etc.) and good reading for mental renewal, and service to society for spiritual renewal.

The central theme in all of the personal excellence theory frameworks is that the ability to manage one's feelings, thoughts, and behaviors both intra and interpersonally requires skills that can be taught and learned; while some may be more innate than others, and there are certainly individual differences in abilities, self-management can be developed through practice.

Demonstrating Emotional Intelligence: Practicing Self-Management

The concepts of self-management as well as the results of both managing and not managing oneself are outlined above. The process of, and strategies for, practicing self –management are presented below.

The **A**ffect, **B**ehavior, **C**ognition (ABC) Model

Based on the work of Arnold Lazarus (1989) and evidence based practices in the field of psychology, O'Keefe and Berger (1999) developed a model for self- management they called the ABC model and applied it to the college student population. The strategies they discussed for managing one's affect, or feelings, behavior, and cognition, serve to empower individuals in their efforts to be the masters of their own lives.

Affect

Many take for granted that our feelings are simply reactions to stimuli and are beyond our control. So often students claim to recognize they are responsible for the behaviors that result from their feelings, but the feelings themselves "are what they are." We've often heard, "you can't control how you feel, but you CAN control how you behave." And yet, as Epictetus, the Greek philosopher, taught: men are disturbed not by the things that happen, but by their opinion of the things that happen. This indicates we *can*, in fact, manage how we feel, if we control how we think. The value of positive thinking not only mediates negative emotion in the present, Lightsey (1994) found positive automatic thoughts buffer stress and predict future happiness. In fact, people who had higher levels of positive thoughts measured by the Automatic Thoughts Questionnaire – Positive experienced less depression in the face of negative life events, suggesting positive thinking serves as a protective factor for the individual and helps build resilience, both of which are necessary for empowerment. Drago (2004) reported that cognitive abilities were maximized when students were able to manage their emotions and this ability was predictive of academic success and retention in college. Conversely, as affect management declined, behavioral difficulties increased (Meyer, Salovey, & Caruso, 2004). Van der Zee, Thijs, and Schakel (2002) also found negative correlations between indicators of academic and emotional intelligence, and yet emotional intelligence was found to predict academic and social success more so than traditional measures of academic intelligence.

Whether one argues the relative importance of affective compared with cognitive management, at the most fundamental level of empowerment is the management of the self. The process of increasing individuals' capacity and ability to make decisions about their lives, to invest in them the power to master their own destinies, must first come from within themselves. Opportunities within one's environment are maximized when one has the ability to manage oneself. Therefore, the following section describes strategies for managing feelings or emotions.

Techniques for increasing positive and decreasing negative emotions

Managing one's life (behavior) begins with the belief (cognition) that one is able to do so, and such beliefs generate positive emotions (affect). Negative thinking, or believing one is incapable or otherwise unable to be in charge of his or her own life results in negative emotions such as stress, depression, anxiety, and anger. **Cognitive restructuring**, a component of Cognitive Behavioral Therapy, is a specific process by which individuals challenge their erroneous beliefs (Ellis, 1969), recognize the faultiness of those cognitions, and replace them with more adaptive ideas in an effort to reduce the negative affect they are experiencing. The process for doing so is outlined below in the *Cognition* section, however, there are many ways of changing one's thinking, often called **cognitive reappraisal**, that directly impact one's emotional experience, or affect and will be discussed here in the *Affect* section. It is important to appreciate that the effectiveness of various approaches to affective regulation depends on whether or not the individual *believes* in its validity. For example, Myers et. al. (2012) found exercise was only effective as a coping strategy for those graduate students who believed in its efficacy. These findings further reinforce the power of cognition.

In his social broadening research, Ong, et al. (2012) studied African

American students and found positive emotions were significantly increased when students wrote about their perspectives regarding the first African American President of the United States, Barack Obama. Their experience of realizing a person of color could be elected president impacted their cognitions about their race, and ultimately, themselves. Contrary to early childhood socialization when racial pride is not fostered (Schmidt & Nosek, 2010), Ong et al. (2012) reported various study findings that indicate positive emotion is correlated with positive racial attitudes for African Americans which resulted in positive academic outcomes and higher self-esteem. He encouraged the use of **expressive writing** for six consecutive days as a technique for perspective development. The process of writing enabled students to clarify their thinking and more accurately articulate their feelings about what this election meant to them, and how it may have changed their thinking about the professional limits (or lack thereof) imposed by their race – if Barack Obama can be elected President, perhaps they too have the opportunity to achieve professional success.

Acting as if, sometimes referred to as "fake it 'til you make it" is a behavioral technique that can be utilized when individuals hold beliefs about a particular ability they perceive they are lacking. For example, when I was first asked to teach a course for my colleague who was on sabbatical, I was absolutely sure I was unable to do so, that I would look incompetent and the students would see me for the imposter I was. I had never taught anything before and I believed I surely did not have the skills or knowledge to be a college professor; I had terrible "stage fright." However, I also did not wish to disappoint a colleague I respected a great deal, so I *acted as if* I were a good teacher. I prepared my lectures thoughtfully and thoroughly; I attended to detail, provided excellent examples, and created interesting supportive materials I could hand out to the students. When delivering my lectures, I *acted as if* I were enthusiastic about the material and completely comfortable engaging with the students, rather than letting them see how terrified I was. About the third lecture, I realized I was no longer faking being a good teacher; I *was* a good teacher. I was excited about the class, and I was comfortable; my anxiety was gone. The experience enabled me to change my perceptions about my inability to teach because I now had evidence of behavior that was contrary to my erroneous beliefs.

Acting as if can also be used when individuals experience decreases in their motivation. Those who are most successful share the common trait of being able to do whatever is necessary whether or not they *feel* like it. I often tell my students that behavior is easy to manage when the activity is something they *want* to do. What separates the truly self-managed from those who are not is the ability to "get the job done" when they're not in the mood – when they *don't feel like it*. This type of acting as if refers to the pretense of actually wanting to do something when one is not motivated to do so, and is similar to the Nike slogan "just do it." Many of us have utilized this technique when the motivation to complete our dissertations disappeared; we knew we must "just do it." Through the process, we restructured our cognition, reinforced our beliefs in our ability to complete a task we did not wish to perform, and generated feelings of self satisfaction.

Deep breathing relaxation is one of the easiest physiological approaches to lowering stress in the body (Murray & Pizzorno, 2006) because breathing deeply sends a message to the brain to calm down and relax. The brain then sends this message to the body and the physiological responses to stress, such as increased heart rate, fast breathing, and high blood pressure, all decrease as the individual breathes deeply to relax. Payne (2005) outlined the following simple steps to relieve stress and relax.

1. Sit in a comfortable position.
2. Put one hand on your belly just below your ribs and the other hand on your chest.
3. Take a deep breath in through your nose, and let your belly push your hand out. Your chest should not move.
4. Breathe out through pursed lips as if you were whistling. Feel the hand on your belly go in, and use it to push all the air out.
5. Do this breathing 3 to 10 times. Take your time with each breath.

(http://www.webmd.com).

Progressive relaxation, another physiological exercise can be used to relax muscles that have become tense as a result of stress. Muscle tension often leads to headaches, backaches, neck pain, and both fatigue and inability to sleep well. Many prefer using an audio recording to help keep focus on each muscle group, however, the following steps outline the process. Choose a place where you won't be interrupted and where you can lie down on your back and stretch out comfortably.

1. Breathe in, and clench both fists (hard but not to the point of cramping) for 4 to 10 seconds.
2. Breathe out, and suddenly and completely relax the muscle group (do not relax it gradually). Repeat 2 times.
3. Relax for 10 to 20 seconds.
4. Breathe in and close eyes tightly. Wrinkle the forehead and press head as far back as possible without causing discomfort. Rotate head clockwise and then counter clockwise.
5. Relax and repeat 2 times.
6. Breathe in and arch back and shoulders. Breathe out and let back and shoulders relax into forward position. Repeat 2 times.
7. Move to a sitting position and straighten and lift legs, point toes toward face. Tighten thighs and buttocks and hold for 5 seconds, then release and place feet back on the floor.

Repeat 2 times.
(http://www.webmd.com).

Behavior

"Pulling one's own strings" or being master of one's own destiny not only implies, but requires one to act, or behave accordingly. Empowerment doesn't emerge from passivity, rather it is an active process by which the individual engages in self- management behaviors. According to Cattaneo and Chapman (2010), the process of empowerment involves acting purposefully toward accomplishing a personally meaningful goal. While taking such steps, by critically evaluating their efficiency and effectiveness, the individual develops self-efficacy (Bandura, 1982) and competence. The outcome is a personally significant increase in the individual's power.

Goal attainment is best accomplished by first, operationally defining a personally meaningful goal. For example, the goal of personal happiness is more likely to be realized when the individual identifies the specific indicators of the goal, or the components that signal "happiness" has been accomplished. I have often asked students "how will you know it when you see it?" to help them identify goal or outcome indicators. These indicators are idiosyncratic in that "happiness" may mean a six figure salary for one, and eight weeks of vacation per year for another; therefore, they need to be defined. The next step in goal attainment is to determine whether or not the goal is reasonable given the resources available to the individual. An individual who has poor financial literacy skills will have a difficult time obtaining economic independence without first learning financial management. If the operationally defined goal is reasonable, and the individual has the tools and ability to accomplish it, s/he should then identify the measureable steps needed to proceed. Many have learned the hard way that failure can come from poor planning and unrealistic expectations regarding accomplishing goals, rather than something inherent in the goal itself. In fact, many have applied the 80/20 rule to goal attainment suggesting 80 percent of one's effort should be in the planning and 20 percent should be in the execution to ensure a successful outcome.

Time management is also critical in effective goal attainment and often reflects our values and beliefs; if we wish to know what we value, we just need to examine how we spend our time. Students may not realize that while the time they spend socializing with friends, for example, inhibits their goal of academic excellence, it reflects the importance of their friendships. The chapter on values clarification contains helpful activities for determining values and may enable students to consider ways of allowing seemingly conflicting values to be more complimentary such that they support divergent goals. For example, the student may choose to use the study-buddy approach which reflects the value of interpersonal support to accomplish his valued goal of academic excellence.

As time is our greatest asset and we must choose how to spend it, I often suggest students keep a time log for one week from the time they get up until the time they go to bed to assess how they are currently using their time. This will enable them to identify how and when they spend time on activities that are contrary to goal attainment and make productive changes. They are often surprised by the results of these time logs and develop insight regarding wasted time and more appropriate scheduling practices.

Example of a Time Log:

Answer the following questions after noting all activities for one week.

1. Were there any surprises?
2. Would you judge this to be a typical week?
3. What patterns could you identify in your time wasters or interruptions (excessive worrying, being indecisive, being unorganized, procrastinating, etc.)?
4. What part of the week would you consider most and least productive?
5. What time of the day was most and least productive?
6. What activities would you like to eliminate? What would be the cost of doing so? What is the cost of not eliminating them?
7. Which activities do you deem most rewarding? Would you like to spend more time doing them in the future? What is your plan for doing so?
8. Which activities keep you on track with accomplishing identified goals? Would you like to spend more time doing them in the future? What is your plan for doing so?

Finally, have someone review your time log. An objective observer may be able to point out discrepancies or patterns that you did not see.

Organization is another important aspect of time management as disorganization and poor planning are tremendous time wasters. Continually having to start over or refocus activities impedes progress. Prioritizing by creating a to-do list in order of importance that includes deadlines is critical. Deadlines are essential; without a deadline, it's just a discussion. Reasonable schedules that can be adhered to go a long way toward accomplishing short and long term goals, but because surprises occur, a good schedule builds in flexibility for when additional time is needed.

Perhaps one of the greatest saboteurs of time management for goal attainment is **the inability to say "no"** when necessary. Over committing to too many obligations derails schedules and non-priority activities are engaged in at the expense of goal directed behavior. While it is often hard to say "no" to requests from others, requests should be considered relative to importance and the extent to which they conflict with one's own agenda.

Reinforcing desired behavior (Skinner, 1969) is another behavioral strategy for strengthening self management and maintaining a time schedule. Very often we can motivate ourselves to stay on task by using a reward system that includes tangible or non-tangible reinforcements. When the reward is contingent on the behavior occurring, the behavior becomes more likely. As Skinner indicated, rewarded behavior is also more likely to be repeated, meaning reinforcing desired behavior predicts its future occurrence.

Effective time management skills are developed with practice. The process does not end with the creation of a to-do list; it takes trial and error of strategies, monitoring progress, and self-analysis to identify what works and what doesn't work for the individual. Ultimately, the way we spend our time is the way we spend our lives; we need to make it count.

Cognition

Lazarus (1989), Ellis (1969), Miller (1962), and many other theorists have written extensively on the primacy of cognition in human experience and self-management is an excellent example. In the *affect* section above, the relationship between emotion and cognition is outlined, and information is provided regarding the management of feelings using cognitive approaches. *Behavior* is also discussed above from the perspective that actions begin with cognitive processes called thoughts. In addition, cognition was addressed in the *behavior* section as attitudes and beliefs are often changed using strategies such as *acting as if*. While the interaction between affect, behavior and cognition have been previously described, this section further outlines the cognitive aspects of self-management, particularly as it relates to empowerment.

The practice of managing oneself and empowerment are reciprocally related in that one's belief in one's power to manage one's self and to be in charge of one's experience is at the core of self-management. And the more one engages in self-management, the more empowered and efficacious (Bandura, 1982) she or he becomes. Therefore, it is important to establish and reinforce the set of beliefs that serves as the foundation of empowerment, such as valuing a feminist perspective that advocates for the rights of all people regardless of race, age, gender, etc. Other beliefs that serve to empower individuals are:

a. I, as well as others, deserve to be treated with dignity and respect;

b. I am responsible for my own happiness;

c. Being wrong sometimes provides me with the opportunity to learn new things;

d. Failure is not as bad as never taking chances; and

e. I have the right to make decisions about my life and the responsibility to own the consequences of those decisions.

Cognitive distortions, on the other hand, are disempowering and lead to maladaptive affect and often, inappropriate behavior. Sometimes called *stinking thinking*, these distortions tend to be automatic thought processes (McKay, Davis, & Fanning, 2011) that require using specific techniques to help individuals change the way they think. Some of the common cognitive distortions that lead to negative affect are:

Polarizing: looking at things as either right or wrong, all or none, or black or white.

Example: "I failed my test; I never get anything right."

Filtering: focusing on the negatives of a situation without appreciating the positive aspects.

Example: "New York is terrible; there are too many people; traffic is horrible; and it's dirty."

Overgeneralizing: applying conclusions about one event to all similar events.

Example: "No one will ever ask me out on a date."

Personalizing: blaming yourself for something that isn't entirely your responsibility, or is not your responsibility at all.

Example: "If I were a better daughter, my mother wouldn't drink as much alcohol."

Emotional reasoning: thinking that is based on feeling.

Example: Because I "feel" stupid, I must *be* stupid.

Labeling: personally identifying with a behavior.

Example: Rather than "I lost the tennis match"; thinking "I am a loser."

Catastrophizing: always thinking the worst; expecting disaster.

Example: I failed my math test, I just KNOW I am going to fail the whole year!"

Being right: continually defending your opinions or behavior;

being right is more important than accepting you may have made a mistake.

Example: "I don't know why it didn't work; I just know I did NOT make a mistake!"

Mind reading/ Jumping to conclusions: you make assumptions about others' thoughts and feelings with no basis for such judgments.

Example: "I can just TELL she doesn't like me."

Shoulds, musts: absolute rules we hold that would be more realistic (less distorted) if less rigid. Example: "I am overweight; I should stop eating" could be replaced with "Working out will help me get in shape and feel better."

Irrational thinking: refusing to consider evidence contrary to your opinion.

Example: "Climate change is a hoax manufactured by politicians. I don't care if scientists say it's real; they're just paid off anyway." (Burns, 1989; O'Keefe & Burger, 1999)

Changing erroneous thinking can be an arduous task because thought patterns tend to be automatic, fairly stable and consistent, and people often don't realize their negative thinking is impacting their ability to accomplish goals and experience positive emotions. As Ellis (1969) noted, people for the most part disturb themselves, therefore, strategies for improving negative thinking and practicing more positive, purposeful thinking are important components of education.

Variations of Albert Ellis' (1969, 2003) **Rational Emotive Therapy** are most commonly used for cognitive restructuring and the steps can be taught easily to students to assist them in developing their ability to manage themselves. Teed and Scileppi (2007) used the example of a student experiencing test anxiety to illustrate the how the cognitive restructuring process allows her to change her response to the test:

1. *Evaluate self talk (statements an individual tells him or herself about an event or about him or herself), and analyze distorted thinking.* For example: the student is probably telling herself:

I'm a terrible student.
That professor gives unfair tests.
My parents will be angry when I fail.
There's no point in studying when I'm going to fail anyway.

2. *Challenge negative thinking.* For example: the student could dispute his negative self-statements by telling herself:

I may not be a straight-A student, but I do alright.

I know this professor gives hard tests, so I'll set aside extra time to prepare.

Even if I do poorly and my parents are disappointed, it won't be the end of the world.

3. *Exchange negative with positive self-statements.* For example, the student could use such statements as:

I've done well in the past on other exams.

Because I know this will be difficult, I'll prepare myself as well as I can so I will be confident about doing well.

My parents will be pleased when my GPA is higher this semester.

In addition to positive thinking and self-statements, **reframing** is a technique that allows the individual to view a troubling situation as a challenge or opportunity. In the example presented above, the anxious student could choose to interpret the situation as an opportunity to perfect her study skills and improve her time management skills (Teed & Scileppi, 2007). She could also reframe the exam as an opportunity to demonstrate to her teacher all she has learned. In putting a "positive spin" on the negative event, the student reduces her anxiety, develops her self-management skills, enhances her self confidence and becomes a better student. Each of these significant outcomes is a direct result of empowering herself to take charge of her experience.

Leadership Through Self-Management

From a philosophical point of view, it is interesting to contemplate what makes someone a leader? Is s/he a leader because s/he was appointed to serve in that capacity? Or is s/he a leader because others choose to follow? For educators who believe leadership skills are an important result of empowerment, some consideration for how these abilities can be developed is warranted. Campbell, Smith, Dugan, and Komives (2012) remind educators that mentoring student leadership development through faculty role modeling and community service participation has been empirically demonstrated, meaning faculty may foster leadership skills in students first by being role models themselves.

Cooper and Sawaf (1997) indicated emotional intelligence is necessary for leadership, particularly as it relates to the ability to influence and relate effectively to others. Goleman (2002) added that emotional control, adaptability and optimism were important leadership qualities, and Labby, Lunenburg, and Slate (2012) reported Mayer, Salovey, and Caruso's findings determining EQ was the most important aspect of effective leadership. Assuming one cannot effectively lead others if one cannot "lead" or manage himself, fostering self-management skills, then, is critical in efforts to empower individuals.

Affect

Emotional control, particularly stress management, is required of leaders. Agitation, restlessness, anxiety, irritability, and general unhappiness negatively impact one's ability to accomplish his or her own goals rendering him or her a poor model for others to emulate. In addition, those in leadership positions experience "power stress" which "is part of the experience that results from the exercise of influence and sense of responsibility felt in leadership positions." (McKee, 2005) When people are in a leadership positions, they must influence others to make things happen and they are under continuous scrutiny and evaluation. Typically, when under pressure, leaders work harder rather than reach out to others, and because there is less affiliation, it is often "lonely at the top."

Goleman, Boyatzis, and McKee (2002) reported the sources of leadership power stress were: making important decisions with complex and conflicting information; attempting to influence others over whom they have little authority; continually generating positive outcomes; managing multiple stakeholders; managing crises; and taking responsibility for even uncontrollable events. In addition, leaders are pressured to place the good of organization above their personal needs, and often work for organizations that undervalue renewal, recuperation, and relaxation. The physiological stress associated with leadership further exacerbates the psychological stress making the requirement for demonstrating self control even more taxing. Therefore, a leader must purposefully attend to stress prevention, reduction, and recovery as motivating others is difficult, if not impossible if one is not optimistic, positive, and energized.

Behavior

As our lives are the sum total of how we spend our time, excellent time management is also critical for leaders. In addition to the strategies presented above in the section on time management, leaders often practice specific strategies to maximize their effectiveness and productivity. For example, prioritizing activities in order of importance, appreciating that not all tasks are of equal significance, and delegating responsibilities when appropriate enable leaders to maintain ownership of their time.

Taking care of one's physiological needs (Maslow, 1970) such as ensuring proper nutrition, sleep, and exercise enable leaders to function optimally. Scheduling breaks during work, such as taking a ten minute "time out" every few hours with no interruptions, serves as rejuvenation. Making time for fun and relaxation is also important as doing so enables the leader to be in a better position to handle life's stressors when they inevitably come. Leaders don't get so caught up in the hustle and bustle of life they forget to take care of their own needs. Leaders laugh; they appreciate the importance of their position without taking themselves too seriously (Quinn, 2012) with the recognition nurturing oneself is a necessity, not a luxury.

Cognition

Effective leadership begins with one's thinking and one's belief that his or her responsibility is to foster more leaders, not more followers; in effect, this is the basis of empowerment. Leaders believe in a vision and in their people's ability to make the vision a reality. They have realistic expectations of themselves and of others, and they understand they do not "control" their world, particularly the people in it. Instead, leaders recognize the world is imperfect and filled with flawed individuals who have limitations and make mistakes, but they believe they have the responsibility and privilege to empower others to maximize their potential. They prefer to influence others rather than use authority, and in many ways, being a leader is a mindset like being a teacher; it reflects who you are, not what you do (Quinn, 2012). Covey (1989) cautioned leaders only to advise after empathically understanding a person's situation; otherwise the advice isn't likely to be heard. In this way, effective leaders aren't dictators; rather they practice the art of compromise and continually demonstrate their respect for others.

A relatively new concept in leadership research is the idea of lifespan development proposed by Murphy and Johnson (2011). These theorists recommend age appropriate activities that foster self-management to empower youth to become leaders. As early as pre and elementary school, students can be taught how to manage themselves in ways that enhance their emotional intelligence giving them social capital which makes them obvious leaders. In preschool, Murphy and Johnson (2011) encourage teaching communication skills and emotional regulation such as delaying gratification. In elementary school, students can be encouraged to help others, be classroom monitor, act appropriately in social situations, be responsible for fundraising or coordinating teams, and to develop public speaking skills. During early adolescence, in middle school, Murphy and Johnson (2011) recommend goal setting, self observation and evaluation, serving in elected office or other student government activities, coordinating student or peer projects, and public speaking as a leader to gain support for a cause. As students enter high school and college, their leadership skills can be further developed through organizing more complex projects, establishing grassroots organizations, becoming politically active, mentoring others, volunteering their services, and being given supervisory responsibilities in clubs and internships. The better able students are to manage themselves and the greater their social competency or emotional intelligence is, the more likely they will be to take on and be successful in leadership roles.

In summary, leaders foster the empowerment of others by practicing effective self management and being a model for others to emulate. For example, leaders appreciate that others take their cues from them so they model stress management because displaying stress or anxiety will likely trigger uncertainty or anxiety in others. Leaders also demonstrate passion for and commitment to defined goals which they believe are valuable. They prioritize success and have well developed strategies for accomplishing goals and they energetically execute those strategies. Perhaps most importantly, excellent leaders appreciate the fact that few accomplish great things alone; leaders acknowledge the support and help of others who made their success possible. Their recognition of and praise for the efforts of those they lead empowers those individuals.

8

Gender Equity in Education:
The Societal Benefits of Empowering Females

Elizabeth Quinn

Those who control the resources control the power.

For much of civilization, knowledge has been used as a tool of oppression and has often been considered dangerous. One can trace the roots of this back to the Bible's Book of Genesis when it is said that Adam and Eve were forbidden by God to eat from the tree of knowledge and after having done so, were banished from the Garden of Eden. Fareed Zakaria (2015), in defending liberal education, proposed that the biblical fall of man (which was caused by a woman) was a result of the quest for knowledge and has left persistently inquisitive humans "fearful of the consequences of its curiosity." (p.135)

    For centuries, a major source of knowledge – namely education in schools – was restricted to men. Beginning with the last century, women have advocated for and have begun to achieve the right to education in many societies. Perhaps most notable, was the Nobel Prize winning Malala Yousafzai, the Pakistani schoolgirl who stood up to the Taliban and defended her right to an education. It has often been said that knowledge is power, and in the simplest terms, education serves to empower women by increasing knowledge, providing opportunities for skills building, and enabling them to develop competencies such that they may actualize their potential in personal and professional activities. While the goals of education are similar when students are male, females face different gender related expectations within many societies that must be addressed through education if potential is to be actualized. The University Grants Commission's (UGC) National Policy of Empowerment of Women of 2001 endorsed the National Policy of Education (NPE) 1986 which emphasizes the need to use education as an agent of change in the basic status of women. Specifically, the Policy prescribes: equal access to education for women and girls; elimination of discrimination; universalize education; eradicate illiteracy; create a gender-sensitive educational system; increase enrollment and retention rates of girls; improve the quality of education; development of occupation/vocation/technical skills by women; and reducing the gender gap in secondary and higher education.

While the benefits of education are well documented, the International Center for Research on Women (ICRW) (2005) reports the role of education in promoting gender equality and empowerment of women is not well understood.

The Value of Empowering Women

Kofi Annan (2006), then UN Secretary-General, said it is impossible to realize our goals while discriminating against half the human race. As a tremendous amount of research indicates, he said, there is no tool for development more effective than the empowerment of women. In 1865, William Ross Wallace wrote about motherhood as the most significant force for transformation in the world in his poem *The hand that rocks the cradle is the hand that rules the world*. Notably, according to the UN (2012), the status of women is highly correlated with the well-being of families. When women's status is low, families are marginalized and fail to thrive. Leigh (1998) also found mothers' education level has a greater influence on children's health than that of fathers. In studies discussed by Namara and Tormey (2011), adolescent illegal drug use, low birth weight babies, and poor health of children are all more prevalent in families where the mother has less education. Therefore, the empowerment of women is strongly correlated with higher levels of education and economic opportunities for their children, thus benefiting families and the next generation.

Health

Women die prematurely and unnecessarily from issues related to reproductive health in developing nations; infant mortality is also higher than in more highly educated populations. Teenage births are higher among girls with less education (Kiernan, 1997) and girls whose mothers have less education. Educated women throughout the world are also more likely to practice safe sex and use condoms, and are less likely to contract sexually transmitted diseases (Higgins, Hoffman, Graham, & Sanders, 2008).

Pulkki et al (2003) found differences in smoking habits between those who were educated and those who were not: those with less education were eight times more likely to smoke than those with more education. Specifically, Arnold et al (2001) reported women with less education demonstrated less knowledge about the hazards of smoking, particularly during pregnancy.

Wolfe and Havemann (2002) found education was correlated with better lifestyles in general and better health in particular. In addition to participating in prevention programs such as cancer screenings (Chiu, 2003; Sabates & Feinstein, 2005), those with more education were less likely to be overweight and more like to exercise regularly (Kenkel, 1991; Arnold, et al, 2005). Perhaps this is because women tend to put into immediate practice whatever they learn about nutrition as well as what they learn about preserving the environment and natural resources (ICRW, 2005).

Economic empowerment

More women than men live in poverty and this results in more children living in poverty. In India, as well as many other countries, the economic benefits of secondary education for women were found to be twice what they were for men (ICRW, 2005). According to Kajiado (2000), the most significant tool for fighting poverty is education, and for a middle class life, a college education is crucial. Anthony Carnevale, Director of Georgetown University Center on Education and the Workforce (2012) found a college education is the distinguishing factor between the middle class and the growing number of low income families in the United States.

Greenstone and Looney of the Brookings Institute (2011) reported "higher education is a much better investment than almost any other alternative for the Class of the Great Depression (23-24 year olds)". They further indicated a 4-year degree nets a 15.2% return on this investment annually.

Educational empowerment

Around the globe, lack of education is a strong force for oppression. Women are the most highly impacted with 66% of the illiterate adults in the world being female (UN, 1998). Some of the main causes of educational disparities between males and females are: early marriages, pregnancy, lack of gender appropriate facilities at schools, belief systems that include placing a low value on the education of girls, lack of resources (money and transportation), and low self esteem (Merang, 2010). Furthermore, men still earn the majority of PhDs and MDs (King, 2010).

Political and Social Empowerment

Social scientists believe the cultural values and attitudes of any society are revealed in the central documents of that nation. Teed et. al. (2007) describe the US Declaration of Independence as a seminal and sacred political statement that reflects Americans' view of themselves and others. Jefferson's 1776 statement, "We hold these truths to be self-evident: that all men are created equal..." demonstrates the belief that access to resources, including education, should be equitable, not based on gender, race, or social or economic status. To test the practical application of this theory, the US Congress charged sociologist James Coleman and his colleagues (1966) with evaluating the extent to which educational funds and resources were being allocated equitably to schools, and whether or not reallocation of those resources would improve students' academic performance. The results of this study indicated access to educational resources was disproportionately favorable to affluent students, compared to economically disadvantaged minority students. Therefore, differences in academic performance were attributed to limited access to educational resources and opportunities. If politics is ultimately the art or science of distributing resources, empowerment is a direct outcome of civil rights.

The worldwide civil rights movement between 1950 and 1980 was focused on ensuring equality under the law. Whether it was the

1964 Campaign for Social Justice in Ireland to end discrimination and to ensure a representative government through voting policies, or the 1968 French uprising that began with students and workers but was quickly joined by citizens across all ethnic, economic, social, age, and class boundaries, human rights issues were at the core of these movements. In the US, the Supreme Court decision in Brown v Board of Education in 1954 made segregation illegal; the Civil Rights Act of 1964 banned discrimination based on race, color religion, or ethnicity; the Voting Rights Act of 1965 restored voting rights; and Feminist Movement between roughly 1963 and 1982 advocated for economic, reproductive, and educational equality.

While there are many examples of important progressive advancements, perhaps most relevant to the topic of gender equity in education is the Patsy T. Mink Equal Opportunity in Education Act, often referred to as Title IX, passed in 1972 which bars gender discrimination in education. In addition, the Lilly Ledbetter Fair Pay Act of 2009 amends the Civil Rights Act of 1964, by essentially removing the 180-day statute of limitations for filing lawsuits regarding pay discrimination in an effort by President Obama to defend the right to equal pay for women.

The impact of women's right to vote has also been influential in fostering the empowerment of women. Verba, Schlozman, and Brady (1995) as well as Green, Preston, and Sabates (2003) found a person's level of education is highly correlated with his or her active political engagement, including voting, serving on governing boards, and membership of political organizations. The quality of such community service is further improved by the well-developed social engagement skills (organizing, advising, communicating, etc) possessed by more highly educated people (Bynner et al 2001). Furthermore, the example of positive civic engagement provided to children by their parents' behavior is likely to result in intergenerational empowerment.

Education as a Tool for Empowerment

While education can be empowering for women, Namara and Tormey (2011) indicate it is less likely to liberate and more likely to indoctrinate the student into the socio-cultural values within a society. Often, education is the process by which "elites reproduce themselves" (p 128), because it fails to challenge societal inequalities, and as Carr (1998) described, education can be more of a socializing institution than a method for fostering independent thinking. "Education either functions as an instrument that is used to facilitate the integration of the younger generation into the logic of the present system and bring about conformity, or it becomes 'the practice of freedom', the means by which men and women deal critically and creatively with reality and discover how to participate in the transformation of their world." (Shaull cited in Freire 1996). It is critical for educators to recognize education, in general, can serve to maintain the status quo, therefore efforts should be directed toward presenting education as a tool for change. More specifically, female education was found to produce greater social benefits than male education due to the degree to which education empowers women to participate in social development (Mareng, 2010).

Freire (1970), and Arnot (2002), discussed education for liberation as a process by which democratic and feminist ideals such as freedom, equality, and social justice for all people become the driving forces in society. In addition to teaching the theoretical basis of these ideals and their accompanying values, methods for realizing them such as developing independent thinking skills and destroying structures of social inequality, must also be practiced by students. Termed "conscientisation" by Freire (1996) these critical thinking skills enable students to become aware of oppression, how it robs individuals of their identities, and how this serves oppressors. Namara and Tormey (2011), in explaining Giroux's perspective said "liberational education should be a form of political intervention capable of creating opportunities for social transformation, while teaching should be a moral and political practice premised on the assumption that learning is not about processing received knowledge, but about actually transforming this knowledge as part of a more expansive struggle for individual rights and social justice. This implies that liberational education should help students to expand, and deepen their understanding of economic and political democracy, and social relations of power, and how such an understanding can be used to liberate the oppressed." (p.153) Because this insight alone is not sufficient for change, Giroux (2003) further advocated for progressive educators to use a "problem solving education" whereby students are given opportunities to think independently, dialogue with others, and develop skills by actively participating in solution-focused exercises. When these academic experiences are successful, the classroom mirrors a collaborative, democratic, prosocial environment where freedom is practiced and transformation occurs; it is a microcosm of the larger world.

The timing of education that has the greatest potential for being a catalyst for change is secondary or post-secondary education (ICRW, 2005). The ICRW review of the impact of female education revealed improved options, opportunities, and outcomes for women were only associated with higher education. While this finding is not surprising, it points to the need to address issues in primary education that may prevent females from participating in secondary education. For example, in Kenya, early marriages and female genital mutilation have been identified as the leading causes of female dropout rates (Mareng, 2010). Ultimately, the empowerment of women begins with the education of girls.

Among the empowerment differences between women and girls are their experiences with sexually transmitted diseases, particularly; HIV, intimate partner violence, and female genital cutting. Jewkes, Levin, and Penn-Kekana (2003) found that among females in Africa and Latin America, primary education improved their ability to ask for condom use and discuss sex with a partner, while secondary education increased their knowledge of risky sexual behavior and their ability to refuse unwanted sex. ICRW (2005) reported secondary education has a stronger effect than primary education on reducing intimate partner violence, and a woman's ability to safely leave an abusive relationship. In addition, in many parts of Africa, women with primary (45%) or no (48%) education are significantly more likely to be victims of this practice than are women with secondary (23%) education. El-Gibaly (2002) also found women in Egypt who had some secondary education were four times more likely than their primary education counterparts to contest the female genital cutting of their daughters and granddaughters.

In addition to the timing and amount of education, the context in which it occurs is an important factor in its impact on empowerment. For example, the benefits of education, such as improved health outcomes, fail to be maximized when mobility and access to services are limited. In many developing countries, where availability or quality of healthcare is problematic, education cannot mitigate these circumstances. Context is relevant as well: in Nigeria, Kritz, Makinwa-Adebusoye, and Gurak (2000) found when family structure, gender role expectations, and employment opportunities for women did not support female autonomy, education failed to benefit those women. However, higher levels of education are associated with positive societal change and community transformation such that mobility, access to healthcare, and gender equality are more likely to be improved when women in those communities advocate for such change.

Education Serves to Empower the Oppressed

Theoretical Basis for the Empowerment of Women in Higher Education
Feminist theorists concerned with the dominance in patriarchal institutions, including academia, and the reduction of women to subordinate positions, advocate for women to assume leadership positions at all levels in educational institutions. The relationship of gender and schooling, patriarchy, hegemony, and androcentrism are thought to foster the inequalities between men and women.

Each theoretical framework representative of feminist ideology (liberal, radical, and socialist) acknowledges the necessity of major transformation as a condition for social justice (Melenyzer, 1991).

Liberal feminism maintains that equal opportunity is possible within existing educational systems and focuses on sex stereotyping and bias. This theory is often criticized for maintaining a narrow focus because it fails to recognize the social and economic conditions that control the ways schools operate.

Radical feminists claims women's situations are dominated by class oppression under capitalism, which must be exposed before their situations can be changed.

Social feminists attend to the social and/or economic analysis which impacts the origins of the practices and other structures of power and control that affect what goes on within schools.

Maher's (1987) model of personal agency and public effectiveness holds that women experience a different, more expressive, subjective, and participatory mode of learning than is validated by traditional models of education. Empowerment is viewed as freedom from oppression of the dominant exploitative ideology. Women's oppression in the paid workforce and in domestic work is reproduced through what happens in the schools.

Themes of Empowerment

Melenyzer presented the following themes of empowerment at the Annual Conference of the Women's Consortium of the Pennsylvania State System of Higher Education in 1991.

Collective Action and Critique

Social feminists recognize that traditionally, education has been organized to encourage isolation and competition among teachers and that teachers and administrators must seek out ways of working collectively and collaboratively. Teachers should attend to history, organize to support their skills and rights, and defend progressive and critical teaching as well as curricular practices. Teachers would also benefit from forming coalitions with other groups, such as nurses, social workers, etc., who are experiencing similar situations. Feminists say the lack of opportunities for women to work collectively and collaboratively has fostered their sense of disempowerment.

Gender and Power

Feminist theorists most often consider issues of gender to be central to the reconstruction of educational theory and the practice necessary for emancipation for all women, not just a few. Power derives from an ability to realize potential and enable the accomplishment of aspirations and values. The goal of empowering women in educational settings focuses on issues of gender and power. The goal is not to increase women's status relative to men but to empower women through a redistribution of power. This redistribution of power should be accomplished by acknowledging that for women to share power, power structures must be changed as described below.

Reform and Feminist Voice

The feminist concern for a change in the gendered power structures within educational institutions to include women's experiences and mechanisms for women to speak is echoed by feminist writers such as Biklen (1987), Noddings (1989), and Shakeshaft and Nowell (1984). Biklen notes "the standard male model of professionalism" is reinforced by "competition" and "elaborated credentialing systems." She offers a model for "feminist professionalism" in which teachers participate in defining the nature of their particular school; promote an articulate, participatory workforce that will enable teachers to interact with each other around decisions that affect their lives; and view human activity as what both men and women do rather than what men do. Gilligan (1982) points out the voice of women is grounded in an "ethnic care, the tie between the relationship and responsibility," and there is a mistaken assumption that "there is a single mode of social experiences and interpretations."

Caring, Community, Connectedness and Equality

This perspective stresses the collaborative nature of the research process as one in which all participants see themselves as members of a community. They suggest these issues have implications for feminist concerns of "connectedness, equality, and caring" and empowerment. Empowering relationships involve feelings of 'connectedness' that are developed in situations of equality, caring and mutual purpose and intention. The necessity of time, relationship, space, and voice in establishing a collaborative relationship is important. Noddings (1989) interprets women's power and empowerment as the realization of interdependence and the joy of empowering others. Melenyzer (1991) describes Berman's philosophy of teaching as an example of caring because it involves fostering and building knowledge by liberating and empowering individuals to make decisions that will benefit themselves, others, or their communities. Feminist researchers believe most research in the social sciences reflects the male bias to the exclusion of women's voices and experiences in our cultural values. Gilligan (1982, p.6) writes, "The differences between the sexes are being rediscovered in the social sciences. This discovery occurs when theories formerly considered to be sexually neutral in their scientific objectivity are found instead to reflect a consistent observational and evaluative bias. We begin to notice how accustomed we have become to seeing life through men's eyes." Establishing women's studies was an outgrowth of the consciousness raising of women in the late 1960s and as a result, women came to see what the social reproduction theorists assert: the producing and legitimating of knowledge through educational institutions is a major instrument of cultural reproduction.

Feminists envision empowerment as a project of possibility and as emancipatory, educative, and resulting from collective action. Different meanings and practices of empowerment are recognized, most notably are the distinctions between empowerment as "power with" and "power over," independence and interdependence, and collaboration and competition. Women are disempowered by the exclusion of the historical role of women as teachers and their own voice in educational reform and research, and they have called for collective and collaborative efforts within and beyond the schools. It is through our schools and universities that we can teach, train and model the experiences and share the voices of women for other generations. Only then can qualities such as collaboration and critical critique, caring, and the spirit of community become alternatives to competition and "power over" which dominate many of the current hierarchical structures in today's schools.

Education as a Method of Challenging Beliefs about Power, Equality and Gender Differences

Cultural norms and attitudes about power, equity, and gender differences within any society are learned and are often realized simply based on compliance with cultural expectations. This suggests that to create a more democratic, equitable, prosocial, gender-inclusive culture requires concerted efforts to change attitudes about power and gender differences. One method for doing so is to challenge the assumptions and theories presented historically, and to reframe our understanding of the dynamics of power and oppression as they relate to gender. The well known theories presented by Kohlberg and Freud are examples of how established assumptions can perpetuate erroneous beliefs about gender differences. The biased nature of Kohlberg's theory on moral development (1981) and the lack of female moral maturity and poorly developed sense of justice postulated by Freud (1925) were discussed by Walker (1984). Historically, theorists have considered the moral development of males to be superior to that of females, particularly after puberty when formal logic in males becomes more apparent. However, Gilligan (1982) addressed this misconception in her analysis of two eleven year old children, one male and one female, and their reaction to Kohlberg's famous moral dilemma experienced by the man named Heinz. In this particular moral dilemma, Heinz contemplated whether it is acceptable to steal medication needed by his dying wife that he does not have the money to buy. Kohlberg complicated, or perhaps clarified, the dilemma by adding Heinz asked the pharmacist to reduce his price for the drug so he can afford it, but the pharmacist refused. Kohlberg indicated the moral reasoning differs between males and females as the boy, Jake, arrived at his decision through logic and the girl, Amy, through consideration of relationships. For Jake, the moral decision is to steal the medication because the law that prohibits theft was developed to maintain social order, and preserving life trumps the need for order – all quite logical. However, Amy, according to Kohlberg, appeared to have more difficulty determining right from wrong, and was more inclined to take her direction from others rather than critically evaluate the situation and make her own determination. Kohlberg reported she was unsure of herself and failed to use logic in her determination. Gilligan indicated Amy believed Heinz should not steal he drug, not because he would violate the law, but rather in doing so, he would jeopardize his ability to care for his sick wife. She reasoned the consequences of his theft could be incarceration which would render him incapable of helping his wife, resulting in her becoming sicker, and it would leave her alone as she approached death. Instead, Amy advocated for Heinz to find other ways of acquiring the drug such as borrowing the money he needed, or compromising with the druggist.

Gilligan's (1982) analysis illustrates the difference in each child's definition and interpretation of the problem. Jake saw Heinz's dilemma as a conflict between life and material property, whereas Amy saw it as a relational problem that could be resolved through effective communication. As much as Jake's resolution demonstrated his ability to apply logic to the problem to reach a solution, Amy demonstrated a well-developed ability to consider the consequences inherent in choices made. Gilligan's perspective is that females' moral development is simply *different from* as opposed to *less than* males'.

Noddings (1998) also pointed out that what has become known as Gilligan's *different voice* in moral reasoning reflects emotions and issues related to quality of life. In *Philosophy of Education,* Noddings reminds us knowledge is established by power, therefore the power differential between males and females must be addressed in education if it is to be effective as a method for empowering females. Similar male oriented assumptions in contemporary education such as the value of completion among students as represented by grading and ranking policies is better than cooperative learning and assessment need to be studied and debated.

Create an environment where creativity can flourish and progressive opportunities can be realized

Research has demonstrated gender biases, likely unintentional, occur in elementary school classrooms that result in less favorable academic performance on standardized tests among females compared with their male counterparts. For example, King (2006) found females are more likely than males to have completed college preparatory courses in math and science, with the exception of calculus and physics, but they do not perform as well as males on either the verbal or math subscales of the SAT (Corbett, Hill & St. Rose, 2008). Sadker, Sadker, and Zittleman (2009) propose this difference is the consequence of teachers' reinforcement of males' classroom behavior. They report that teachers are more likely to resolve problems experienced by females when struggling with academic problems, but are also more likely to encourage males to continue struggling with the problem until they are able to resolve it on their own. This difference in teachers' responses to academic difficulties may enable males to develop more self-efficacy than females as they learn they are capable of solving problems independently. In addition, Sadker, Sadker, and Zittlemann found teachers wait longer for males to answer questions posed which may communicate teachers' beliefs that males will come up with the correct response if given time to do so while females will not.

Innovative Strategies for Promoting the Success and Empowerment of Women

The value of education in an effort to empower women globally cannot be overstated. The ICRW (2005) has identified the following as important to the maximization of educational benefits:
- Invest appropriately to achieve universal primary education within 10 years;
- Increase investments to achieve gender parity and higher levels of enrollment in, and completion of secondary and tertiary education;
- Improve the context, quality, and relevance of education through curriculum reform, teacher training, and other actions aimed at transforming attitudes, beliefs, and gender-biased social norms that perpetuate discrimination and inequality; and
- Provide women and girls better health care services, social services, decent employment, and other support so they are better able to reap the full benefits of education.

Strategies for maximizing the benefits of education include gender-specific education for girls, science, technology, engineering, and math (STEM) education for girls and women, and continuing with microloans and microcredit.

Gender-Specific Education

Jenkins (2006) reported co-educational schools negatively influence girls' attitudes about achievement, course enrollment and career choices. This may reflect gender-related cultural norms and expectations as girls reported being less comfortable speaking in co-ed classes compared with their counterparts schooled in same sex classrooms who were more comfortable demonstrating their intelligence (Kirschenbaum & Boyd, 2007). Jenkens also found girls were identified as gifted at younger ages than boys, but by high school, those same girls were less likely to be in gifted programs. She theorized this may be a result of the social pressure on girls to dumb down their intelligence in the presence of boys. Carol Gilligan famously stated, "girls are confident at 11 and confused at 16".

The benefits of gender specific classrooms include a greater sense of empowerment reported by girls, and without the distraction of boys they were more focused on learning (Flowers, 2005). In addition, Flowers found girls in single sex classrooms highly valued academic excellence. A 2001 Daily Post article reported professors Nolen and Booth divided their economics students into mixed gender groups and single gender groups and found the all girls group experienced a 7.5% increase in their average compared to no change in the mixed gender or all boys groups.

While the outcomes of general education for girls are better in single sex classrooms, in the specific areas of math and science, academic differences between the types of educational settings are most pronounced. In traditional, co-educational classrooms, the American Association of University Women (AAUW) (1992) reported girls were not expected nor encouraged to take higher level math and science, which leads us to the importance of STEM education for girls.

STEM (Science, Technology, Engineering, and Math) Education Targeting Girls

Perhaps one of the best ways of encouraging girls to pursue education in STEM specifically is for women to model similar interest. While women continue to be underrepresented in these fields (Gorman, Durmowicz, Roskes, & Slattery, 2010) in 2005-2006, women were the recipients of more than half of all doctoral degrees awarded in social sciences, life sciences, and humanities, but far fewer in physical sciences (28%), engineering (20%), and business (39%). In addition, Snyder and Dillow (2010) report that in 2007, while 46% of all full-time faculty members were women, less than 30% were tenure track professors at research institutions. The positions held by women are less secure, lower paying, and the least prestigious (West & Curtis, 2006), and the National Science Foundation reported 31% of full time STEM faculty and 27% of department chairs and deans, respectively, are women.

While different from the national norm, Stevenson University was discussed at the 2010 Forum on Public Policy as an example of "what works" in STEM education and the empowerment of women in academia. Specifically, all of the academic leadership positions in STEM at Stevenson are held by women and the full time STEM faculty is comprised of 71% women. This has led to large enrollment increases in the School of Science such that it now represents approximately one third of the University's undergraduate population. Not surprisingly, Lee, Marks, and Byrd (1994) also found there was significantly less sexism at schools that aggressively encourage gender equity in enrollment and in the hiring of faculty.

In 2009, US President Barack Obama launched "Education to Innovate," a nationwide initiative designed to increase STEM literacy, especially critical thinking skills and in depth learning; to support Americans in becoming global leaders in advancement in STEM fields in the next decade; and to focus on STEM learning and access to careers for under-represented populations, particularly women and girls. When Obama called for "all hands on deck," the private sector formed partnerships with the US government to develop STEM learning opportunities for girls. Some examples include Girls, Inc. which focuses on STEM programming, Girl Scouts, US, and Mocha Moms Inc. (a national network of Moms of color) which provides STEM mentors, and the Entertainment Industries Council which strives to develop pathways for women to pursue careers in media. The National Girls Collaborative Project (NGCP) joins organizations committed to informing and encouraging girls to pursue careers in STEM and the American Association of University Women (AAUW) advocates for breaking through barriers that prevent girls and women from advancing in STEM. AAUW also stresses the importance of sponsors and mentors (www.aauw.org) to support such advances in STEM fields. Their Tech Trek: a week long camp for 8th grade girls involving student and professional role models, and Tech Savvy: a daylong seminar for 6th through 9th grade girls and their parents about careers in STEM, are designed to promote interest and participation in science and engineering in an effort to develop the innovative workforce needed to build the industries of the future.

In addition to various public and private sector partnerships, individuals such as actress Danica McKellar, are also creatively contributing to the effort to increase math literacy among girls. Ms.

McKellar is best known for her role as Winnie Cooper in the popular television show *The Wonder Years,* but after becoming a mathematician and pledging to Congress in 2000 to be an ambassador of math, she has become a *NY Times* bestselling author of math books for girls. Using her celebrity, she designs the covers of her books to look like teen magazines so girls get the message "these books are for you; math is for you". Her titles, *Kiss My Math; Math Doesn't Suck; Hot X; Algebra Exposed;* and *Girls Get Curves: Geometry Takes Shape,* are also appealing to girls. Content is disguised as fun and practical. For example, snow angels' armpits are used to teach the degrees of angles such that acute angles are smaller than 90 degree angles because they are small and cute; obtuse angles are bigger than 90 degrees because they are obese. McKellar dispels the notions math is too hard, is not a subject for girls, and is irrelevant for girls by teaching mathematical concepts related to topics of interest to girls. For example, she addresses ways to attract boys, and methods for improving self-esteem, and uses personality and body image quizzes to teach girls "you don't have to be a nerdy outcast; you don't have to choose between being a fun and fabulous girl and being a smart girl who knows what's up. You can be both." (www.danicamckellar). She also includes testimonials from successful women in an effort to provide mentors and role models for girls.

Microcredit

Winning the Nobel Peace Prize in 2006 for his revolutionary microfinance project, Muhammad Yunus may be the most influential champion of women's empowerment of our time. He began the Grameen Bank in Bangladesh for the sole purpose of providing loans for poor women, and was an important mentor to Roshaneh Zafar who established the Kashf Foundation. "Kashf's mission is to **alleviate poverty** by providing quality and cost effective microfinance services to low income households, especially women, in order to enhance their economic role and decision-making capacity." (http://www.kashf.org).

Kristof and WuDunn (2009) tell the inspirational story of Saima, a Pakistani woman who was poor, physically and emotionally abused by her husband, and who had to give up her daughter because she could not feed her. When she subsequently had another daughter, the extended family encouraged her husband to take another wife who might bear him a son. Saima realized this would further exacerbate the family's financial situation and result in less money to feed and educate her children, so she turned to a women's support group affiliated with Kashf. She took a $65 loan to purchase beads and cloth and created enough embroidery products to earn sufficient money to support her household, bring her eldest daughter home, and to make payments on her husband's debt. Being the sole wage earner in her home gave her status whereby she was able to demand respect and the beatings stopped. Her position in the community was also elevated as she was unable to keep up with the demand for her products so she hired 30 families to work for her, in addition to putting her husband to work. This prosperity has enabled her to lend money to her neighbors, pay off the family debt, renovate and connect running water to her home, buy a television, and most importantly, educate her daughters.

As with most cultural change, the societal pushback was great. The empowerment of women was not well received by many but with time, perseverance, and the positive outcomes that resulted, Kashf began expanding rapidly (Kristof & WuDunn, 2009) and even branched out into offering life and health insurance. The effectiveness of micro financing can be measured in the fact that currently, there are 157 Kashf branches, more than 500,000 families have been aided, and 265 million dollars have been loaned. The repayment rate is also significant with nearly 100% repaid in full. The loans have directly contributed to upward mobility with 34% of borrowers moving above the poverty level by the time they have taken their third loan. In spite of this level of success, Roshaneh told Kristof and WuDunn, "microfinance is not a panacea; you need health. You need education. If I were prime minister for a day, I would put all our resources in education." (p. 191)

Summary

The challenge will be to also empower women to maintain a feminist perspective. Chodorow (1989) wrote about women becoming more like men to be competitive in the workplace, and yet this results in losing the diversity of the feminine point of view. In addition, the empowerment of women through education must include appreciation for the centrality of motherhood in the lives of many women – that empowerment and motherhood are not mutually exclusive.

Education, in and of itself, may not be empowering as discussed by Freire in *Pedagogy of the Oppressed* (1966), yet lack of education or ignorance has rarely been found to be transformational. Therefore, education is necessary but may not be sufficient for achieving gender equality and improving women's well-being. However, the extent to which education is empowering and used as a tool for advancing our world may be influenced most by educators. Many in the field are examining what they need to do to encourage a culture of intellectual curiosity, discovery, and creativity for the purpose of disrupting the status quo. Regardless of intellectual ability, many students report being bored, challenging the educational system to develop pedagogical approaches that maximize intellectual curiosity using appropriately distributed resources such that education serves to empower all students, particularly those historically disenfranchised from the existing system.

9

Case Studies of Empowerment in Primary and Middle School

Barbara Ruggiero and Linda Dixon-Dziedzic

The implementation of empowerment strategies in schools may be difficult to conceptualize. Therefore, the following case studies have been provided as possible approaches to creating academic programs designed with student empowerment as an outcome. Both reflect the important ideas of Ruby Payne and demonstrate the Search Institute Developmental Assets in practice.

Children's Community School – Elementary School
"where learning and self-empowerment are the keys to a brighter future"

Barbara Ruggiero

A Children's Community School (CCS) graduate from two decades ago stands before the small group of current graduates to address them as they nervously anticipate saying goodbye to a school that has been home to them for the last seven years. She is tall, really tall, and she tells the kids she was a basketball player through high school and college. She looks the part. But more importantly, she tells them she knows where they come from. Raised by a grandmother because of drug and incarceration problems with her own parents, she is like so many of the kids who attend CCS. She, like them, was a poor child growing up in an inner-city neighborhood in an unsettled family that had experienced generational poverty. But then she entered CCS where things began to change for her. She learned the skills she needed for academic success but, as she told the young graduates, she had learned something equally important. She had learned that deep inside her, she had what it would take to achieve personal success. Her teachers had taught her well. She learned how to study but she had also learned that she had the emotional strength to weather life's challenges and to create for herself a meaningful life both in terms of her work as well as her personal relationships. She was a model for those young students showing them that if she had the power within her to take her rightful place as a productive member of her community, so did they.

Children's Community School was incorporated in 1969 by a group of religious sisters and community activists in a public housing project in Waterbury, Connecticut, an old industrial city that reveals traces of its once prosperous past in the many empty and crumbling factory complexes that are scattered throughout its core. Today, the unemployment rate for the overall Waterbury Labor Market area is the highest in the state and close to a third of children under 18 years of age live below the federal poverty level. Eighty percent of school age children in the city qualify for free/reduced lunch. More than half of the city's adults function at a low literacy level which means they do not have the skills necessary to function on the job or in society (United Way of Greater Waterbury Community Status Report, 2012). CCS serves 150 students grades pre-k through grade 5; classes are small with no more than 18 per class and there is only one class per grade level. Students are predominately black with an increasing number of Latinas and 90 percent of the school's students receive free or reduced price lunches. The original founders of the school were addressing issues of poverty that have only become more serious with the passing of the last four decades.

Ruby Payne, in her breakthrough book, *A Framework for Understanding Poverty* (2005), offers a working definition of poverty which includes but extends beyond the financial. She describes poverty as "the extent to which an individual does without resources" (p. 7) which include, among others, emotional and mental resources, as well as relationships and role models as resources. Two of these are internal to the person while the other is external. She defines these resources like this:

Internal:
Emotional - *being able to choose and control emotional responses, particularly to negative situations, without engaging in self-destructive behavior. Shows itself through stamina, perseverance, choices*
Mental – *Having the mental abilities and acquired skills (reading, writing, computing) to deal with daily life*
External:
Relationships/Role Models – *having frequent access to adult(s) who are appropriate, who are nurturing to the child, and who do not engage in self-destructive behavior*

Payne also talks about other resources such as financial, which a school cannot directly fix, but the three resources named above have a direct connection on what can and what does occur in successful urban schools that empower students. Children's Community School is a case in point. CCS empowers children from poverty by providing the cognitive as well as the non-cognitive emotional and social skills to insure the success of each child.

For our purposes, the following working definition of "empowerment" is put forth. **Empowerment,** for school children, is a process by which children gain the necessary skills and knowledge that will allow them to create for themselves a meaningful and fulfilling life.

The Problem for Poor Children

Emotional: Some of the most compelling work to date which underscores the significance of emotional resources for children is the Center for Disease Control (CDC) ACE Study. The study concludes: "Childhood abuse, neglect, and exposure to other traumatic stressors which we term *adverse childhood experiences* (ACE) are responsible for what pediatrician Nadine Burke Harris (2011) calls "trauma spectrum disorder". It's not post-traumatic stress disorder because it is not linked to an event but rather represents life lived with chronic stressors. The short- and long-term outcomes of these childhood exposures include a multitude of health and social problems." Using ACE scores, Nadine Burke Harris, M.D. (2011) demonstrated a clear link between childhood trauma and learning and behavioral problems.

Many environmental factors which do not qualify as "trauma" but reflect a generally chaotic home environment also have a negative effect on learning. A previous study found the elements of the household chaos scale that measure order and routine predict early reading skill (Johnson et al., 2008). Chaotic living conditions statistically predicted helpless/hopeless responses and withdrawal from academic challenge – an effect partially mediated by disrupted and inconsistent sleep patterns (Brown & Low, 2008).

As has become increasingly evident, *stress* has potentially damaging effects on all of us. Stress activates our fight or flight response and is vital when we experience acute threats. But it is not healthy for us when it is a response to a chronic situation. Early adversity causes stress to developing bodies and brains. The effects are physical as well as cognitive. Fifty one percent of patients with Adverse Childhood Experiences (ACE) scores of four or higher, have learning or behavioral problems. Stress physiologists know why: stress affects the prefrontal cortex of the brain which is critical to self-regulation including our ability to regulate our thoughts. Children who grow up in stressful situations have trouble concentrating, recovering from disappointing or difficult situations, and sitting still and following directions in class, all of which affect school performance. Pre-kindergarten teachers strongly believe a young child's social-emotional developmental is far more crucial to positive school outcomes than knowing the alphabet. Developing a strong self-regulatory capacity is essential to learning.

Cognitive: There is recognition that low socio-economic status (SES) students start school at a disadvantage particularly in terms of language development. The seminal work of Hart and Risley (1995), demonstrated that language acquisition among children differs dramatically by socioeconomic class both in quantity and kind of language and that exposure to language in early childhood, correlates strongly with academic outcomes. Therefore, low SES students are behind in school even before they begin.

Waterbury, like most urban school districts, reflects the well-documented achievement gap that exists for children of poverty when compared to their economically better off peers. All academic performance measures for Waterbury public school children lag behind corresponding measures of students statewide. For instance, in Connecticut, over 62% of 4th grade students are meeting the state goal for reading while in Waterbury just over 42% are meeting that goal.

Education pays and is the key to ending the cycle of poverty. Education pays in higher earnings and lower unemployment rates and empowers people with choices that lead to meaningful lives. For underserved, urban students, a good education that provides the skills to compete with more affluent peers is an elusive goal.

Relationships/Role Models

According to Payne (1995), the development of emotional resources is crucial to student success. The greatest free resource available in schools is the role-modeling provided by teachers, administrators, and staff. Many studies support this notion and demonstrate that the primary factor in resilience for children is having caring and supportive relationships. Relationships that provide role models, and offer encouragement and reassurance help bolster a child's resilience.

So many of the students at CCS have challenging home lives where the significant adults in their lives have made choices that have led them away from achievement and into a life of limited resources and options. Many live stressful lives that limit their ability to offer their children the appropriate nurturance and secure

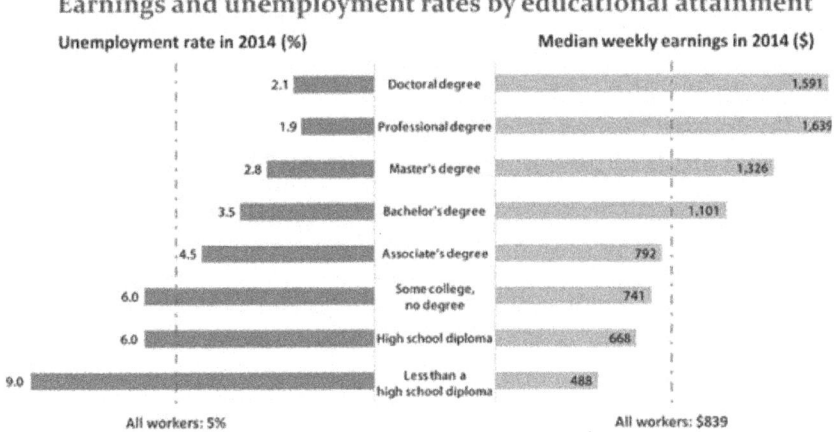

attachment that are foundational to healthy development. The choices they have made early on – early pregnancies, dropping out of school, and drug use have not only been self-destructive but have caused them to be unavailable to their own children. Many homes are headed up by single moms who work fulltime and attend school while transferring the responsibility of caring for their own children to others. One father, when losing his hard sought after job, turned to drug dealing and his children witnessed his arrest. Another father, hoping his son would seize the opportunities he himself missed out on, beat him with a belt because he did not complete his homework. Many CCS fathers have a series of children from several women and are not present to their children in a positive and predictive way. These parents are unable to be the role models their children need in order to develop the resilience that will help them secure a bright future. Some students at CCS are in foster care and face a future of multiple placements and a childhood of uncertainty and chronic disruption.

A Solution

As stated previously, CCS is the place where learning and self-empowerment are the keys that allow children to create for themselves a meaningful and fulfilling life. Many aspects of the school contribute to an environment that supports positive emotional development, provides for the development of strong academic skills, and fosters positive relationships with adults who are indeed positive role models. Our core beliefs are the guideposts for all we do and for the successes our students enjoy:

- **High expectations, combined with a supportive environment, affect student outcomes.** There is robust evidence to support the far-reaching benefits of high expectations for students in terms of academic outcomes. CCS teachers believe in the intrinsic worth and ability of each child and do not believe demographics determine destiny. We believe students can achieve success if teachers hold them to high standards and provide classrooms rich in intensive language instruction as well as with experiences they might not access outside of the school. Students are also empowered in classrooms to contribute to decision making including creating the classroom's rules. An afterschool program that offers enrichment activities and a full summer program that provides both academic and enrichment activities to prevent the well documented "summer-slide", contribute to student success. We also know the importance of early childhood experiences so CCS offers full day/full year a PreK for three and four year olds. A recent review of scores in reading on the Fountas and Pinnell Benchmark Assessment, a widely used system for evaluating reading levels, revealed 85 percent of students in grades 1 through 5 were reading at or above grade level and of those students, 50 percent were above grade level. The 15 percent of students below grade level were not more than a half a year behind expectation, and of those students, 50 percent were designated learning disabled. Our inputs result in extremely favorable outcomes when compared to reading scores for local public school children. CCS also cultivates a supportive environment. The Search Institute has designed a survey of the "developmental assets" which are considered the building blocks of healthy development. The students at CCS were surveyed using their instrument and the deficit most consistently reported by students was in the area of believing people listened to them and that they were heard. Once CCS staff members identified this concern, they decided to address this issue by implementing the Responsive Classroom model which calls for each day to begin with a "morning meeting" during which time the classroom community comes together to begin the day by sharing information about important events in each student's life. This is a powerful way to greet one another and to believe one matters and has something important to say. In addition, a school counselor is available for children who might need to talk as well as for parents who may need social services. In order to support students in their transition to middle school, every 5th grader is given a mentor at the beginning of the year who follows him or her through middle school and beyond. One outstanding CCS graduate who is now in graduate school credits his mentor for her continued support from middle school through college. Research shows that positive mentoring relationships have a direct and measurable impact on children's lives. With high expectations for students and a supportive environment, CCS consistently boasts an over 90 percent on-time graduation rate from high school which stands in marked contrast to the city's much lower rate.

- **Academic skills alone do not insure future success; social and emotional learning are critical.** CCS has had a long tradition of care for the whole child and in providing character education that permeates the entire curriculum. Current research points to the importance of teaching character development and to helping students develop resilience. The school counselor introduces a character trait each month which is discussed in morning meeting and which then infuses the classroom discussion and activities each day. Students are recognized for demonstrating "good character" such as persistence, integrity, and respect. Students are also offered opportunities to contribute to their communities and to experience the power of knowing they can make the world a better place for others. For example, a food pantry is situated in the school basement and students contribute regularly to that bank. The school's adoption of The Responsive Classroom approach also supports social and emotional learning by having teachers facilitate a set of social skills: cooperation, assertion, responsibility, empathy, and self-control which are linked to success in the classroom as well as to students' future achievement.

- **Committed, mission driven, high quality teachers and school leaders are essential to the success of students.** The staff of CCS is compensated far less than local public school teachers but the teachers are committed to a school that truly makes a difference in the lives of students. Teacher retention is extremely high and this consistency for students is crucial for children who experience unpredictability in their lives outside of school. A clear mission that all embrace and a collaborative work environment create a supportive work community. Teachers and staff regularly participate in professional development from in-class coaching in reading, to seminars on the most current research on brain development and its application to learning, in order to hone their skills. The school values its staff and believes the single most important factor affecting student achievement is teachers. This is particularly true for low SES students who are very dependent on their school experience for their future outcomes.

- **School resources matter, especially for children in low SES areas.** A small school with small classes allows every student to be known, connected, and engaged. CCS is small by design and rich in human capital. Each class averages 16 students and each class has both a teacher and an assistant. Teachers are able to differentiate instruction to meet each child's individual learning needs. The STAR (Student Teacher Achievement Ratio) Study, conducted in Tennessee 1985-1998, found students who had been placed in small classes in grades k-3 continue to outperform others right through high school, with higher graduation rates, higher grade point averages, and a greater likelihood to be headed towards college. In particular, attendance in small classes in the early grades cuts the gap between minority and white students taking college entrance exams in half. Seventeen percent of inner-city students who had been placed in small classes in the early grades were held back through the ninth grade, compared to 44 percent of those from similar backgrounds who had been put in regular sized classes.
This important finding underscores what CCS has known and practiced all along. In addition to its paid staff, CCS is profoundly lucky to have many volunteers who participate regularly in the life of the school. Most particularly, volunteers work daily under the direction of the classroom teacher tutoring students so that students receive one-on-one academic assistance as well as the support and attention of a caring adult.

- **Parental involvement is important for the success of a student.** The mission of CCS includes the statement: "… and encourages strong parental support to ensure the success of each child." CCS strives to create a welcoming environment for parents. Research shows strong parent – school ties have a direct effect on student participation in class, on motivation, and on long term outcomes. Each school year begins with parents, students, and teachers sitting down together to discuss the expectations for the year and then signing contracts pledging support for the educational process in the ways that are appropriate for each party. Teachers promise to do whatever it takes to support a child's learning; parents promise to support the school and supervise nightly reading and homework; and students promise to work hard and approach their learning with seriousness of purpose. Three times annually parents and students return to meet with teachers to review progress. CCS frequently boasts one hundred percent participation in these conferences which sends a strong message to students that school and family are working together to ensure their success. In addition to formal meetings, teachers maintain regular contact with parents throughout the school year. Very importantly, a strong parent teacher organization (PTO) creates opportunities for community building through activities as well as by providing a forum by which parents' voices concerning school issues can be heard.

- **Community partnerships and involvement are vital to the life of the school**. CCS has always been proud of its outstanding support in the community. The friends of the school are the reasons CCS has been able to thrive for the past 40 plus years. Community foundations, corporate supporters, and individuals contribute both financially to the school and by their active participation in service to the school. Bankers paint. Scientists judge science fairs. Business leaders teach entrepreneurship. And children's eyes are opened to a bigger world. CCS also welcomes many volunteers from the local high schools and colleges and partners with those schools so students can experience a college campus or dance in a school's dance studio affording opportunities they might not otherwise be available to them.

As was stated earlier, **empowerment,** for school children, is a process by which children gain necessary skills and knowledge that will allow them to create for themselves meaningful and fulfilling lives. Children's Community School, for more than four decades, has adopted a philosophy that understands, has concerns for, and realistically acknowledges difficulties of children who grow up in poverty. However, it does not permit those difficulties to become obstacles to learning. Each day, the faculty and staff of CCS work to compensate for those resources that are lacking for its children – emotional and mental resources as well as the resource of relationships and role models. By embracing and realizing core beliefs that have propelled the school to fulfill its mission, young students leave CCS at the end of 5th grade to face the challenges of middle and high school with a solid foundation so learning and self- empowerment will indeed prove to be the keys to a brighter future.

Arlington Central School District

Linda Dixon

The Arlington Central School District (ACS), located about 75 miles North of New York City, is comprised of about 8 elementary schools, 3 middle school and 1 high school, and is a district that covers an area of 114 square miles. There are close to 9,300 students in the Arlington School District. Student achievement is particularly high with approximately 90% of graduating students continuing on to college, while 10% enter the military service or work force. http://www.arlingtonschools.org/pages/arlington_schools

For the purpose of operationalization, ACS defines empowerment as facilitating students by "letting their power out from that which they possess from within."(Blanchard, Carlos, & Randolph, 2013) Wikipedia describes empowerment as the process by which students gain the skills, knowledge, and wisdom to overcome personal, professional, and societal challenges throughout their lives. The Arlington Central School District mission is to empower all students to be self-directed, lifelong learners, who willingly contribute to their community, and lead passionate and purposeful lives."

There are many strategies that have been used to empower students in the Arlington District. The focus of this chapter is to share how middle school students have been empowered to overcome obstacles in life, and gain the skills to achieve academically, socially, emotionally and behaviorally. The following "Core Values" are the underpinnings or foundation of the empowerment strategies implemented:

All students have inherent value

"Life long" learning is essential for growth

A community thrives when all members embrace their interdependence with compassion and empathy

Potential can only be attained through commitment, resilience and high expectations

All people can learn

Change is essential to progress

Communication of these values is critical when empowering students, as is the importance of institutionalization. Accordingly, ACS established the following goals and objectives:

Goals:

To develop systems that are clearly and consistently applied across the organization that promotes interdependence, efficiency and trust that contributes the strategic mission

To develop a trusting collaboration of interdependent relationships to empower students, teachers and administrators to support and contribute to the strategic mission.

Objectives:

Students will continually pursue knowledge and skills by developing a deeper understanding/skill in a topic of their interest.

Each student will demonstrate initiative, responsibility and action toward a goal of their choosing

To accomplish such goals and objectives, ACS committed to *adopting only new programs/services that are aligned with or contribute to the mission, and accompanied by resources needed for effective implementation.*

Lagrange Middle School (LMS)

LaGrange Middle School is home to over 900 students. Programs which incorporate the core values, objectives and delimiters of the strategic empowerment plan include primary, secondary and tertiary preventive levels. The US Preventative Services Forces Guide to Clinical Preventative Services (UPSTF) defines primary prevention measures as "those which are provided to individuals to prevent the onset of a condition. Secondary intervention is seen as those which identify/treat asymptomatic persons who have risk factors but have not developed a condition; while tertiary intervention involves the "care of disease, to alter or restore function, and/or to minimize the effects or prevent further disease." (Fitzgerald, 2013)

Empowering students at LaGrange Middle School is done through a variety of methods. One of which is a demonstration or pilot program designed to communicate that students have inherent value with teachers demonstrating compassion and empathy called Positive Behavioral Intervention Support Program (PBIS). It is a school wide program that was utilized to teach expectations to students upon their entrance into 6th grade.

This primary intervention was a school-wide positive behavioral support program that was incorporated at LMS in 2007. Students watched a short video on the first day of school in the cafeteria that identified and discussed appropriate class and school wide behaviors. Scripted by the PBIS team, which included a school psychologist and a multi-disciplinary group of teachers. A group of drama students volunteered to portray real life scenarios in the middle school. Teaching expectations to reduce misbehavior in high-incidence problematic settings can most effectively be shown when students teach students how to behave in the gym locker room, cafeteria, hall way, and class room. When students were "caught being good," they were given positive cards that had the school wide expectations that were coded in mnemonic "BOLTS" form. This reinforced the students' knowledge that "BOLTS" stood for the following expectations: "Be prepared (B), Organize yourself (O), Listen/Learn (L), Try Your Best (T) and Show Respect (S). Students were told they could put their earned BOLTS cards in the main office in a raffle to win prizes. This program also included short lessons in classrooms with activities used to foster the BOLTS expectations. Booster activities were used to support positive behaviors in the school. As LMS was a pilot site for PBIS, the video has been used to teach other schools' personnel how to implement PBIS. In addition, members of the LMS PBIS team presented the video nationally to guide other schools in the use of best practices.

Another example of a primary intervention and method of empowerment stems from the core value that all students have inherent value. The recent June 2013 New York State Dignity for All

Students' Act mandates that the "curriculum include instruction that supports the development of a school environment free from discrimination and harassment. It also requires schools to amend their code of conduct to include prohibition of discrimination and/or harassment against students or employees and to include provisions to respond to such acts. In accordance with New York Dignity for All Students Act (2013) LMS utilizes trained staff who accept incident reports, investigate and notify police enforcement when harassment, bullying or discrimination may constitute criminal misconduct.

Secondary intervention and empowerment strategies target "at risk" middle school students who have developed risk factors, such as beginning to fail academically, socially, behaviorally and/or emotionally. Students in this category are often perceived as being from economically disadvantaged environments, culturally deprived, or abused/neglected backgrounds. In Ruby Payne's breakthrough book, *A Framework for Understanding Poverty*, the lack of finances is not what defines impoverished students. In fact, Payne goes on to define poverty as, "the extent to which an individual does without resources...which include, among others, emotional and mental resources, relationships, and role models." (Payne, 2005, p. 8-9) Resources, according to Payne would help to teach students how to develop their own "emotionally internal" resources such as: being able to choose and control emotional responses to negative situations without engaging in self-destructive behavior. This produces empowerment with behaviors such as: stamina, perseverance and making positive choices. "

Primary intervention empowerment strategies would include exposure to social skills groups that teach: decision making, problem-solving, anger management, friendship skills, and basic communication. Academic empowerment occurs when students receive **core classroom instruction** that is differentiated, universal, and provided all academic year to all students with bi-yearly monitoring of progress. In comparison, secondary intervention strategies would provide **supported targeted interventions** to those students (typically 10-15% of the population), who are identified by educational teams as demonstrating significant trouble in academic areas. In terms of emotional functioning, those students recovering from loss through divorce or parental death would be included recipients for support through group counseling. Academic empowerment would include intervention programs that reinforce math, writing and/or language concepts that provide daily re-teaching in small groups of 1:5 for at least 9-30 academic weeks with bi-weekly monitoring of progress. "At risk" students would likely benefit from interacting with adults who are nurturing to the student such as with a mentoring program such as "Eye to Eye," which will be discussed later in this chapter.

Tertiary prevention and empowerment strategies in the middle school include providing special education support, or *intensive targeted intervention* to students who have failed (typically 3-5% of the population). This would include individualized instruction for a period of 15-20 weeks with weekly monitoring of progress. Based on recommendations presented in "Response to Intervention" (2010) for Guidance Documents in New York school districts, emotional support can be provided through individualized counseling and functional plans of analyses (FBAS)/behavior improvement plans (BIPs) that target the environment and provide individualized supports to minimize adverse academic, social, or emotional behaviors.

To *encourage students to create for themselves meaning and fulfillment,* the role of teachers should be to nurture positive emotional development, offer rigor to challenge academic development and strong core skills. What might be most meaningful is the strong connections that are developed with positive adults who become mentors and role models. Core beliefs that are behaviorally modeled by adults may be the most important lesson students receive in school. Core beliefs are the foundation and guideposts for all we do and those fostering empowerment strengthen the process or the journey, such that successful living results.

The combination of *high expectations* coupled with *a strong supportive environment* is positively correlated with student outcomes. The Dutchess County Children's Services Council (2013) integrates developmental assets into its projects for children and youth to develop their decision making skills and improve social competencies. These developmental assets are considered the healthy blocks of human development to help children grow up caring and responsible. They were developed by the Search Institute (1997) and highlight eight domains of internal and external assets necessary to predict emotional and behavioral health in responsible youth. These external assets are comprised of four domains which include: support, empowerment, boundaries/expectations, and constructive use of time. Internal assets include the four domains which are commitment to learning, positive values, social competencies and positive identity. For more than 50 years, Search Institute has been a leader and partner for organizations around the world in discovering what kids need to succeed. Their research, resources, and expertise help partners in organizations, schools, and community coalitions solve critical challenges in the lives of young people (Benson, 1993). The following are the developmental assets as postulated by the Search Institute:

Developmental Assets for Middle Childhood (ages 8-12) that help young people grow up healthy, caring, and responsible.

External Assets

Family support—Family life provides high levels of love and support.

Positive family communication—Parent(s) and child communicate positively. Child feels comfortable seeking advice and counsel from parent(s).

Other adult relationships—Child receives support from adults other than her or his parent(s).

Caring neighborhood—Child experiences caring neighbors.

Caring school climate—Relationships with teachers and peers provide a caring, encouraging environment.

Parent involvement in schooling—Parent(s) are actively involved in helping the child succeed in school.

Community values youth—Child feels valued and appreciated by adults in the community.

Children as resources—Child is included in decisions at home and in the community.

Service to others—Child has opportunities to help others in the community.

Safety—Child feels safe at home, at school, and in his or her neighborhood.

Family boundaries—Family has clear and consistent rules and consequences and monitors the child's whereabouts.
School Boundaries—School provides clear rules and consequences.
Neighborhood boundaries—Neighbors take responsibility for monitoring the child's behavior.
Adult role models—Parent(s) and other adults in the child's family, as well as nonfamily adults, model positive, responsible behavior.
High expectations—Parent(s) and teachers expect the child to do her or his best at school and in other activities.
Creative activities—Child participates in music, art, drama, or creative writing two or more times per week.
Child programs—Child participates two or more times per week in co-curricular school activities or structured community programs for children..
Religious community—Child attends religious programs or services one or more times per week.
Time at home—Child spends some time most days both in high-quality interaction with parents and doing things at home other than watching TV or playing video games.

Internal Assets

Achievement Motivation—Child is motivated and strives to do well in school.
Learning Engagement—Child is responsive, attentive, and actively engaged in learning at school and enjoys participating in learning activities outside of school.
Homework—Child usually hands in homework on time.
Bonding to school—Child cares about teachers and other adults at school.
Reading for Pleasure—Child enjoys and engages in reading for fun most days of the week.
Caring—Parent(s) tell the child it is important to help other people.
Equality and social justice—Parent(s) tell the child it is important to speak up for equal rights for all people.
Integrity—Parent(s) tell the child it is important to stand up for one's beliefs.

Honesty—Parent(s) tell the child it is important to tell the truth.

Responsibility—Parent(s) tell the child it is important to accept personal responsibility for behavior.

Healthy Lifestyle—Parent(s) tell the child it is important to have good health habits and an understanding of healthy sexuality.

Planning and decision making—Child thinks about decisions and is usually happy with results of her or his decisions.

Interpersonal Competence—Child cares about and is affected by other people's feelings, enjoys making friends, and when frustrated or angry, tries to calm her- or himself.

Cultural Competence—Child knows and is comfortable with people of different racial, ethnic, and cultural backgrounds and with her or his own cultural identity.

Resistance skills—Child can stay away from people who are likely to get her or him in trouble and is able to say no to doing wrong or dangerous things.

Personal power—Child feels he or she has some influence over things that happen in her or his life.

Self-esteem—Child likes and is proud to be the person that he or she is.

It might well be from the modality of group counseling at the Lagrange Middle School where embedded in the safe haven for these children are opportunities for them to develop these assets. Paramount to any intervention is the need for ***committed, mission driven, high quality teachers who believe in their students.*** Consistency of teachers appears to be medicinal since the backgrounds of those students in the greatest need have been fraught with abandonment and instability. Collaboration creates support and high morale within the work community, and research is rich to corroborate that those teachers that participate in professional development from "in-class co-teaching for example in reading," and seminars in research of most effective teaching practices are better equipped to help students.

Finally, it is with community support (partnerships) paired with quality and supportive teachers that blend the most promising ingredients towards achieving developmental assets in youth. LaGrange Middle School partners with multiple community agencies to assist students who need community based assistance. Partnerships include: teachers, parents, PTA, home-based interventionists, private therapists, day treatment centers and psychiatric hospitals. Every teacher serves a role in being a collaborative team member communicating about his or her children in an effort to receive help and outreach. It is true that "it takes a village to raise up a child."

LMS also will be initiating a national mentoring program called "Eye to Eye" which has impressive empirical support in the area of empowering our students. Eye to Eye is a network of 51 local chapters driven by dynamic community partnerships with public and private schools, colleges, universities, and local businesses. The mentor/mentee model is very straightforward - coming together once a week to create art projects specifically designed to share similar experiences. There is a clearly defined set of principles that focuses the work and distinguishes the program as one of the most innovative movements in the country in support of students labeled with language, reading, and math based learning disabilities (LD) and/or attention deficit hyperactivity disorder (ADHD). The Eye to Eye Mentoring program helps middle school students to develop their strengths, understand their weaknesses, manage their expectations and build their self-esteem. Mentors are not tutors but are role models who provide a safe, fun and empowering community for students labeled with LD/ADD/ADHD.

A Secondary Intervention for Empowerment: Destiny: A Case Study on Empowerment After Losing a Friend to Death:

I loved the small country feel, the smell of coffee beans in the air, but could do away with the pungent aroma of cow manure that remained dense in the air. That was my journey of over one hour each way from my residence to the Pine Plains Central School District. Those three short years I worked as a school psychologist in the elementary school there and then I transferred to ACSD in September 2001. I felt many mixed emotions upon leaving Pine Plains. My first year at the Seymour Smith elementary school was the initiation by fire and was marked by the 9/11 horrific event. My first experience dealing with grieving students in mass numbers was going class to class to support kindergarten through sixth grade students who were traumatized by unspeakable tragic events and feared they would be the next victims. That fear became a reality for a second grade student named Destiny (not her real name) who witnessed a horrible car accident in which her best friend was killed. A loss of this magnitude is felt throughout the whole community and the school community was no different. Many second grade students were impacted by this tragedy and I found myself initiating grief groups in the classes as well as in my office. Destiny visited me for the next four years each day-checking in with me for assurance and comfort. Not one day went by that she did not speak about her dear friend.

Destiny had a profound sense of helplessness that resulted in her feeling quite powerless and insecure. She was trying desperately to make sense of something that made no sense. She came to me for answers to the tough questions and learned that even adults can't explain some things in life. As the school psychologist, I could only listen to her, help her to identify her feelings, and comfort her, in an effort to empower her to use her grief in a constructive way. By conveying she had inherent value, showing compassion and empathy, believing in her and her ability to go on, Destiny, too, began to believe she can grow, change and progress. I knew she was beginning to heal when she organized a community tribute to her friend. Because her friend loved reading and gardening, the entire second grade class honored their fellow student by creating a book drive from which money was raised to plant vegetables and flowers at the school. This tribute to their lost friend enabled the students to celebrate her life. Years later I received a very moving poem from Destiny with her thanks for helping her through this very difficult time. I am forever reminded of the important role school personnel have in the opportunity to support the empowerment of young people to not only actualize their potential, but to overcome some of life's most difficult experiences.

When I started to work at LaGrange Middle School, I realized many students were experiencing devastating losses either through parental divorce or illness-related deaths. I decided to assist students by empowering them to coauthor a book with me on divorce and loss. Together, we wrote about identifying and exploring those feelings that were common to middle school students who just lost their original family through divorce or separation, as well as death.

The book contained information about marriage and divorce, the loss process including the stages of grief, and how one moves forward after these life events shatter their equilibrium. The students believed their work would empower others who are struggling so they wanted to "share it forward here"

The Lagrange Middle School Divorce Recovery Book

Separation, death and divorce are traumatic events for families. The experiences are defined as "Our Journey." Coping with loss and change requires identifying and communicating feelings and thoughts that only those who experience this situation can identify with. Some reactions are unpleasant; they need to be expressed in order for us to heal from pain and unresolved conflict. Without healing, issues will continue to surface bringing on poor resolution.

Most of the remainder of this chapter consists of excerpts from the book. They are presented as practical applications of how a school psychologist or counselor can empower students encountering challenging experiences such as divorce or the death of a loved one. Recall that the book includes many contributions of students eager to assist other students who are coping with and understanding loss.

Separation, through divorce or death are traumatic events for families. Coping with these losses and changes requires communicating feelings and thoughts that can be unpleasant. But experiencing the feelings and expressing them enables us to heal from the pain and resolve the conflict we feel. You may not believe this right now, but you can become stronger and more resilient through the process of dealing with this loss.

Divorce
   A divorce is when two people who are married choose to end the marriage. Parents must go in front of a judge to have the marriage legally ended.
   A divorce is not between children – only parents. Divorce does not end your father being a dad or mother being a mom.
Children

Parents have children for many reasons: My parents had me because _____

Family

Family is made up of unique individuals. At times, conflict can create tension in the family. At the time of this writing, the following drawing is of my family. I live with one parent and visit with the other. The parent I live with is _____; I visit with my other parent _____.

Drawing of my family

Here is a drawing of my family. These are the members of my household. I have described my relationship with each member by giving them a rating of 0 (needs improvement) to 10 (excellent). I am continually working on my relationships so I can have some impact on my situation.

The Loss Process

Divorce is like a death. The stages or feelings one goes through are similar. These are the stages I have gone through and will continue to go through in different ways: denial, anger, bargaining, depression, and acceptance.

Denial – denial is the refusal to accept what is happening. Avoiding the situation enables us to escape the pain of the loss. Sometimes we deny the reality of what is happening because we don't know how to deal with it.

Anger – anger results when we feel as if our lives are changing in ways we don't want them to. We sometimes even convert our sadness into anger because being mad can feel less painful than being very sad.

Bargaining – bargaining happens when I make a deal. Sometimes children think if they would "be better," parents would not fight. The thought is "if parents do not fight, then they would not get divorced." We have no control over parents who fight or divorce.

Depression – depression occurs when we have no control over situations, feel hopeless and helpless, and give up. Everyone gets depressed now and then, but we can choose to feel sad and then choose to heal. Healing takes time. I give myself permission to grieve and feel sad. I choose to be gentle on myself.

Acceptance – acceptance is my choice to deal in the reality of here and now. I have come to terms with the separation/divorce of my parents.

Students learn, through accepting the loss they have experienced, they are then better able to share their strength with other members of the group. They make meaning of the experience by realizing the loss helps them to better understand others who are hurting. They also learn helping others through their depression empowers them as individuals to "move on."

Moving on – Moving on is the process of evaluationg where I have been and thinking about where I need to go. I have a vision of hope and success for my life and I can make plans to overcome the loss I have faced. I am a person who thrives in spite of my heartaches; I am also a person who understands bouncing back is a slow process. I give myself permission to work at my own pace.

My Moving on Plan

I have a vision. I want to be _____ in 5 years. I want to be _____ in 10 years. I am committed to attending school daily, making good grades, and pursuing a healthy home and school life.

My Healthy Lifestyle Plan

My plan to have a healthy family looks like this:

My plan to have a healthy school life looks like this:

Death

Death means the end of physical life on earth. A loved one's death makes us feel terribly sad, afraid, angry and confused. Death is inevitable. The moment we are born we age and in the process of time will die. It is a natural part of life; it is the end of the physical life cycle. We live in bodies that naturally get old and no longer work

Frequently Asked Questions:

Does death hurt?

Doctors tell us death is not usually painful. When old people die, it is usually quiet. When people die in accidents, death usually happens quickly and they do not feel pain. When someone is sick or hurt for a long time before death, medication and treatment usually take away much of the pain.

Is death punishment for something bad someone did?

Death is never punishment. It is natural. Time wears out important parts of the body. After many years the parts no longer work. Sometimes sickness makes the body stop working before a person reaches an old age. A person may die accidentally but this is not punishment either.

Why did someone I love have to die?

Death is not fair; but it is inevitable. Almost everyone will be missed when he or she dies and everyone loses people they love.

How can I stop feeling so sad?

It is natural to feel sad and miss the person who has died. At first it hurts so much, but then you learn to live with the loss and begin to move on. But moving on takes time; give yourself permission to work at your own pace.

Why can't doctors stop death?

Doctors can help people live long lives; people often live well into their 80's and in past generations, they often only lived into their 60's. Sometimes people make lifestyle choices that make their illnesses hard for doctors to treat. And some illnesses do not get better no matter what the doctor does.

Memory Book

A memory book helps us to remember our lost family member or friend. We can dedicate a place to write about our loved one, and we can write to the person in our book. This helps us to express our feelings and stay connected to the person who is no longer with us.

Whether students have experienced loss through separation, divorce, or death, their experiences often result in empowerment and resilience if school staff are able to be responsive to their needs at the times of these crises. Below are some examples of the important effects of timely and appropriate interventions.

Marissa is a 12 year-old 6th grader who had experienced parental separation for one year. She shared that her father left her mother and her. She was told it was because of her mother but she recently found out her father left for another woman. She completed the divorce recovery class by attending weekly counseling "Banana Splits" groups for 10 months. She shared with the group "I learned to keep fighting and don't give up because what you say does matter; I learned I am happier that I have spoken out instead of keeping it to myself; I learned that my friends have problems too and I am not the only one, and they all help you when you need it the most."

Marissa learned how to share with the group. The group identified rules to keep her safe. She learned to be a self-advocate and spoke to her parents about feeling lied to. She deals with a constant fear of abandonment that causes her to not be assertive for fear she will be rejected and disappointing to others. She continues to use her strategies, shares with the group and does homework exercises using role-playing among her peers. She has learned that group is give and take. She can share from her experiences to help others and allow others to help her.

Robbie is an 8th grader who lives with his mother. His father has a girlfriend. When Robbie is with his father, he perceives that his father's girlfriend puts him down and his father allies with her. Robbie feels betrayed by his father and does not want to see him again. Robbie shared with his group that he learned how to accept people who are ignorant, that he learned that God made him who he is, and that kids go through worse. In this instance, group helped him to cope with struggles, accept himself for who he is and to minimize his problems thus "shrinking them to the size of a postage stamp" which is a visual exercise using cognitive behavioral therapy.

Lauren is an 8th grader who was in a foster home. Her father never met her and her mother used drugs. Lauren learned others have been through more than she has and she was more angry than she thought. She reported she was good at playing basketball and wanted to talk more in group. Lauren graduated to 9th grade and learned she could talk her feelings out and trust in a group of like-minded students.

Oliver is a 7th grader who lived with his mother and step-father. He visited his father on weekends. Oliver's grades went up in the past year. He shared with his group how to deal with divorce, that he can get good grades despite coming from two homes, that he was funny to others, and that he loved getting together with his group for a banana splits party. For Oliver, support helped to identify his strengths and to overcome his weaknesses.

Raymond is a 6th grade student who lives with his mother. He does not see his father. He learned people have a lot of problems and we need to come together to solve them. He learned it is okay to be angry at times but he needs to control himself. He learned he is not defined by his autism. He learned others can be sensitive and that bullies are sad. He enjoyed sharing his stories and learning about others.

Melissa lost her mother to brain cancer approximately one year ago. She graduated 8th grade to move into the high school. She lived with her father and step-mother. Initially, she refused to accept the death of her mother, and her step-mother as a parental figure, as she believed she was trying to replace her mother. Her academic and social behaviors plummeted. At the beginning of the group, she cried each period for weeks. At the end of the Loss Recovery group she stated she learned how to accept her mother's death. She also shared with her group that she learned to love her step-mother. She learned she is a student who is caring and giving, that people support, that the group accepted her and did not judge her and she enjoyed attending. Melissa plans to start another group in her high school with a teacher who will agree to be a club advisor. In this case, Melissa was empowered to move on. She also received an award for most improved and resilient.

Kerri is an 8th grader who lost her mother after a negative reaction to a drug she was taking for her heart. It had been 5 years since this loss. Initially, Kerri would not talk. After hearing others speak about their losses, Kerri shared her story and brought in pictures of her mother. She learned it is okay to be upset, that she is stronger than she thought, that there are others out in the world and in the school who have experienced losses, and she was able to share things with people and they would just listen. She wished the group would meet more often. Her plan of empowerment was to pass these lessons forward by pairing up with Melissa and starting a Loss Recovery group in her high school.

Theresa is a 7th grade student who suffers from anxiety. Her parents just split up and she lives with her mother 3 days per week and her father the other 4 days. Her parents are both dating. Theresa is angry at her mother and believes she is responsible for the divorce. She is often upset and mean to her mother because she wants to see her punished. She refused to attend group but after agreeing to come once and listen to others, she began to attend regularly. At the end of group she learned ways to cope with problems. She shared with her group that she can face problems to make them better. She learned that others face similar problems. She reported to her group that people support each other like her group members supported her. Social support is an important aspect of empowerment. Countless other students shared that they were struggling with their own feelings of loss, abandonment, and rejection, but the support of others enabled them to feel less alone, cared for, and accepted. They also reported having a new belief that life will move on and they will be alright.

Additional Ways a School Psychologist or Counselor Can Empower Students Experiencing Crises

As practicing counselors, it is important to use resources that have empirical support. In the words of Albert Einstein, "It is the supreme art of the teacher to awaken joy in creative expression and knowledge." Stated by Henry Brooks Adams, "a teacher affects eternity; he can never tell where his influence stops." I never imagined school psychology was about teaching, mentoring and much more. After receiving a note that said, "The 8th grade class students came to an important realization that without the help and support of someone like you, they would not be who they are today," I understood that the beginning of power is knowledge. The knowledge students possess about themselves is life defining, and the appreciation of their ability to change results in serenity, "to accept the things they cannot change, courage to change and the wisdom to know the difference."

In summary, I would like to present the following outline for the Self-Control, Self-Awareness, and Communication Module of the Social Skills Group I facilitate as it is a useful method for developing students' empowerment skills:

1) Identify what makes you angry
2) Identify what your body feels like when it is angry
3) Visualize what your body feels like when it is angry
4) Identify what you do when you are angry
5) Identify an angry situation in your life
6) Identify how you feel when you are in trouble, what is lost and what is gained
7) Identify how things would be different if you did not get in trouble

8) Identify your commitment to change old behaviors that don't work

9) Understand what anger is and facts

10) Anger is a signal that you, someone you care about or something you care about is being hurt or threatened

11) Anger warns us that something is wrong

12) "I" messages state how "you" feel without blaming, insulting, calling names or threatening

13) "You" messages involve blaming, threat or/and name-calling

14) Power talk is a way to communicate your feelings without blaming

15) Power talk reruns are ways of replaying a situation using power talk

16) Power talk communicates good feelings

17) Anger gets stuck in the body. Ignoring or calming are good techniques but do not get rid of anger

18) Dissolving (getting rid of) anger can be done by taking deep breaths, walking, an activity, changing thoughts and feelings and then behavior

19) Shrinking the picture involves drawing a picture of something that made you mad and then reducing the situation to the size of a post stamp

20) Using a daily peace plan is committing to a strategy to change thoughts and behaviors

21) A daily peace plan can include: ignoring people when they make you angry, walking away, reminding yourself of the consequences of losing your temper, talking to an adults, talking to a friend, using power talk, distracting yourself by doing schoolwork, distracting yourself by doing something fun or exercising

22) Qualities for good friendships do not just mean the absence of anger but a positive state of working on relationships. This includes: being honest, showing kindness, allowing time apart, helping, returning items you borrow, talking about feelings, using I messages, being able to say no, not believing messengers, keeping promises, and knowing your strengths

23) Things that break up friendships include: breaking promises, being jealous/possessive, not spending time together, being

dishonest, hiding true feelings, being a messenger, spreading gossip and/or rumors, using you messages (blaming), using the silent treatment, being late, threatening, and hitting

24) Writing feelings down is a great way to deal with good and bad feelings. Writing your feelings down is like talking to a trusted friend. You can share your journal, hide it or throw it away

25) Thoughts come before feelings and thoughts cause feelings

26) Identify what you think about yourself so that you can change these thoughts

27) Identify how you feel about yourself so that you can change these feelings

28) Develop affirmations to change your negative self-talk

29) Understanding what is important in life to you is called a value

30) Using a chart to monitor your commitment to change helps to visualize your change

31) Problem solving is a technique used to change a situation it involves 5 techniques: Identifying a problem, brainstorming solutions, picking the best one, trying it and reviewing the outcome

32) Study skills are behaviors done to keep control of and keep up with assignments they involve doing classwork, homework and completing tests.

10

Improving Self-Efficacy Through Cultural Competence:

The Role of International Study Abroad in Empowerment

Gavin Webb and John Peters

> We must go beyond textbooks, go out into the bypaths and untrodden depths of the wilderness and travel and explore and tell the world the glories of our journey.
> —*John Hope Franklin*

Study abroad professionals tend to be highly passionate about their work, and there is no lack of either enthusiasm or (on balance, engaging) eccentricity in study abroad alongside this passion. We believe in what we do, and our life's work is that of finding ways to do it better.

Extolling the virtues of study abroad has become commonplace. Former (and current) presidents of nations, CEOs, and leading academicians now provide a healthy supply of laudatory quotations ripe for use in study abroad promotional materials, and college mission statements are incomplete without reference to international engagement.

Empirical support for the benefits of study abroad extends to the academic literature as well. Maddux and Galinsky (2009), for example, explore the link between living abroad and creativity and, through five psychological studies, find strong evidence across a range of measures that time living abroad promotes creative thinking and problem solving. The large-scale GLOSSARI Project (Sutton & Rubin, 2004), analyzing ten years of study abroad data throughout the 35 campus University of Georgia system, has produced some interesting findings as well. For example, even after controlling for student self-selection for study abroad, socioeconomic background, and a host of other factors, it was found that students who study abroad have improved academic performance upon returning to the home campus. Four-year graduation rates were also higher among study abroad students, and study abroad improved students' functional knowledge of cultural practices. Similarly, analyzing data from the Study Abroad for Global Engagement (SAGE) project, Paige et al. (2010) suggest that study abroad positively supports ongoing global engagement, which is defined as civic engagement, knowledge production, philanthropy, social entrepreneurship, and volunteering.

Thus to the question, "does study abroad promote empowerment?" we offer what is perhaps an unexpected answer: *study abroad may promote empowerment. But then again, it may not.*

At first glance, our "it depends" answer reads wishy-washy, but this is precisely the central argument of the chapter. *Study abroad, done well, is a powerful methodology for promoting empowerment, but this empowerment, however defined, does not automatically come simply by virtue of studying abroad.* Rather, best practice articulation of study abroad and empowerment is purposeful, and requires iteration, reflection, and in many cases, a facilitative hand or voice.

This chapter provides a working definition of student-focused "empowerment" in study abroad, and concretizes this definition by connecting it to examples of best-practice application. In terms of the latter, we provide an overview of Marist's international programs (including discussion of the Marist Florence Branch Campus), and offer a detailed case study of the "Marist in Ghana" summer program. Many of the components of these programs were specifically designed to maximize opportunities for student empowerment, and as such it is our hope that the methodologies, programming, and assignments discussed herein inspire readers toward new ideas and insights for other student empowerment projects and programs.

Marist College's Emphasis on Student Empowerment in the Context of Study Abroad

Marist College is a private liberal arts college of approximately 4,500 undergraduate and 900 graduate students in Poughkeepsie,

New York, located on the east bank of the Hudson River halfway between New York City and the capital city of Albany.[1] Through the institution's partnership with Istituto Lorenzo de' Medici (LdM)[2], Marist offers a branch campus in Florence, where study abroad, as well as full bachelor's and master's programs are offered in fields particularly suited to the artistic and historical context of Florence and Italy.[3]

Marist leverages the Florence branch campus as well as additional international sites, locations, and affiliations as a central internationalization strategy. In recent years, Marist has enabled over 40 percent of its students to study abroad at least once during the eight semesters of their undergraduate education. To put this percentage in perspective, currently, approximately five percent of incoming freshman at all institutions of higher education in the US can be expected to study abroad in their undergraduate years. Hence, Marist has worked hard to make study abroad a possibility for students and a priority for the College, through the following policies: the ability for students to use financial aid to help fund study abroad, significant pre-program support by international programs staff, clear course and credit transfer policies, and a faculty and administration supportive of facilitating international and intercultural experiences for students.

While there are many ways to define "empowerment," Marist International Programs (MIP) utilizes the College's mission statement as the starting point and organizational framework for student empowerment: "Marist is dedicated to helping students develop the intellect, character, and skills required for enlightened, ethical, and productive lives in the global community of the 21st century." As such, students therefore demonstrate empowerment through study abroad where they increasingly take responsibility for their own intellectual, character, and skills development. This implies an active rather than passive orientation, and commitment to knowledge accumulation, reflection, and active experimentation. Nurturing an ongoing passion for learning, a desire to see and appreciate the world from multiple points of view, and a drive to connect with people and the world in enlightened, ethical, and productive ways are indeed the goalposts of study abroad from this perspective.

Students can thus be said to be empowered through study abroad where they increasingly: (a) accumulate information on a topic (content knowledge, language abilities, etc.) that enables understanding on a deeper level and to make interconnections *(intellect)*; (b) demonstrate an optimistic orientation to new situations and environments and seek to connect to people and the world in positive, respectful ways *(character)*; and (c) develop flexibility, a problem-solving orientation, resilience, and an attitude of expecting the unexpected *(skills)*.

This active orientation toward empowerment and taking responsibility for one's education and development is not only part of MIP's study abroad program, but is paralleled in the Marist Florence Branch campus bachelor's and master's degree programs as well. As is explored in detail below, a most powerful methodology to ensure strong opportunities for empowerment through study abroad is to adopt an experiential methodology, with programming well-grounded in local cultural contexts. The degrees offered in Florence, e.g., conservation studies and museum studies, lend themselves particularly well to this, with classroom learning integrated with experiential components such as hands-on restoration of centuries-old works and internships in leading museums, respectively. Another key strength of the Marist-LdM offerings that encourages strong connections between empowerment and study abroad is that the programs are culturally embedded. That is, branch campus offerings do not take place within an institutional or cultural bubble, but rather the curriculum and co-curricular activities that comprise the programs operate within the rich cultural, human, and physical context that is Florence, Italy, and Southern Europe.

Pedagogical Considerations

Study abroad takes many forms, including but not limited to: direct enrollment at an overseas institution through bilateral agreement; direct enrollment overseas with additional educational services provided by a US study abroad "provider"[4]; participation in (often) smaller programs, tailored to the needs of US study abroad students and often thematically-focused[5]; and an institution's own overseas programs, sometimes offered in collaboration with educational affiliates and partners in the host country. In this chapter, we draw upon the last of these types of programs, in order to explore how Marist's overseas programs uniquely support student empowerment. First, we offer an overview of the Florence Branch Campus degree offerings; and second we undertake a detailed case study of the Marist in Ghana summer program. While the Italy and Ghana programs are vastly different in terms of structure, size, and scope (the former offering full Bachelor's and Master's degrees in Florence and the latter being a summer study abroad program in Ghana), they share pedagogical space, specifically in their goal to integrate theory and practice in a context-rich environment, and to support a student's cognitive, affective, as well as social or psychological development.[6]

The pedagogical orientation of these programs is experiential. We seek to purposefully link theory and practice in the curriculum and to facilitate exploration and reflection on this dynamic. For this, we can start with Kolb's (1984) theory of experiential learning, equipping students with the framework of the experiential learning cycle of concrete experience, reflective observation, abstract conceptualization, and active experimentation. Honey and Mumford (2000) re-state this as having an experience, reflecting on it, drawing conclusions, and then putting the new understanding into practice to determine (through discussion/observation/participation) if it better explains events or experiences. Drawing inspiration from John Dewey's (1897) emphasis on "learning by doing," the learning process is ongoing, cumulative, active, and integrative through successful experiential learning cycles.

It is through successful iterations of experiential educational cycles, then, that students become increasingly empowered. Please note, however, that empowerment defined as the development of a useful and integrated body of knowledge; optimistic and enthusiastic orientation; and an emphasis on resilience and problem-solving skills, may not be realized if there is blockage anywhere along the cycle. One can have an experience, but if not adequately reflected upon, much of its meaning and significance is lost. Even if reflected upon, students might not take an experience to the next level by abstracting and trying to make theoretical sense out of it. Or, a student may come up with a new pet theory as to why something happened that they experienced in the host culture, but leave it at that, and not "test" the theory or new understanding by "experimenting" with it through talking with local experts, further observation and participant observation, etc. And then finally, it is not guaranteed that students will always take forward and bring to bear the cumulated wisdom of reflection, theorizing, and active experimentation to each new experience.

It is here that the crux of the chapter's argument is made: study abroad may be empowering, but one does not automatically become empowered simply by virtue of studying abroad. It depends on if our student embarks upon a journey of becoming a reflector, a theorist, a pragmatist, and finally, an activist, through the myriad (potentially) educational experiences that one has–inside and outside of the classroom–while studying abroad. In many cases, students are successful in this regard; thousands of students have empowered themselves on all types of study abroad programs, from direct enrollment at a large university overseas to small, tailored study abroad programs. They have also experienced interacting with a multitude of local staffing structures, from large staffs supporting a student's academic and cultural adjustment, to a small, understaffed international office with which the study abroad student may have little contact.

If our goal is to maximize opportunities for student empowerment through study abroad, however, there is a strong theoretical as well as empirical case for eschewing laissez-faire for a more purposeful, facilitative hand in the process. Following a review of recent research in study abroad, for example, Vande Berg, et al. (2012) conclude that student learning is most successful where purposeful, facilitative interventions are made in the learning process. The research shows that programs are most consistently successful (using a variety of qualitative and quantitative measures of educational outcomes) where particular strategies and methodologies are emphasized, including: in-situ cultural mentoring; active and facilitated reflection; and well-designed and assessed experiential curricula including internships, volunteering, and guided research.

As such, empowerment in study abroad needs to be nurtured: "a critical reflection process that generates, deepens, and documents learning does not occur automatically—rather, it must be carefully and intentionally designed." Thus, it is not enough to tell students "it is now time to reflect" (Welch 1999, p.1). Eyler et al. (1996) note that reflection "need not be a difficult process, but it does need to be a purposeful and strategic process" (16). Especially given how unfamiliar most students are with learning through reflection on experience, they often need structure and guidance to help derive meaningful learning when outside the traditional classroom setting. Otherwise, reflection tends to be little more than descriptive accounts of experiences or venting of personal feelings (Ash & Clayton, 2009).

Case Study: Marist in Ghana

Since summer 2011, Marist College has offered a summer study abroad program in Ghana focused on a variety of themes depending on the particular year and/or cohort. Economics, community-health, psychology, and history are some disciplines and fields that have been involved in the project. New fields are under development for the future, including a program for teachers-in-training as well as an option for environmental science students. The specific disciplines and foci of the program vary by year, with different tracks enabled through a modular format and delivery. A specific faculty member is assigned to each track being offered in a particular year, and students in the program participate in some shared lecture, discussion, and excursion activities, as well as more tailored programming in the particular topic/discipline in which the student is receiving credit. Following an (on average) weekly on-campus session during the spring semester to help students learn about Africa, Ghana, and the program emphasis from an interdisciplinary perspective, students travel to Ghana for three weeks with their professors and undertake an integrated experience of lectures, seminars, excursions, and activities in a variety of Ghanaian cities, towns, and villages. As noted, focus and disciplinary rigor is brought to the program as the different thematic cohorts engage in some shared activities while allowing time and space for specialization.

    In broad strokes, everyone is together in the beginning of the program, as the group builds knowledge and context and starts to engage in empowerment activities and assignments. Mid-way through the program, the cohorts split so as to be able to take full advantage of local resources and opportunities tailored to the cohort theme, e.g., the group studying education will locate at a public school, those interested in development will partner with local non-governmental organizations, the community health students shadow health workers in the field or conduct participant observation in clinics, etc. Then as we approach the end of the program, ideally the cohorts come back together to debrief, share experiences across themes, and further process what individuals and groups have learned about the country, culture, and topics under study. In these final few days there is also emphasis on reflection and processing of what individual participants have learned about themselves, and what they now want and plan to do with these new insights going forward in their academic, personal, and professional lives.

Empowering students in the context of a study abroad program in Africa can be difficult as students come to grips with post-colonial realities about the continent and its history that entangle critical issues such as racism, colonial legacies, the historically-rooted nature of economic disparity and north-south relations vis-à-vis global power. Without positioning oneself properly, these important features of Africa's history and contemporary circumstances can be disempowering to students as they become reticent or hesitant to engage with the continent and its people for the fear of replicating neocolonial behaviors and prejudices. The opposite end of this behavioral spectrum is equally problematic, where students arrive on the continent with little understanding of Africa's colonial and postcolonial history and therefore little capacity to make connections between Africa's present and past. As faculty and facilitators we empower students in this respect through arranging curriculum content and learning approaches designed to inform, provide an opportunity to work through the psychology of guilt, and facilitate a cognitive shift from feelings of culpability to the process of bridge-building for intercultural discussion and dialogue. Below we explore four program components which support student empowerment in this regard, each designed to foster empowerment of the student: (1) excursion to the castle-dungeons of Elmina and Cape Coast; (2) the "Welcome to Ghana" assignment; (3) homestay; and (4) community engagement. The last three of these program components can be applied to nearly any study abroad location, and while the first component (visits to the castle-dungeons of Elmina and Cape Coast) is highly context dependent as a site of human exploitation, the educational methodology and pedagogical framework of the excursion has broad applicability to other study abroad programs as well.

Cape Coast and Elmina Castle Dungeon Excursions

While the history and complexity of the Trans-Atlantic Slave Trade (TAST) is beyond the scope of this discussion (as is the politics of preservation and issues of representation in Ghana), site visits to the castle-dungeons[7] at Elmina and Cape Coast are powerful ways of engaging students in the myriad issues rooted in the history of West Africa and the African Diaspora, as well as a way for young American students[8] to make important connections with their own past through this type of "contact zone" where issues of race, colonization, inequality, violence, and power are "on display" (Pratt 1992, 6; Richards 2005, 618). However, simply having American students visit the dungeons at Elmina and Cape Coast is not in and of itself a way to get them to effectively engage in the history of the TAST and to assemble some understanding of this watershed moment in human history. It requires greater intentionality, with the site visit supported by readings, a briefing session to prepare the students for what they are about to experience prior to arriving at the sites, an informative visit allowing for structured and unstructured time, and a debriefing session (or series of sessions) after the visit to begin processing the experience and to place into an appropriate context.

As sites that challenge us to think about what life must have been like to live in fear of being kidnapped, shackled, beaten, and transported off the continent for four centuries, as well as the brutality and rape that occurred within the compound walls, the potential emotional impact of the experience needs to be clearly articulated to the students. This statement may appear to be a truism, but it presents an opportunity for faculty and facilitators to create an ethos of support among students and to prepare them for a broad range of emotional responses. Failing to do this, to simply let the experience of the castle-dungeons present itself, leaves open the opportunity for emotional responses that conflict with the intended learning outcomes and potentially compromises future group processing sessions where additional layers of learning occur. Finding flexibility to accommodate particular needs within the group, such as experiencing both Elmina and Cape Coast castle-dungeons individually or in smaller groups, reinforces the ethos of group support so long that it is done with respect of other group members.

The debriefing sessions that occur after the castle-dungeon site visits are also a critical part of the experiential and intercultural learning, and are carefully designed with a few aims in mind, specifically: to provide additional historical information on the TAST; to make essential connections between this watershed period and important features of contemporary society in postcolonial countries such as Ghana; and to discuss the multiple interpretations and meanings embodied in the two edifices between the "three broadly defined categories of visitors: local people, most of whom are school-age youths on field trips; Europeans; and diaspora [sic] Africans, that is, black people from the historic, slave-derived diasporas of the Caribbean and the United States as well as from newer diasporas, constituted by economic and/or political instability and war." (Richards 2005, 620) A fourth and equally crucial aim for the debriefing is to allow students an opportunity to take an active role in shaping the direction of the debriefing that is facilitated by a recognized speaker in the subject area, thereby further attempting to empower students through reorienting the session away from a teacher-centered learning environment to one which privileges student discourse in shaping the direction and content of the debrief.

When schedules are properly aligned, there are two separate debriefs with two different facilitators that occur after the site visits. Each of the sessions is organized in the same manner – a short discussion by the facilitator on a relevant theme followed by group discussion. The effectiveness of the group discussion is often determined by the group dynamics and what the students bring to the table. In addition to the expertise of each of the facilitators, their individual identities play an important part of the overall design;

in the case of the Marist in Ghana program, one of the facilitators of the castle-dungeon debrief is a Ghanaian, and the other an African American deeply involved in the African American repatriation movement in Ghana. While identity formation is complex and typically multifaceted, their status as African and African American respectively does impact the narrative, emphasis, scope of opening discussion, nuanced perspectives on the TAST, and the perspective of how this continues to be felt in contemporary Africa and the African Diaspora.

While readings, briefings, lectures, visits, and debriefings of the castle-dungeon excursions can be an intense experience for individuals and the group, it can also be an empowering experience. Students begin to better, and in more concrete terms, understand how Ghana's past shapes the present, and offers ways to think about some of the features of Ghanaian social, cultural, and economic life: why many people adopt "Christian" (read European/American) names; the hole in the education system for superficially dealing with the TAST; the psychological impact of slavery and colonization; the non-linear nature of development, neocolonialism, the artificial nature of national borders on the continent; and contemporary articulations of centuries of human and natural resource depletion in Africa that helped fuel the development of Western economies[9]. This is not to say, of course, that all the challenges, contradictions, or seeming paradoxes of Ghanaian life can be directly connected to the TAST, but it does underscore that the TAST is not an historical footnote but a foundational phenomenon in the development of both African and Western socioeconomic life. For young Americans this lesson is all the more potent as they reflect on their own society's history of slavery and economic development through experiencing and processing this reality at a key source.

For this experience and learning opportunity to be empowering, it must be enabling rather than debilitating. Therefore the debrief of the experience must be led with the critical objective of empowering students so that they can engage with Ghanaian society as informed citizens and agents of social change and armed with a more critical pedagogy. By extension, ideally this educational experience should be equally integrated into students' lives back home, informing their actions and responses in the context of inequalities based on race, gender, and class in one's home country. The experiences at the castle-dungeons, and subsequent debriefing sessions, are an important moment where students often engage the study of Ghanaian life and culture with renewed vigor. Through journal entries and other writing and discussion assignments that encourage reflection and synthesis, students demonstrate an increased capacity to connect the experiences of the TAST and subsequent colonization with modern Ghanaian life and society. Students' increased understanding has a direct impact on the development of intercultural curiosity and understanding as well, namely through demonstrating analytical thinking and the re-evaluation of assumptions about the socioeconomic features of Ghana in light of this new experience.

Developing Confidence through Field Assignments – Welcome to Ghana!
News reports of exotic diseases, war torn regions, failed states, and poverty coupled with pre-departure medical briefings of potentially deadly ailments such malaria, Ebola, and HIV clearly have an impact on people's perceptions of the African continent, despite the diversity of lives and livelihoods found in practice. There are of course many well-informed students who are knowledgeable on regional and/or country-specific realities of these and other health issues. Nevertheless, anyone familiar with leading groups of foreign students to and within Africa knows well that it is not uncommon for students to be overly concerned with their physical well-being when coming to Africa in contrast to parts of the world more frequently traveled in study abroad circles. An additional layer to this phenomenon is the unfortunate connection of Africa with the mystical, primitive, exotic, and "other" that clouds people's understanding, requiring a guiding hand to help people shed negative perceptions, further the process of demystification, assist in the development of contextual understanding, and better empower students toward effective intercultural engagement.

One highly effective way to do this is to begin the process of cultural immersion and "field study" as early as possible. To this end, the somewhat tongue-in-cheekily named "Welcome to Ghana" assignment is an effective co-curricular component to the study abroad experience that gets students out of their comfort zone, kick starts the process of intercultural study and engagement, familiarizes them with essential features of daily life such as transportation or the market, and provides a facilitated experience in small groups aimed at building confidence and capacity to function independently and effectively in Ghana (and elsewhere).[10]

As a component listed in the program schedule, students are often curious to know exactly what the exercise entails and so tend to ask about it after receiving the program itinerary. As faculty and facilitators, not divulging too much information about the exercise ahead of time becomes an important way to nurture students' comfort with ambiguity–an important skill students come to learn under the right conditions in an experiential learning context. Similar to other academic and co-curricular program components, the exercise is preceded by a briefing and followed by a debriefing session(s) for program participants.

For the exercise students are split into small groups (typically three people), with each group being given an envelope containing a set of instructions and a small sum of money. The students are taken by bus to select locations, dropped off, and asked to perform a particular task (or series of tasks) appropriate to the respective location, and to return to the program base at an agreed time. The money contained in the envelope is earmarked for public transport back to the program site. Students are typically dropped at locations around town, told to return to a central location 4 hours later, and are encouraged to use the language skills they have developed up to that point and to think about some of the cultural issues discussed in the orientation phase at the beginning of the program. After the short briefing session where students begin to move towards the bus that will take their groups to town, one often sees that many feel apprehensive, unsure of themselves or what to expect, nervous, or hesitant about going into town on their own. As facilitators it is important to recognize that this is a crucial moment in the process of developing intercultural competency, and that these types of anxiety-laden responses and the discussions that ensue are often part of the process of developing the capacity to function independently in Ghana.

The final phase of the exercise, after the students have returned from their experiences in town, is the debrief, which typically takes about two and a half hours for a group of 15-20 students. Here each group (and individual) has a chance to share experiences with program participants, faculty, and staff, and to offer "findings" of their short (and early) field-study assignment on their group's particular theme. The first thing that becomes strikingly apparent in the debrief is an overall sense of excitement and energy on the part of the students after having a first experience "alone" (without local staff, faculty or facilitators). Some eagerly chat with their friends about what happened on the trip, while others show off what they purchased during their adventure. Each group is called upon to present their experiences through the lens of their assigned task, and within the group each student takes a turn describing what occurred and what was discovered. What follows from this design is a series of anecdotes, questions, (mis)interpretations, and observations that provide faculty and facilitators with the materials to build discussions around various aspects of Ghanaian society and culture with the aim of increased intercultural understanding and the building of each student's level of comfort with cultural immersion. Empowering students to develop a level of self-confidence to be able to have intercultural experiences in Ghana without the need for immediately-present staff support is a key measure of success and an essential learning outcome. As students return to the central location, they have greater self-confidence in their abilities to navigate an unfamiliar town in an unfamiliar country, and are increasingly prepared (or increasingly empowered!) to take on the challenge of exploring "the world."

In addition to learning more about Ghanaian society, infusing a high-energy and fun (if sometimes exhausting) experience early into the curriculum, and helping students to build self-reliance, flexibility, and confidence, the "Welcome to Ghana" assignment also provides an early gateway to discussion of how one formulates a research question, collects data, and puts it together into a coherent story. For example, a group assigned to research "education" might be dropped off close to a school. But how the group should best go about researching "education" from there, is not at all obvious, and can be linked to interesting methodological and epistemological questions and issues.

For our group assigned to examine "education," simply barging into the school is problematic, as one has to negotiate the terrain of entry respectfully. Even if one does enter the school, who do they speak with, and how do they explain themselves? What questions do they ask of the people they meet? Do they ask the same questions of everyone? What do the various responses mean? Or maybe students take another angle and do not enter the school gates at all, but rather sit on the sidewalk and observe – number of students and teachers visible, how they are dressed, timetables, who enters and exits the school and their modes of transport, etc. Here, students have an early chance to try out not only semi-structured interviewing, but also observation and possibly participant observation as well.

The perhaps more astute of groups given the "school" assignment will dig further, not only collecting data from the immediate context of the school grounds, but also taking a look at the surrounding community. Are there kids walking around the area who do not seem to be part of the school, and if so, why are they not in school? Do they go to a different school, or perhaps no school at all? And if the latter, why? The assignment thus nudges students toward the complexities of research methodology and epistemology, and sets an early "inquisitive" tone for their studies.

Homestay

Homestay is another key component of the Marist in Ghana program, in terms of building into the program opportunities for student empowerment. And indeed, homestay is a key pedagogy of study abroad, and can be quite powerful in its ability to help students gain an insider's view of culture and family life, to practice language, and to learn more about the country's politics, economics, and history. Homestay also often leads to life-long intercultural friendships, solidifying the value of the study abroad experience for decades to come in very practical terms. There are simply conversations that take place around the household, over dinner, in front of the television, while doing chores, going food shopping with family members, etc. which offer our students cultural insights that would never be possible in a hotel, hostel, or apartment complex designed to house international students. Homestay can be a most effective breaker of the US student cultural bubble, and a successful homestay component effectively achieves this objective.

While some students are drawn to programs due to the integration of homestay experiences in their design, the experience of moving in with an unknown family can be an intimidating (but ultimately, empowering) one. Will my family like me? Will they speak English? What if I don't like the food? What if they are strict and forbid me going out to meet my friends in the evening? Will they have children my own age? These are some of the many questions or fears that students can bring to the experience, and so as with other program components in the context of study abroad, it is the responsibility of facilitators to ensure that students are carefully and purposefully guided to a mental space that prepares them to embrace the experience.

Failure to properly supervise and manage a homestay component can lead to unrealistic expectations, a lack of preparedness to embrace the challenges that come with living in a new family in the host culture, simple and unnecessary cross-cultural mishaps, insufficient information or strategies on how to deal with common intercultural issues in the home, or even potential safety and security issues. These types of situations can be disempowering to students and have a profoundly negative effect on the abroad experience, hence underscoring the importance of strong facilitation and ongoing nurturing of the homestay component.

Equally essential to the success of the homestay experience is giving adequate time and attention to the families hosting students so that they also have clear expectations and the requisite understanding of aims and objectives, knowledge of some of the idiosyncrasies typical of young American students, and the ability to articulate to faculty and facilitators their own expectations and desires. The entire homestay component, in fact, is best approached in a reciprocal, balanced way; just as one must work with the group of students to appropriately set expectations, one also works in partnership with the group of families offering their homes to the young students from abroad to ensure the best fit and experience possible.

The briefing given to homestay families and students provides the space to address many issues of potential concern, and creates a level of preparedness needed to make the experience a positive one. For the families, informing them about issues such as vegetarianism or veganism, the more open culture regarding LGBT (lesbian, gay, bisexual, transgender) issues, young American expectations regarding freedoms and outings, or common dietary concerns are some essential types of information that families should be armed with prior to hosting a student. As an important learning outcome for the homestay is to try to increase students' language abilities, families are asked to encourage students to speak some *fante*[11], however basic, in the household. For the students, in addition to fielding the many questions they have, the homestay briefing covers strategies for building rapport with the family, dealing with dietary issues or feeding portions, how to present gifts to homestay family members, understanding the nature of the extended family system, thinking about what it means to be a good guest, and reviewing some of the nuances of typical Ghanaian family life. Also critical to the briefing session is to rearticulate the aims and objectives of the homestay experience for students so that they are reminded of what learning outcomes are envisioned for this component of the program. At times this important feature of the homestay can be forgotten as students mentally prepare for the experience.

Finally, and perhaps most crucially, the briefing session for students is an opportunity for facilitators to move students into a headspace where they are prepared for whatever experiences they might encounter. As we strive to enrich our classrooms by getting students involved in knowledge creation, the homestay context furthers this dialogue and focuses discussion on active learning and taking responsibility for shaping the learning experience, and this is re-emphasized as students enter the homestay. While this can be challenging to some students who initially find it difficult to make the psychological and epistemological leap towards this type of learning, it is a necessary cognitive shift that potentially empowers students to take ownership for individual situations as well as their overall learning experience. "Only you can take responsibility for your learning experience" is a common statement for exploration at homestay briefings, usually with positive effect. Homestays teach students the art of human relations (among other things), and therefore cannot be reduced to an experience that is "bought" as a product and "consumed" with predictable expectations in mind. It must be navigated by the student with the ongoing support of the facilitators.

One way in which this ongoing support is afforded to students is through the debriefing session that occurs after the first night of the homestay experience (and at less frequent intervals thereafter). Students gather at the program site in the morning, and a formal processing session is carried out by way of each student sharing their individual experiences with the rest of the group. This manner of debriefing the experience is effective for a number of reasons: it allows peers to provide support or recommendations to one another to overcome perceived obstacles; offers a chance for "less positive" students to witness positive attitudes or behaviors on the part of their peers; provides good material for the facilitators to further engage students to move beyond their comfort zone; and alerts facilitators to red flag situations. Debriefing and processing of the homestay experience, continued at select portions of the program, ensures that the potentially empowering nature of the homestay experience doesn't become a disempowering one due to the lack of guidance and intentionality that is required to give the students the emotional and intellectual support they need to successfully navigate the experience. When done well, students develop further resilience and an increased capacity to deal with intercultural situations through the homestay. They also learn to balance anxiety with intellectual curiosity, and are able to further practice these emotional and behavioral skills in order to navigate new and relatively unstructured intercultural and interpersonal relationships.

Community Engagement

The "capstone" of the Marist in Ghana program is a week of community engagement projects that are designed to harmonize with the student's major and/or the program theme (students also have the option to stay on in Ghana to engage in an extended, facilitated internship experience upon completion of the program). Participants have worked with schools, community health organizations, social welfare groups, and environmentally-focused non-governmental organizations. While the principles of community empowerment and reciprocity are important values to the study abroad program in Ghana, with respect to this component, these values must be weighed against the capacity of students and their depth of knowledge about the language, culture, and social features of the people. It is for this reason that the students are prepared for what is regarded as *community engagement* rather than *internship*, with the former better capturing the spirit and nature of the experience and ensuring that student expectations and perceived outcomes are realistic.

Community engagement also conveys a sense of humility on the part of students who are encouraged to see their role as seeking to understand and support what is happening within the institutions they are being placed in rather than viewing their role in paternalistic terms, i.e., coming to "help" or to "solve" particular problems. Embedded in this type of experience, as well as in study abroad more generally, are critical ethical issues concerning the responsibilities international educators have towards their hosts and the various communities in which their programs operate, and how these types of experiences optimally lead to the "development of non-exploitative relationships between people of different cultures" and promote "collaboration with the local community to ensure that their relationships are built on mutuality and reciprocity and not any kind of exploitation" (Lutterman-Aguilar & Gingerich 2002, 70). Students might reflect on the problems faced in this community engagement and creatively consider both how those in the host country as well as the home country confront similar issues. As one of the goals of a liberal arts education, this helps to "liberate" students from having only one narrow perspective to problem confrontation.

A point of departure here (and a point which is underscored at various points of the program, including pre-departure) is that participants are not coming to "help" anyone. It is not the role of the program or its participants to "help" Ghanaians overcome their problems, as Ghanaians (or especially as program participants) see them. Rather, the purpose of the program is to help facilitate and build bridges for broader and deeper cultural understanding and dialogue. Program participants undertaking the community engagement component, therefore, seek reciprocal exchanges, discussions, and relationships with program partners, institutional affiliates, and individuals. While there is scope for the student to be part of, and in some cases assist, ongoing successful activities of the partner organizations, this is an added benefit. We seek this as an ideal in practice, but make clear to students that they do not travel to Ghana as "aid workers," however defined. This emphasis helps program participants to eschew paternalistic notions in favor of positioning themselves and the program as partners ready to share and learn from one another for mutual benefit, which indeed are the goalposts for successful study abroad.

In terms of on-site briefing, just prior to moving into their respective sites the group again reviews the aims and objectives of the community engagement component of the program, offering participants a chance to share any fears or expectations they might have before beginning their assignments. As with some of the other key components of the program, the perception of ambiguity relating to students' roles in the host institution, not knowing the full scope of their duties and responsibilities, and being uncertain of their capacities to integrate effectively gives context to faculty and facilitators of what types of materials to cover in the briefing session. Students are made aware that although a lot of thought and planning has gone into developing and organizing the community engagement assignments, students need to bring the qualities of flexibility, patience, humility, enthusiasm, tolerance for ambiguity, and self-motivation in order for their experiences to be fulfilling and positive. The crucial point students should come to learn through the briefing session is that the experiences in community engagement are organic, and requires one to be ready to respond to whatever is presented. Approaching their engagement experiences from this perspective, and remembering the short-list of qualities needed to successfully navigate the experiences is an important way to empower students and to open the door for intercultural learning and understanding of the institutions and organizations with which we work.

Students are given opportunities to share their thoughts and experiences after the first full day of the community engagement experience, with additional sessions scheduled strategically throughout the program. This initial debriefing session is a critical time in the community engagement experience for students to be able to combine knowledge gained in the field with that of the classroom, thus encouraging them to begin closing the gap between theory and practice in their course of study. This also provides students with opportunities to process what they have experienced and observed, thereby moving them intellectually from an observer's perspective to an analytical one. Additionally, this is the time where faculty and facilitators can address particular challenges students may be having in their placements, and to share with the entire cohort strategies for overcoming them. Empowerment from this perspective comes through providing students the necessary support they need to overcome particular obstacles, and to assure them that dealing with these types of challenges is an essential feature of the learning process and a critical element of intellectual, personal, and positive emotional transformation.

In essence two types of learning are occurring simultaneously through community engagement experiences that will appeal to both departmental faculty and international education professionals whose outcomes overlap in many cases. From the perspective of faculty, students are using their community engagement experiences to broaden their understanding of their discipline, provide comparative understanding of topics or critical issues appropriate to their majors, or in the case of medical science students working in Ghana, beginning the process of understanding national policies, local procedures, cultural perspectives on health, and spheres of provision in Ghana's public health system. From the perspective of international education, students are additionally acquiring important intercultural skills, a more global perspective, an integrated academic environment that connects the student and university with local communities, increased language capacities, and skills that will enhance their resiliency, problem-solving abilities, tolerance, curiosity, empathy, and confidence.

As we approach the end of the community engagement component, the group debriefs and individual writing assignments also tend to become much more cumulative, as students continue to process and work to deepen connections between program components, readings, seminars, excursions, assignments, chance encounters, etc. Many discussions by this phase have now turned the corner from initial exploration of competing interpretations of experiences toward the drawing of new conclusions (or more accurately described, evolving understandings), and this "lens" of ever-evolving intellect, character, and skills can then be employed in a fresh iteration of the experiential learning cycle.

The closing days of the program not only involve a great deal of introspection and individualized writing assignments, but as noted, group debriefs as well, thus offering students a variety of pathways to process the significance of the experience and to approach the question of "ok, now what?" On the last of these points, where possible, the program offers opportunities for the different thematic tracks to report back to one another, thus not only offering additional opportunities for the honing of presentation skills, small group work and cooperation, etc., but for all program participants to gain insight into the various themes offered by the program in a particular year. These final group assignments, activities, and discussions also help to set a positive tone for the idea that the learning does not stop here, but continues post-program, by way of students focusing future research papers on Ghana, by talking about the experience and becoming unofficial ambassadors for Ghana back home, making campus presentations (in many cases facilitated by Marist faculty and international staff), joining international clubs and seeking out international students from Ghana, Africa, and elsewhere on the home campus, etc.

Conclusion

The professionalization of international education has led to increased awareness on the part of those who advocate for it to better articulate and measure the benefits of education abroad to those yet convinced. This feature of the field's development is also reflected in the design of programs, methods of assessment, expansion of program models, and the nature and degree of intervention on the part of program directors and faculty. Empowering students by developing their self-confidence in a new setting, by giving them a critical view of the country and depth of understanding of the people with which they interact, and by drawing on experiential educational models that enable eager students to become active, immersed participants requires innovative and creative programming on the part of faculty and study abroad professionals. It is therefore something that needs to be fostered through intentional, logically, and cumulatively planned programs incorporating opportunities for reflection and the guiding hand of the study abroad program director or faculty member to make the right kinds of interventions to maximize the opportunities for transformative learning experiences. Most importantly, fostering empowerment as an outcome for a study abroad program must be purposeful and built into the curriculum and design of the program–it is not something that necessarily occurs by simply crossing a national border.

Study Abroad Programs of any type, be they of a few weeks duration, a semester or year of study, or even multiple-year programs, and whether in a cosmopolitan city in an industrial nation or in a rural town in a developing country, stand the best chance of facilitating student empowerment where the program utilizes strategies for students to take reasonable journeys outside their comfort zone while exploring the host culture. Thus to maximize opportunities for student empowerment, facilitators should ensure ample programming and curricular support for students all along the experiential learning cycle: get them out there having a variety of experiences both in and outside of the classroom; design or otherwise ensure writing and/or other assignments requiring reflection on those experiences and to begin to formalize new understandings and interpretations; and create environments where students are then challenged to put these new understandings to experimentation and further practice. And, crucially, look for opportunities along the way to underscore with students that their development, or their empowerment, is holistic, and extends to one's intellect, character, and skills.

Notes

1   As one of the chapter's authors is Dean of International Programs at Marist College while the other has experience with the institution as a study abroad consultant, examples of empowerment through study abroad are drawn from Marist's international programs.

2   LdM, celebrating its 40th year in 2013, offers a variety of study abroad and degree opportunities to US American and other international students, with particular strengths in the arts, in addition to Italian language and culture. A rich selection of liberal arts courses is available as well. Programs are offered in Florence, Tuscania, Rome, and Venice.

3   In addition to semester, academic-year, and short-term study abroad, key offerings on the Florence branch campus include four-year Bachelor's degrees in Studio Art, Art History, Conservation Studies, Digital Media, Fashion Design, Interior Design, and Italian Language. An MA in Museum Studies is also offered on the Florence branch campus.

4   Examples of US-based study abroad providers include Academic Programs International (API), Knowledge Exchange Institute (KEI), SIT Study Abroad (SIT), and the Council on International Educational Exchange (CIEE).

5   An example here would be the School for Field Studies (SFS), which immerses its students in environmental science/studies contexts with a heavy emphasis on student (primary data) research projects.

6   Readers will recognize these learning objectives as they are found in a slightly altered form in Bloom's Classification of Learning Domains (1956, updated 2000) that was devised as a way to compel educators to think of education from a more holistic perspective.

7   The term "castle-dungeon" here is borrowed from Rabbi Kohain Halevi, an African American living in the community of Iture between Cape Coast and Elmina who not only has been one of a handful of people able to help students debrief their experiences at the UNESCO World Heritage sites, but who also is the Executive Secretariate of PANAFEST and active in the African American repatriation community in Ghana. The term "castle-dungeon" instead of "castle" to signify these sites better captures the history and function of the edifices. For usage in print see Richards (2005).

8   It is crucial to note here that the term "American students" has a level of ambiguity in it, particularly as US study abroad enrollments as a whole are still disproportionately represented by white, affluent female students. As Simon and Ainsworth (2012, 2) suggest "despite recent improvement in diversity, enrollment in study abroad continues to be largely restricted to White, affluent, middle-, or upper-middle class fe-

male students, who study the humanities or social sciences. A significant proportion of the US college population, including blacks and lower socioeconomic status students, don't typically participate in study abroad programs. For example, in 2004/5 among students at four-year institutions, while white students comprised 66% of the population, their representation in study abroad programs was 83% compared to a meager 3.5% black student representation from a college population of 12.5%."

9   In Karl Marx's identification of slavery as an economic category, he wrote "Direct slavery is just as much the pivot of bourgeois industry as machinery, credits, etc. Without slavery you have no cotton; without cotton you have no modern industry. It is slavery that gave the colonies their value; it is the colonies that created world trade, and it is world trade that is the precondition to large-scale industry. Thus slavery is an economic category of the greatest importance" (1847, 94).

10   Study abroad professionals will recognize this as a common methodology used by programs to help empower students early on in a program. The authors first learned of the method as "The Drop Off," as formulated and termed by SIT Study Abroad (both authors previously worked for SIT).

11   While students are given some instruction in *twi*, a lingua franca in the country, the homestay experience takes place in Cape Coast, a traditionally *fante* speaking area. Both *twi* and *fante* fall under the linguistic umbrella of *akan*, and are therefore mutually intelligible in many respects.

References

Introduction
Ritchie, A.T. (1885, republished 2011). *Mrs. Dymond*. London: British Library, Historical Print Edition.
Zakaria, F. (2015). *In defense of a liberal education*. New York, NY: W.W. Norton & Company.

Chapter 1
Arendt, H. (1958) *The human condition*. Chicago: University of Chicago Press
Balducci, E. (2005) *L'uomo planetario* (in English: The planetary man). Firenze: Giunti Editore.
Balducci, E. (1986) *Cittadini del mondo* (in English: citizens of the world). Milano: Principato.
Bauman, Z. (2005) *Liquid Life*. Polity.
Bergson, H. (1911). *Creative evolution*. (A. Mitchell, tr.). New York: Henry Holt.
Boulding, K. (1989) *Three faces of power*. Newbury Park, California: Sage Publications.
Burton, J. (1990) *Conflict Resolution and Prevention*. New York: St. Martins Press.
Capitini, A. (1999) *Il potere di tutti* (in english: The power of all). Perugia: Guerra edizioni.
Chardin, T. (2004) *The future of man*. New York: Image books.
Commission of the European Community (2001). Making a European area of lifelong learning a reality. Retrieved on September 14, 2015 from http://eur-lex.europa.eu/LexUriServ/LexUriServ.do?uri=COM:2001:0678:FIN:EN:PDF.
Diamond, J. (2005) *Collapse: How Societies Choose to Fail or Succeed*. New York: Viking Press.
Dolci, D. (1981) *Sicilian Lives*. Pantheon Village.

Eibl-Eibesfeld, I. (1996) *Love and Hate: the natural history of behavior patterns.* Aldine Transaction. Empowerment (nd). In Wikipedia. http://wikipedia.org/wiki/Empowerment.

Freire, P. (1992) *Pedagogy of the Oppressed.* New York: Continuum.

Friedman, J. (1992) *Empowerment: the politics of alternative development.* Oxford: Blackwell Publishers.

Fromm, E. (2006) *The art of loving.* New York: HarperCollins.

Harari, Y. N. (2015) Sapiens: a brief history of humankind. New York: Harper.

Hicks, D. (2001) *Dignity: the essential role it plays in resolving conflicts.* New Haven, CT: Yale University Press.

Hofstede, G. and Hofstede, G. J. (2005) *Cultures and Organizations: Software of the Mind.* New York: McGraw-Hill.

Kelman, H. C. (1996) Negotiation as interactive problem solving. *International Negotiation: A Journal of Theory and Practice.* 1(1):99-123.

Koestler, A. (1983) *The yogi and the Commissar and other essays.* Hutchinson: Danube edition.

Kristof, N. and Wu Dunn, S. (2009) *Half the Sky: Turning Oppression into Opportunity for Women Worldwide.* NY: Alfred A. Knopf.

Maslow, A. (1970). *Motivation and personality* (2nd ed.). New York: Harper and Row.

Maturana, H. R. & Varela, F. J. (1980) *Autopoiesis and Cognition. The Realization of the Living.*
Dordrecht, Holland: D. Reidel Publishing Company.

Mirable, M.E. & Mullings, L. (2009). Let nobody turn us around: African American anthology. New York: Rowman & Littlefield.

Naraghi-Anderlini, S. (2007) *Women Building Peace: What They Do, Why It Matters.* Boulder, CO: Lynne Rienner Publishers.

Nussbaum, M. (2010) *Not for profit. Why democracy needs the humanities.* Princeton, NJ: Princeton University Press.

Pinker, S. (2011) *The better angels of our nature: why violence has declined.* New York: Viking Books.

Putnam, R. (2000) *Bowling Alone.* New York: Simon and Schuster. Sen, A.K. (1985) *Commodities and Capabilities.* Oxford: Oxford University Press.

Todorov, T. (1999) *The conquest of America. The question of the other.* Norman, OK: University of Oklahoma Press.

UN Resolution 1325 (2000, October). Women, peace and security. http://www.un.org/en/ga/search/view_doc.asp?symbol=S/RES/1325%282000%29

Chapter 2

Batini, F. (2011), *Storie, futuro e controllo. Le narrazioni come strumento di controllo del futuro,* Napoli: Liguori.

References

Batini, F. & Del Sarto, G. (2005). *Narrazioni di narrazioni. Orientamento narrativo e progetto di vita*, Trento: Erickson.
Batini, F., Del Sarto, G., & Giusti, S. (2007). *Narrazione e invenzione. Manuale di lettura e scrittura creativa*, Trento: Erickson.
Batini, F. & Giusti, S. (2008), *L'orientamento narrativo a scuola*. Trento: Erickson.
Batini, F & Giusti, S. (2009). (Eds) *Le storie siamo noi. Gestire le scelte e costruire la propria vita con le narrazioni*. Napoli: Liguori.
Butturini, E. (1993). Antichi valori e nuovi impegni educativi, in M. Mascia (Ed) *Per una pedagogia della pace*. Fiesole: Quaderni dell'Istituto Internazionale J. Maritain.
Carofiglio, G. (2010) *La manomissione delle parole*. Milano: Rizzoli.
Colzi, G. (1990). Moderno, postmoderno e fede cristiana, in *Aggiornamenti sociali*, N. 12.
Cortelazzo, M. & Zolli, P. (1992). *Dizionario etimologico della lingua italiana*. Vol. II, p. 382. Bologna: Zanichelli.
Curtis, A.M. 1930). *Il nuovo misticismo*. Torino: Fratelli Bocca Editori.
Dallago, L. (2006). *Che cos'è l'empowerment*. Roma: Carocci.
Dolci, D. (1998). *Gente semplice*. Scandicci: La Nuova Italia.
Dolci, A. & LaFata, V. (2002, April 19-20). (Eds.). Atti del seminario: *Giornata Maieutica. Il metodo nonviolento nell'esperienza di Danilo Dolci*. Palermo: Santa Maria dello Spasimo Palermo.
Fabbri, M. (2005). *Empowerment e nuove tecnologie*. Bergamo: Edizioni Junior.
Galimberti, U. (2009). *I miti del nostro tempo*. Milano: Feltrinelli.
Ghiani, G. (1995). Ecosofia e non violenza, in *Sviluppo equo e solidale. Scelte e percorsi di formazione: l'apporto degli obiettori di coscienza*, edited by P. De Stefani & M. Stambellini. Padova: Fondazione E. Zancan.
Giusti, S. (2010) *Imparare dalle narrazioni*, a cura di F. Batini. Milano: Unicopli.
Giusti, S. (2011) *Insegnare con la letteratura*. Bologna: Zanichelli.
Givone, S.(2012). *La metafisica della peste. Colpa e destino*. Torino:Einaudi, 2012.
Heyes, C. (2010). Mesmerzing mirror neurons. *Neuroimage, 51.2*, 789-791.
Keysers, C. (2009). Mirror neurons. *Current Biology, 19*, R971-973.
Orlandi, M. (2005). *Costruire la terra. Avventure di vita Giorgio La Pira – Léopold Sédar Senghor*, Firenze: Anscarichae Domus.
Pasolini, P.P. (1995). Nuove questioni linguistiche. in P.P. Pasolini, *Empirismo eretico*, pp. 5-24. Milano: Garzanti.
Pasolini, P.P. (2007). *Scritti corsari*. Milano: Garzanti.
Piccardo, C. (1995). *Empowerment*. Milano: Raffaello Cortina Editore.
Pinker, S. (2010) *L'istinto del linguaggio. Come la mente crea il linguaggio*. Milano: Mondadori.
Porta, L. (2004). (ed.). *Autobiografie a scuola: un approccio maieutico*. Milano: Angeli.

Praszkier, R. (2014) Empathy, mirror neurons and SYNC. *Mind and Society*. doi 10.1007/S11299-014-0160x.
Pulina, G. (2008). *L'angelo di Husserl. Introduzione a Edith Stein*, Editrice Zona: Pieve al Toppo.
Putton, A. (2010). *Empowerment e scuola. Metodologie di formazione nell'organizzazione educativa*, Roma: Carocci.
Stein, E. (2005). *La donna*. Roma: Città Nuova.
Stein, E. (1997). *La ricerca della verità. Dalla fenomenologia alla filosofia cristiana*, edited by A. A. Bello. Roma: Città Nuova.
Tosolini, A., Giusti, S., & Papponi Morelli, , G. (2007). (Eds.) *A scuola di intercultura. Cittadinanza, partecipazione, interazione: risorse della società multiculturale*. Trento: Erickson.
Yrigaray, L. (1997). *Il respiro delle donne*. Milano: Il Saggiatore.

Chapter 3

Bourdieu, P. (1989). Social space and symbolic power. *Sociological Theory*, 7 (1), 14-25.
Bourdieu, P., & Passeron, J. C. (1977). *Reproduction in education, society, and culture*. (L. Wacquant, Trans.) Thousand Oaks: Sage Publications.
Cannatella, H. (2007). Place and being. *Educational Philosophy and Theory*, 36, 622-632.
Casey, E. (1998). *The fate of place: A philosphical history*. Berkley, CA: University of California Press.
Chandler, P. (2009). Social studies and the color of the empire: a case study of conflict-free pedagogy. Tuscaloosa, Alabama: The University of Alabama.
Cromwell, R. R. (1993). Educators look to the power of words: A reflection on an ethic governing the words and language we use. *NJATE Journal: Issues in Education*, (5), 20-30.
Crossley, N. (2008). Social class. In M. Grenfell, *Pierre Bourdieu: Key concepts* (pp. 87-100).
Deer, C. (2008). Doxa. In M. Grenfell, *Pierre Bourdieu: Key concepts* (pp. 119-130). Durham: Acumen Publishing Limited.
Eisner, E. W. (2002 edition). *The educational imagination: On the design and evaluation of school programs*. Upper Saddle River, NJ: Merrill Prentice Hall.
Erevelles, N. (2002). Voices of silence: Foucault, disability, and question of self-determination. *Studies in Philosophy and Education*, 21, 17-35.
Giroux, H. (1999). *The mouse that roared: Disney and the end of innocence*. Lanham, MD: Rowman & Littlefield Publishers, Inc.
Gordon, T. T. (2012). *How students' interpretation of place relate to educational experiences* (Doctoral dissertation). Retrieved from Proquest Dissertations and Theses (Accession Order No. **UMI** 3539991).

Heath, S. B. (1983). *Ways with words: Language, life, and work in communities and classrooms.* Cambridge: Cambridge University Press.

Kohlberg, L. (1981). *Essays on moral development, Vol. I: The philosophy of moral development.* San Francisco, CA: Harper & Row.

Lantolf, J. P., & Genung, P. (2002). "I'd rather switch than fight": An activity-theoretic study of peer success, and failure in a foreign language. In C. Kramsch (Ed.) *Language acquisition and language socialization. Ecological perspectives (pp.175-196).* London: Continuum.

Lee, B. (1988). *Tao of Jeet Kune Do.* 1975. Reprint Santa Clarita: Ohara Publishing, Inc.

Lofland, J., Snow, J., Anderson, L., & Lofland, L. H. (2006). *Analyzing social settings: A guide to qualitative observation and analysis.* Belmont: Wadsworth, Cengage Learning.

Nardi, B. A. (1996). Activity theory and human-computer interaction. In B. A. Nardi (Ed.) *Context and consciousness: Activity theory and human computer interaction (pp.7-16). Cambridge, MA: MIT Press.*

Newman, J. H. (1952). *The Idea of a University.* South Bend, Indiana: University of Notre Dame Press.

Selinker, L. (1972). Interlanguage. *International review of applied linguistics, 10,* 209-231.

Tuan, Y. F. (1977). *Space and place: The perspective of experience.* Minneapolis: University of Minnesota Press.

U.S. Department of Education, National Center for Education Statistics. (n.d.) Trends in High School Dropout and Completion Rates in the United States: 1972–2009, Compendium Report. Washington, DC. http://nces.ed.gov/pubs2012/2012006.pdf.

van Manen, M. (1990). *Researching lived experience: Human science for an action senstitive pedagogy.* Albany, NY: State University of New York Press.

Wacquant, L. (2004). *Body & soul: Notebooks of an apprentice boxer.* New York: Oxford University Press.

Webb, J., Schirato, T., & Danaher, G. (2002). *Understanding Bourdieu.* London: Sage Publications.

Chapter 4

Adams, D.W. (1995). *Education for extinction: American Indians and the boarding school experience 1875-1928.* Lawrence: University Press of Kansas.

Allington, R.L. 2013. What really matters when working with struggling readers. *The Reading Teacher,66,(7),* 520-530.

Anderson, J.D., (1988). *The education of Blacks in the south, 1860-1935.* Chapel Hill: The University of North Carolina Press.

Anyon, J. (1980). Social class and the hidden curriculum of work. *Journal of Education, 162* (1), 67-92.

Beck, I.L., McKeown, M.G., and Kucan, L. (2013). *Bringing words to life: Robust Vocabulary Instruction*. New York: Guilford Press.

Byrnes, J.P. and Wasik, B.A. (2009*). Language and literacy development: What educators need to know*. New York: Guilford Press.

Cohen, E.G. (1994) *Designing groupwork: Strategies for the heterogeneous classroom*. New York: Teachers College Press.

Delpit, L.(2006). *Other people's children: Cultural conflict in the classroom*. New York: The New Press.

Freire, P. (2000). *Pedagogy of the oppressed*. New York: The Continuum International Publishing Group, Inc.

Goldin-Meadow, S., (1999). The role of gesture in communication and thinking. *Trend in Cognitive Science, 3,* (11), 419-429.

Gutierrez, E., Williams,D., Grosvald, M., and Corina, D. (2012). Lexical access in American Sign Language: An ERP investigation of effects of semantics and phonology. *Brain Research, 1468,* 63-83.

Hirsch, E.D. (2003). Reading comprehension requires knowledge-of words and the world: Scientific insights into the fourth grade slump and the nation's stagnant comprehension scores. *American Educator, Spring,* 10-24.

Hart, B. and Risley, T.R.(1995). *Meaningful differences in the everyday experiences of young children*. Baltimore: Paul H. Brookes Publishing Company.

Hoff, E. (2012). Interpreting the early language trajectories of children from low-SES and language minority homes: Implications for closing achievement gaps. *Developmental Psychology 2013, 49,*(1), 4-14.

Kuhn, M.R. and Stahl, S.A. (1998). Teaching children to learn word meanings from context: A synthesis and some questions. *Journal of Literacy Research 30, (119) doi:10.1080110862969809547983.*

Ladson-Billings, G. (2009). *The Dream keepers: Successful teachers of African-American children*. San Francisco: John Wiley & Sons, Inc.

McClelland, A. (1992). *The education of women in the United States: A guide to theory, teaching, and research*. New York: Garland.

NICHD (National Institute of Child Health and Human Development), (2006). *Report of the National Reading Panel: Teaching children to read.* Retrieved from http//:www.nichd.nihgov/publications/nrp/smallbook. cfm?venderforprints=1

Smith, M. K. (1941). Measurement of the size of general English vocabulary through the elementary grades and high school. *Genetic Psychology Monographs, 24,* 311-345.

Spring, J.,(2011). *The American school: A global context from the Puritans to the Obama era*. New York: McGraw-Hill Companies, Inc.

UNESCO (United Nations Educational, Scientific, and Cultural Organization). 2013. *Education indicators and data analysis*. Paris: UNESCO

UNESCO (United Nations Educational, Scientific, and Cultural Organization). 2005. *Education for all global monitoring report 2006*. Paris: UNESCO

United States Department of Education. (2011). *Trends in high school dropout rates in the United States:1972-2009. Compendium report of the National Center for Education Statistics*. Washington, DC: Author.

Chapter 5

Asher, J.W. (2003). The rise to prominence: Educational psychology. In Zimmerman, B.J., & Schunk. D.H. (eds.) *Educational psychology: A century of contribution*. Mahwah, NJ: Lawrence Erlbaum.

Bandura, A. (1997). *Self-efficacy: The exercise of control*. New York: Freeman.

Bredo, E. (2003). The development of Dewey's psychology. In Zimmerman, B.J., & Schunk. D.H. (eds.) *Educational psychology: A century of contribution*. Mahwah, NJ: Lawrence Erlbaum.

Bruner, J. S. (1966). *Toward a theory of instruction*. Cambridge, MA: Harvard University Press.

Coleman, W.S.E. (2000). *Voices of Wounded Knee*. Lincoln, NE: University of Nebraska Press.

Dewey, J. (1916). *Democracy and education: An introduction to the philosophy of education*. N.Y.: Macmillan.

Dewing, R. (1985). *Wounded Knee: The meaning and significance of the second incident*. N.Y.: Irvington.

Dunn, K., Scileppi, J., Averna, L., Zerillo, V., & Skelding, M. (2007). *The contemporary applications of a systems approach to education*. Lanham, MD: University Press of America.

Gardner, H. (1999). *Intelligence reframed: Multiple intelligences for the 21st century*. NY: Basic Books.

Gary, S. (n.d.) Humanistic approaches to Teaching. Retrieved from http://homepage.ntlworld.com/gary.sturt/human.htm

Golding, W. (1978). *Lord of the flies*. NY: Putnam.

Gutierrez, R. (1992). Achievement effects of the non-graded elementary school: A best evidence synthesis. *Review of Educational Research*, 62 (4), 333-376.

Hall, V.C. (2003). Educational psychology from 1890 – 1920. In Zimmerman, B.J., & Schunk. D.H. (eds.) *Educational psychology: A century of contribution*. Mahwah, NJ: Lawrence Erlbaum.

Industrial Development Department (1975). *Industrial facts/Pine Ridge, South Dakota*. Columbus, NE: Area Development Department, Nebraska Public Power District.

Jackson, P. (1968). *Life in classrooms*. NY: Holt, Rinehart &Winston.

Kanna, P.K. (2010). *Educational psychology*. Jaipur, India: Global Media.

Laird, G. & Chapman, R. (2010). Wounded Knee incident. In R. Chapman (Ed.). *Culture wars: An encyclopedia of issues, viewpoints and voices.* Vol. 2. Armonk. NY: M.E. Sharpe.

Maynard, E. & Twiss, G (1970). *That these people may live: Conditions among the Oglala Sioux of the Pine Ridge Reservation.* Pine Ridge, SD: Indian Health Service.

Meyer, R. E. (1972). *The XL Program.* Chicago, IL: St. Xavier College.

Oglala Lakota College (2010). *College history.* Retrieved from http://www.olc.edu/about/history.

Oglala Sioux Community College (1976). *Lakota Higher Education Center 1976-1977 Bulletin.* Pine Ridge, SD: Oglala Sioux Community College.

_____ (1980). *Oglala Sioux Community College 1980-1981 Catalog.* . Pine Ridge, SD: Oglala Sioux Community College.

Pajares, F. (2003). William James: Our father who begat us. In Zimmerman, B.J., & Schunk. D.H. (eds.) *Educational psychology: A century of contribution.* Mahwah, NJ: Lawrence Erlbaum.

Pitman, C. & Scileppi, J.A. (1971). *New Community: A proposal for total individual learning and community gathering.* Chicago, IL: New Community School of Chicago.

Rowan, J. (n.d.) *Humanistic education.* Retrieved from http://www.ahpweb.org/bibliography/chapter 17.htm.

Sarbin, T.R. (1970).A role theory perspective for community psychology: The structure of social identity. In D. Adelson& B.C. Kalis (Eds), *Community psychology and mental health: Perspectives and challenges.* Scranton, PA: Chandler.

St. Xavier College (1973). *The XL Program.* Chicago, IL: Admissions Office, St. Xavier College.

Scileppi, J.A. (1973). *Fact sheet on XL.* Chicago, IL: St. Xavier College.

Scileppi, J.A. (1976). *Continuing education need study assessment of the Pine Ridge Reservation: Final report.* Pine Ridge, SD: Oglala Sioux Community College.

Scileppi, J.A. (1988). *A systems view of education: A model for change.* Lanham, MD: University Press of America.

Sullivan, A.M. & King, L. (1999). An investigation into empowering students through cooperative learning. *Research in Education.* ERIC accession number: ED430180.

Teed, E.L., Scileppi. J.A., Boeckmann. M., Crispi, E.L., Regan, J., & Whitehouse, D.J. (2007). The community mental health system: A navigational guide for providers. N.Y.: Allyn and Bacon.

Zigler, E., & Child, I.L. (1969). Socialization. In G. Lindzey & E. Aronson (Eds.) *The handbook of social psychology.* (2nd ed). 3. Reading, MA: Addison-Wesley.

Zimmerman, B.J., & Schunk. D.H.(Eds.) (2003). *Educational psychology: A century of contribution*. Mahwah, NJ: Lawrence Erlbaum.

Chapter 6

Casteel, J.D. & Stahl, R.J. (1975). *Value clarification in the classroom: A primer*. Santa Monica, CA: Goodyear Publishing Co.

_____ (1997). *Doorways to decision making: A handbook for teaching decision making strategies*. Waco, TX: Prufrock Press.

Dewey, J. (1916). *Democracy and education: An introduction to the philosophy of education*. New York: Macmillan.

Easterbrooks, S. R. & Scheetz, N. A. (2004) Applying critical thinking skills to character education and values clarification with students who are deaf or hard of hearing. *American Annals of the Deaf, 149*(3), 255-263.

Edwards, A. & Allen, C. (2008). Values clarification used as intervention for urban, delinquent, pregnant adolescents and young mothers. *Journal of Human Behavior in the Social Environment, 18*, 1-14.

Frondizi, R. (1971). *What is value?: An introduction to axiology*. Chicago: Open Court Publishing Co.

Goldberg, K. (1987, March 11). Federal court finds secular humanism a religion. *Education Week, 6*, 24.

Hartman, A. (2011). Judge W. Brevard Hand, Intellectual historian. US Intellectual History, the blog of the Society for US Intellectual History. Retrieved from US-intellectual-history-blogspot.com/2011/09/judge-w-brevard-hand.

Jourard, S.M. (1971). *The transparent self* (Rev. ed.). New York: Van Nostrand Reinhold Co.

Jung, C.G. (1960). The psychogenesis of mental disease. In H. Read, M. Fordham & G. Adler, *The collected works of Carl Jung*, Vol. 3. New York: Pantheon Books.

Kirschenbaum, H. (1977). *Advanced value clarification*. LaJolla, CA: University Associates.

_____ (1985) Values clarification. In J.W. Noll (Ed.) Taking sides: Clashing views on controversial educational issues, 3rd Ed. Guilford, CT: Dushkin Publishing Group.

Mosconi, J., & Emmett, J. (2003). Effects of a values clarification curriculum on high school students' definitions of success. *Professional School Counseling, 7*(2), 68-78.

National Curriculum and Training Institute (1994). The fallout shelter problem. Retrieved from http://www.NCTI.Org//contactcommerce/images/resources/the_fallout-shelter-problem.pdf

Ohlde, C. D. & Vinitsky, M.H. (1976). Effect of values-clarification workshop on value awareness. *Journal of Counseling Psychology, 23*(5), 489-491.

Raths, L.E., Harmin, M., & Simon, S.B. (1966). *Values and teaching.* Columbus, OH: Charles E. Merrill Publishing Co.

Rogers, C.R. (1951). *Client-centered therapy.* Boston: Houghton Mifflin Co.

Rokeach, M. (1968). *Beliefs, attitudes and values. A theory of organization and change.* San Francisco: Jossey Bass.

_____ (1971). Long range experimental modification of values, attitudes and behaviors. *American Psychologist, 26,* 453-459.

_____ (1979). *Understanding human values: Individual and societal.* New York: Free Press.

Scileppi, J.A. (1988). *A systems view of education: A model for change.* (Rev. Ed.) Lanham, MD: University Press of America.

Simon, S.B., & DeSherebenin, P. (1977). Values clarification: It can start gently and grow deep. In C.R. Clarizio, R.C. Craig, & W. Mehrens (Eds.) *Contemporary issues in educational psychology.* Boston: Allyn and Bacon.

Simon, S.B., Howe, , L.E. & Kirschenbaum, H. (1972). *Value clarification: A handbook of practical strategies for teachers and students.* New York: Hart Publishing Co.

Thompson, D.G. & . Hudson, G. R. (1982). Values clarification and behavioral group counseling with ninth-grade boys in a residential school. *Journal of Counseling Psychology,* 29(4), 394-399.

U.S. Department of Education (2002).Fact sheet: The No Child Left Behind Act of 2001. Retrieved from ed.gov/offices/OESE/esea/factsheet.htm.

Zuo, H. & Wei, X. (2008). The intervention experiments on the prosocial behaviors of junior middle school students. *Chinese Mental Health Journal,* 22(9), 669-673, 677.

Chapter 7

Bandura, A. (1982). Self-efficacy mechanism in human agency. *American Psychologist, 37,* 122-147.

Boyatzis, R. & McKee (2005). *Resonant leadership: Renewing yourself and connecting with others through mindfulness, Hope and compassion.* Boston, MA: Harvard Business School Press.

Campbell, C. M., Smith, M., Dugan, J. P., and Komives, S. R. (2012). Mentors and college leadership outcomes: The importance of position and process. *The Review of Higher Education,* 35(4). 595-625.

Cattaneo, L., & Chapman, A. R. (2010). The process of empowerment: A model for use in research and practice. *American Psychologist,* 65(7), 646-659. doi:10.1037/a0018854

Covey, S. R. (1989). *The seven habits of highly effective people.* New York: Simon & Schuster.

Goleman, D., Boyatzis, R. & McKee, A. (2002). *Primal leadership: Realizing the*

References

power of emotional intelligence. Boston, MA: Harvard Business School Press.   http://chronicle.com/article/Todays-Students-Need/125604/ http://www.uic.edu/depts/wellctr/docs/Stress%20and%20the%20College%20Student.pdfhttp://www.ncsu.edu/csleps/leadership/Resource_Sheets/Managing_StressTips.pdf
http://www.webmd.com/balance/stress-management/stress-management-breathing-exercises-for-relaxation#

Horney, K. (1942). *Self –Analysis*. New York: Norton.

Labby, S., Lunenburg, F.C. & Slate, J. R. (2012). *Emotional intelligence and academic success: A conceptual analysis for educational leaders.* NCPEA Publications.

Lightsey, O. (1994). 'Thinking positive' as a stress buffer: The role of positive automatic cognitions in depression and happiness. *Journal of Counseling Psychology, 41*(3), 325-334.

McKay, M., Davis, M., & Fanning, P. (2011). *Thoughts and feelings: Taking control of your moods and your life.* CA: New Harbinger.

Murphy, S. E. & Johnson, S. K. (2011). The benefits of a long-lens approach to leader development: Understanding the seeds of leadership. *The Leadership Quarterly,22*(3), 459-470. doi:10.1016/j.leaqa.2011.04.004.

Murray M.T. & Pizzorno J.E., Jr. (2006). *Textbook of Natural Medicine, 3*(1), St. Louis: Churchill Livingstone.

Myers, S. B., Sweeney, A. C., Popick, V., Wesley, K., Bordfeld, A., & Fingerhut, R. (2012). Self-care practices and perceived stress levels among psychology graduate students. *Training and Education In Professional Psychology,* 6(1), 55-66. doi:10.1037/a0026534

O'Keefe, E. J. & Berger, D. (1999). *Self -management for college students: The ABC approach.* Hyde Part, NY: Partridge Hill.

Ong, A. D., Burrow, A. L., & Fuller-Rowell, T. E. (2012). Positive emotions and the social broadening effects of Barack Obama. *Cultural Diversity and Ethnic Minority Psychology, 18*(4), 424-428. doi:10.1037/a0029758

Payne, R. (2005). *Relaxation Techniques: A Practical Handbook for the Health Care Professional,* 3rd ed. Edinburgh: Churchill Livingstone.

Quinn, E. (2012, Winter). Stress management skills for student leaders. *Champagnat: An International Marist Journal of Charism in Education,* 14(2), 48-53.

Schmidt, K. & Nosek, B. (2010). Implicit (and explicit) racial attitudes barely changed during Barack Obama's presidential campaign and early presidency. *Journal of Experimental Social Psychology,* 46(2), 308-314.

Skinner, B. F. (1969). *Contingencies of reinforcement.* New Jersey: Prentice Hall.

Suval, L. (2012). What Drives Our Need For Approval?. *Psych Central.* http://psychcentral.com/blog/archives/2012/09/20/what-drives-our-need-for-approval/

Teed, E. L. & Scileppi, J. A. (2007). *The community mental health system: A navigational guide for providers*. Boston, MA: Pearson Education

Van der Zee, K., Thijs, M., & Schakel, L. (2002). The relationship of emotional intelligence with academic intelligence and the big fve. *European Journal of Personality*, 16, 103-125. doi: 10:1002/per.434

Chapter 8

American Association of University Women (2010). Why so few women in science, technology, engineering, and mathematics. Retrieved from http://www.aauw.org/files/2013/02/Why-So Few-Women-in-Science-Technology-Engineering-and-Mathematics.pdf

Arnold, C., Bass, R., Carden, D., Davis, T. C., Huang, J., Kennen, E. M., & Yu, H. (2005, January). Tipping the scales: the effect of literacy on obese patients' knowledge and readiness to lose weight. *Southern Medical Journal*, 98(1), 15+

Arnold, G. (1974). Kenyatta and the politics of Kenya. London, England: Aldine Press.

Arnot, M. (2002). Making the difference to sociology of education: Reflections on family-school and gender relations. *Discourse*, 23(3), 347-355.

Biklen, S. K. (1987). Schoolteaching, professionalism, and gender. *Teacher Education Quarterly*, 14(2), 17-24.

Bynner, J. (2001). Childhood risks and protective factors in social exclusion. *Children & Society*, 15(5), 285-301.

Carnevale, A. (2012). *The importance of post-secondary certificates*. Politico, July 31st.

Carr, D. (1998). *Education, knowledge, and truth: beyond the postmodern impasse* (Vol. 4). Psychology Press.

Chiu, L. F. (2003). *Inequalities of access to cancer screening: a literature review*. Sheffield: NHS Cancer Screening Programmes.

Chodorow, N. (1989). *Feminism and psychoanalytic theory*. New Haven [Conn.]: Yale University Press.

Coleman, J. S., Campbell, E. Q., Hobson, C. J., McPartland, J., Mood, A. M., Weinfeld, F. D., & York, R. (1966). Equality of educational opportunity (2nd ed.). Washington, DC: US Government Printing Office.

Corbett, C., Hill, C., & St. Rose, A. (2008). *Where the girls are: The facts about gender equity in education*. Washington, DC: AAUW.

El-Gibaly, O., Ibrahim, B., Mensch, B. S., & Clark, W. H. (2002). The decline of female circumcision in Egypt: evidence and interpretation. *Social science & medicine*, 54(2), 205-220. doi: 10.1016/S0277-9536(01)00020-X

Flowers, C. (2005). With no boys to ogle, we had time to learn. *Newsweek*, 146(Yl), October, p. 26.

References 261

Freire, P. (1970, 1966). *Pedagogy of the oppressed*. New York: Continuum International Publishing Inc.

Freud, S. (1925). Some physical consequences of the anatomical distinction between the sexes. In J. Strachey (Ed.), *The standard edition of the complete psychological works of Sigmund Freud* (Vol. 19). London: The Hogarth Press, 1961.

Gilligan, C. (1982). In a different voice: Psychological theory and women's development.Cambridge, MA: Harvard University Press.

Giroux, H. A. (2003), Public Pedagogy and the Politics of Resistance: Notes on a critical theory of educational struggle. *Educational Philosophy and Theory*, 35: 5–16. doi: 10.1111/1469-5812.00002

Gorman, S. T., Durmowicz, M. C., Roskes, E.M., & Slattery, S.P. (2010). Women in the academy: Female leadership in STEM education and the evolution of the mentoring web. Forum on Public Policy

Green, A., Preston, J., & Sabates, R. (2003). Education, Equality, and Social Cohesion: A Distributional Approach. *Compare*, 33(4), 453-70.

Higgins, J. A., Hoffman, S., Graham, C. A., & Sanders, S. A. (2008). Relationships between condoms, hormonal methods, and sexual pleasure and satisfaction: An exploratory analysis from the women's well-being and sexuality study. *Sexual Health*, 5(4), 321–330.

International Center for Research on Women (2005). Icrw.org

Jenkins, K. J. (2006, April). Constitutional lessons for the next generation of public single-sex elementary and secondary schools. *William and Mary Law Review*, 47(6), 1953+.

Jewkes, R. K., Levin, J. B. & Penn-Kekana, L. (2003). Gender Inequalities, intimate partner violence, and HIV preventive practices: findings of a South-African cross-sectional study." *Social Science and Medicine* 56, p. 125-134.

Kashf Foundation (2015). Vision, mission, and core values. Retrieved from http://kashf.org/?page_id=244

Kajiado, W. E. (2000) Female Genital Mutilation blamed for school dropout. *Inter-church Coalition on Africa*.

Kenkel, D. S. (1991). Health behavior, health knowledge, and schooling. *Journal of Political Economy*, 99(2), 287-305.

Kiernan, K. E. (1997). Becoming a young parent: A longitudinal study of associated factors. *The British Journal of Sociology*, 48(3), 406-428. doi: 10.2307/591138

King, J. 2010. *Gender Equity in Higher Education: 2010*. Washington, DC: American Council on Education.

Kirschenbaum, R., & Boyd, A. (2007). Do students learn better in single-sex classrooms. *NEA Today*, 25(8), 41.

Kohlberg, L. (1981). *The meaning and measurement of moral development*. Worcester, MA: Clark University Press.

Kristof, N. D. & WuDunn, S. (2009). *Half the sky: Turning oppression into opportunity for women worldwide.* NY: Random House.

Kritz, M. M., Makinwa-Adebusoye, P. & Gurak, D. T. *(2000).* Wife's empowerment and reproduction in Nigeria. *In* Harriet B. Presser & Gita Sen *(Eds), Women's empowerment and demographic processes: Moving beyond Cairo (p.* 260-298*).* New York: Oxford University Press.

Lee, V. E., Marks, H. M., & Byrd, T. (1994). Sexism in single-sex and coeducational independent secondary school classrooms. *Sociology of Education, 67,* 92-120.

Leigh, J. P. (1998). Parents' schooling and the correlation between education and frailty. *Economics of Education Review, 17(3),* 349-358. doi: 10.1016/S0272-7757(98)00014-4.

Greenstone, M. & Looney, A. The great recession may be over but American families are working harder than ever. Brookings: July 11, 2011.

McKellar, D. (2008). Math books. Retrieved from http://www.danicamckellar.com/math-books/

Melenyzer, B. J. (1991). Empowerment and women in education: A critique of the feminist discourse. Presented at the Annual cnference of the Women's Cnsortium of the Pennsylvania State System of Higher Education, Shippensburg, PA. November 1991.

Merang, C. (2010). Development of women's education in Kenya. *International NGO Journal,* 5(3), 68-73.

Namara, N., & Tormey, R (2011). *Women, higher education and career choice; Women's experiences of higher education and career choice in Ireland and Uganda.* Saarbrucken, Germany: Lambert Academic Publishing, 2011.

Noddings, N. (1989). *Developing models of caring in the professions.* Presented at the Annual Meeting of the American Educational Research Association, San Francisco, March.

Pulkki, L., Kivimaki, M., Keltikangas-Jarvinen, L., Elovainio, M., Leino, M., & Viikari, J. (2003). Contribution of adolescent and early adult personality to the inverse association between education and cardiovascular risk behaviours: prospective population-based cohort study. *International Journal of Epidemiology,*32 (6): 968-975. doi: 10.1093/ije/dyg097

Sabates, R. and Feinstein, L. (2005) *The effects of education on parenting.* London: Centre for Research on the Wider Benefits of Learning.

Sadker, D. M., Zittleman, K., & Sadker, M. P. (2009). *Teachers, schools, and society.* New York: McGraw Hill.

Shakeshaft, C., & Nowell, I. (1984). Research on theories, concepts, and models of organizational behavior: The influence of gender. *Issues in Education,* 2, (3), 186-200.

Snyder, T.D. & Dillow, S.A. (2010). *Digest of educational statistics.* Washington DC: Center for Educational Statistics.

Teed, E.L., Scileppi, J.A., Boeckmann, M., Crispi, E.L., Regan, J, & Whitehouse, D.J.M. (2007). *The community mental health system: A navigational guide for providers.* NY.: Allyn & Bacon.
United Nations Women (2012, 1998). Commission on the status of women 2012. http://www.unwomen.org/en/news/in-focus/commission-on-the-status-of-women
Verba, S., Schlozman, K.L. & Brady, H. (1995). *Voice and equality: Civic voluntarism in American politics.* Cambridge, MA: Harvard University Press.
Walker, L. (1984) Sex Differences in the development of moral reasoning: A critical review. *Child Development,* 55(3), 677-691. West, M. S., & Curtis, J. W. (2006). *AAUP faculty gender equity indicators 2006.*
Washington, DC: American Association of University Professors.
Wolfe, B. L., & Haveman, R. H. (2002). Social and nonmarket benefits from education in an advanced economy. In *Conference Series; [Proceedings]* (Vol. 47, 97-142). Single-sex classroom 'better for girls'. (2011, Dec 28). *Daily Post,* p. 9. Retrieved from http://search.proquest.com/docview/9 12853393?accountid=28549
www.danicamckellar.com/math-books/
www.aauw.org
www.kashf.org

Chapter 9
Arlington Central School District Home Page: District Profile, "About Us", 2013 http://www.arlingtonschools.org/pages/arlington_schools
Arlington Central School District Strategic Plan: "Overview, Mission, Core Values, Objectives, Definition, Strategies and Delimeters." http://www.arlingtonschools.org/pages/arlington_schools
Benson, P.L. (1993). *The troubled journey: A portrait of 6th to 12th-grade youth.* Minneapolis: Search Institute
Blanchard K.H., Carlos, J.P. & Randolph A. (2013) *Empowerment takes more than a minute.* San Francisco: Berrett-Koehler.
Brown E.D. & Low C.M. (2008) Chaotic living conditions and sleep problems associated with children's responses to academic challenge. *Journal of Family Psychology,* 22, 920–923. doi: 10.1037/a0013652.
Burke, N. J., Hellman, J. L., Scott, B. G., Weems, C. F., & Carrion, V. G. (2011). The impact of adverse childhood experiences on an urban pediatric population. *Child abuse & neglect,* 35(6), 408-413.
"Developmental Assets Profile," Search Institute, (2005)
Dutchess County Children's Services Council, Homepage (2013) http://www.mhadc.com/csc_web/httpdocs/aboutus_whatis_overview htm
Fisher, C., & Lerner, R. Encyclopedia of Applied Developmental Science. Sage Publications. 2005. 343.

Fitzgerald, M. (2013). "Primary, Secondary and Tertiary Prevention in Certification and in Practice," Retrieved from https://fhea.com/main/content/.../fheanews_volume12_issue2.pdf.

Hart, B., & T.R. Risley. (2003). The early catastrophe: The 30 million word gap by age 3. *American Educator, 27(1)*, 4–9.

Johnson A.D., Martin A, Brooks-Gunn J, & Petrill S.A. (2008). Order in the House! Associations among household chaos, the home literacy environment, maternal reading ability and children's early reading. *Merrill-Palmer Quarterly: Journal of Developmental Psychology*, 54, 445–472. doi: 10.1353/mpq.0.0009.

McGhee, K. & McKay, G. (2007). "Insects." *Encyclopedia of Animals*. Washington: National Geographic Society

NYS Education Department, "New York Dignity for All Students Act" (June 2013)

Payne, R. K. (2005). *A framework for understanding poverty* (4th rev. ed.). Highlands, Tex.: Aha!

"Response to Intervention", Guidance Document for NYS School Districts, State University of New York, (October 2010) http://www.bls.gov/
www.cdc.gov/violenceprevention/acestudy/#ACED
www.wikipedia.org/

Chapter 10

Ash, S. L. & Clayton, P. H. (2009). Generating, deepening, and documenting learning: The power of critical reflection in applied learning. *Journal of Applied Learning in Higher Education*, 25-48.

Bloom, B. S. (1956). *Taxonomy of educational objectives: The classification of educational goals*. New York: David McKay Company Inc.

Dewey, J. (1897). My pedagogic creed. *School Journal*, 54, 77-80.

Eyler, J., Giles, D. E., & Schmiede, A. (1996). *A practitioner's guide to reflection in service learning*. Nashville, TN: Vanderbilt University.

Honey, P. & Mumford, A. (2000). *The learning styles helper's guide*. Maidenhead Berks: Peter Honey Publications Limited.

Kolb, D. A. (1984). *Experiential learning: Experience as the source of learning and development*. New Jersey: Prentice-Hall Inc.

Lutterman-Aguilar, A. & Gingerich, O. (2002). Experiential pedagogy for study abroad: Educating for global citizenship. *Frontiers: The Interdisciplinary Journal of Study Abroad*, 8, 41-82.

Marx, K. (1847). *The poverty of philosophy: A reply to M. Proudhon's philosophy of poverty*. New York: International Publishers.

Maddux, W. W. & Galinsky, A. (2009). Cultural boarders and mental barriers. *Journal of Personality and Social Psychology*, 96(5), 1047-1061.

Paige, R. M. (2010). *Beyond Immediate Impact: Study Abroad for Global En-*

gagement (SAGE). Report Submitted to the Title VI: International Research and Studies Program, U.S. Department of Education.

Pratt, M. L. (1992). *Imperial eyes: Travel writing and transculturation*. London: Routledge.

Richards, S.L. (2005). What is to be remembered?: Tourism to Ghana's slave castle-dungeons. *Theatre Journal, 57*(4), 617-637.

Simon, J. & Ainsworth, J. W. (2012). Race and socioeconomic status differences in study abroad participation: The role of habitus, social networks, and cultural capital. *International Scholarly Research Network*, 1-21.

Sutton, R. & Rubin, D. L. (2004). The GLOSSARI Project: Initial findings from a system-wide research initiative on study abroad learning outcomes. *Frontiers: the Interdisciplinary Journal of Study Abroad,10*, 65-82.

Vande Burg, M. (2012). *Student learning abroad: What your students are learning, what they are not, and what you can do about it*. Sterling, VA: Stylus Publishing LLC.

Welch, M. (1999). The ABCs of reflection: A template for students and instructors to implement written reflection in service-learning. NSEE Quarterly, 25, 22–25.

List of Contributors

The authors were chosen for their diverse expertise. Together they form a community of scholars interested in empowering students to succeed.

Branton Burgess Baird, Ph.D. Candidate, is studying Applied Linguistics and Romance Languages at The University of Alabama, Department of Modern Languages and Classics, where he also teaches Spanish as a Graduate Teaching Assistant. He is currently working on his dissertation, which investigates the role of prosodic intonation on interlanguage acquisition of conventional expressions of Spanish second language learners, and is scheduled to defend in the Spring of 2017.

Debra Baird, Ph.D., has been an educator for over 37 years, spending 7 years in the K-12 classroom and then teaching at the University of Alabama, Austin College, the University of West Alabama, Stillman College, and Athens State University. She was an administrator for 23 of those years, including Dean of the College of Education/Executive Director of the Regional Teacher In-Service Center at Athens State University. Currently, she is a Professor in the College of Arts and Sciences, Department of Religious Studies, and her research interests have focused on the challenges and opportunities of the immigrant. She has studied, written, and lectured on the world of multi-racial children, seasonal farm workers, refugee concerns, and at-risk/abused individuals, both adult and children. The spiritual development of children and adults is her current focus.

Ronald Cromwell, Ed.D., now retired and consulting, has 40 year experience in education teaching at all levels. He had been in higher education for over 25 years and served as Provost and Senior Vice president for 13 years. He has received national awards for leadership and for his work as principal in P -12 settings. He has been awarded over 8 million dollars in grants, supervised over 20 million dollars of earmark national research projects and raised over 9 million dollars. He has over 85 publications and national presentations. His research interests have been in enabling all students to reach high standards, learning/personality styles, integration of technology, diversity, and creativity.

Linda Dixon-Dziedzic, MA, CAS, NCC, Ph.D. Candidate, has served as a NYS certified school psychologist for over 15 years and a mental health counselor for over 20. As School Psychologist at LaGrange Middle School in the Arlington Central School District, she consults with educators, evaluates students for special education services, counsels students, and facilitates social skill, divorce/loss recovery groups for middle school students. In addition, Linda is co-founder of Renewed Hope Counseling Center in Fishkill, New York where she is an ordained minister. She is currently completing her doctoral degree in Christian Counseling through the National Christian Counseling Association (NCCA), and is Nationally Board Certified as a Counselor through the National Board for Certified Counselors (NBCC).

Maureen Fitzgerald-Riker, Ph.D., taught at-risk student populations in public schools in Colorado for more than 10 years. In her role as an Assistant Professor of Literacy at Marist College, she prepared pre-service teachers to integrate literacy across various contexts. She has taught internationally in Ghana and in Nicaragua. She is currently principal of Tinmouth Elementary school in Vermont and continues to design and initiate literacy curriculum and practices in Vermont district schools as an educational consultant.

Maurizio Geri, Ph.D. Candidate, is a research assistant in International Studies at Old Dominion University, VA. Originally from Florence, Italy, where he got a BA in Political Science and a MA in Educational Science, he has extensive professional experience in Latin America and South Asia where he worked in the areas of peacekeeping and peace education with different NGOs (to include

Peace Brigades International and Nonviolent Peaceforce). He has been working as a social worker with at-risk youth (in Italy), as a teacher of Italian language (in Italy and the US), and as a consultant on trainings for women mediators (in Indonesia). His most recent research focus is in the area of democracy, in particular the post-Arab Spring and the Muslim democracies.

Tedi Gordon, Ph.D., has been in education for over 30 years. As Assistant Professor in the College of Education at Athens State University since 2009, she teaches the foundations of education courses as well as methods and technology courses. She has also served as internship coordinator, community lab school co-chair, and state department liaison. Early career experiences include the Alabama Reading Initiative-Project for Adolescent Literacy at the state level, secondary literacy coach at the system level, and classroom teacher. She holds a B.S. in Elementary Education and a Masters of Education from Tarleton State University, and a doctorate in Instructional Leadership from The University of Alabama. Research interests include role of "place" in education, teaching practices that promote social justice, academic and transgressive spaces, and collaborative partnerships.

Fabrizio Guarducci, Ph.D., is an art and culture entrepreneur, founder and President of Lorenzo de' Medici: The Italian International Institute, executive film producer and author of two books: *La Parola Ritrovata: Ricostruire l'Uomo Attraverso il Linguaggio* and *Theoria: Il Divino Oltre il Dogma*. He is involved in numerous important projects in the Florentine community and has dedicated his life to helping people, teaching "enthusiasm" and anthropology. Currently, he is working in cinema, developing artistic and historical films. He is also forming a center to help people evolve their spiritual creativity in the world.

John Peters, Ph.D., is Dean of International Programs and Associate Professor of Economics at Marist College. As an undergraduate, he studied for a year in Japan and a year in Zimbabwe, and found this time abroad both pivotal and transformative. As a result of these experiences, John's professional work has taken him (so far) to more 30 thirty countries, and his mission is one of helping to create, facilitate, and connect students with unique and powerful learning opportunities. Of particular interest is experiential learning and encouraging students to think through the significance of the overseas experience for their academic, personal, and professional development. John holds a BA in Economics and Japanese Studies from California State University Sacramento; an MA in Economics and MA in International Studies from Ohio University; and a Ph.D. in Political Economy and Public Policy from the University of Southern California.

Elizabeth Quinn, Ph.D., LMHC, has been teaching for 19 years and is an Associate Professor of Psychology at Marist College, Poughkeepsie, NY. Among other courses, she teaches The Psychology of Women, Counseling, and Chemical Dependency. Her research and psychotherapy practice are directed toward the application of cognitive behavioral therapy, developing self-efficacy, and the empowerment of women, including women in recovery. She has also been invited to give professional presentations to athletes, students, and other clinicians on self-management, leadership, and cognitive behavioral therapy. She has co-authored several books on community psychology and has published in the areas of stress management, military veterans and trauma, and chemical dependency.

Barbara Ruggiero, Ph.D., a founder and current Executive Director of Brass City Charter School in Waterbury, CT whose varied career demonstrates a life-long commitment to children's academic success, was the former Executive Director / Principal of Children's Community School in Waterbury. Dr. Ruggiero is a former licensed child psychologist and an experienced school leader. She has a master's degree from Harvard University and a doctorate from Boston University and completed pre and post-doctoral clinical training in the Department of Child Psychiatry, Tufts New England Medical Center, Boston, MA.

John Scileppi, Ph.D., Professor Emeritus, has served as an educator for over 40 years. In his role as Professor of Psychology at Marist College, Poughkeepsie, NY, he has directed graduate and undergraduate programs and authored three books on education from a systems perspective. He has taught internationally in Barbados, Ghana and Italy. In addition he was a faculty member at St. Xavier College in Chicago where he originated an innovative Freshman Year Experience emphasizing student-oriented learning, and served as academic vice president at Oglala Sioux Community College on the Pine Ridge Native American Reservation.

Gavin Webb, PhD., is a Visiting Assistant Professor of Ethnomusicology at Binghamton University in New York. From 1998 – 2012 he was based at the University of Ghana where he completed both his M.A. and Ph.D. in musicology, with 12 of those years designing and delivering international education programming while affiliated with the Institute of African Studies as a Director and Associate Dean with the School for International Training. An active member of the Society for Ethnomusicology, in addition to his research, teaching and performing activities he continues to work in the field of international education through delivering faculty-led programming and private consulting. He is also currently a consultant with Oceans Beyond Piracy, researching the sociopolitical features of maritime crime and piracy in West Africa. He has had the good fortune to travel extensively throughout Africa, and his love of drumming-based music has led to multiple research trips to Togo, Benin, Nigeria, and Mali.

Index

acting as if 159, 160, 164
active agent 97, 98, 124
Adams, D.W. 88, 253
Adams, H.B. 219
Adler, A. 97, 120, 257
adverse childhood experiences (ACE) 195, 196, 263
Affect, Behavior, Cognition (ABC) Model 157
affluent students 176
Agenzia Formativa dell' istituto Professionale di Stato L. Einaudi di Grosseto 48
L'Abate, A. 49, 50
Ainsworth, J.W. 246, 265
alcohol abuse 136
Algeresque fallacy 90
alienation from self 133
Allen, C. 140, 257
Allington, R.L. 83, 253
American Association of University Women (AAUW) 187, 188, 260, 263
Anderson, J.D. 85, 88, 253,
androcentrism 180
Annan, K. 174
Anyon, J. 89, 253
Appio C. 7, 10
Arendt, H. 11, 249
Arlington Central School District 203, 263, 267
Arnold, C. 175, 260
Arnot, M. 178, 260
Asher, J.W. 104, 255
Associazione Cinema TeartroLux 51

Associazione Pratika 48
at risk middle school students 206,
attention deficit hyperactivity disorder (ADHD) 211
Automatic Thoughts Questionnaire 157
Autopoiesis 9, 250
Averna, L. 96, 255

Balducci, E. 20, 249
Bandura, A. 108, 112, 161, 164, 255, 258
Batini, F 48, 250, 251
Bauman, Z. 17, 249
Beck, I.L. 83, 254
behavior improvement plans (BIPs) 207
behavioral objectives 75
Benson, P.L. 208, 263
Berger, D. 65, 157
Bergson, H. 9, 29, 249
Biklen, S.K. 182, 260
Blanchard, K.H. 203, 263
Boeckmann, M. 113, 256, 262
Bordfeld, A. 155, 259
Boulding, K. 15, 249,
Bourdieu, P. 70, 71, 72, 252, 253
Boyatzis, R. 168, 258
Boyd, A. 186, 261
Brady, H. 177, 263
Brooks-Gunn, J. 264
Brown, E.D. 196, 263
Bruner, J.S. 120, 121, 255
Burton, J. 27, 249
Butturini, E. 43, 251

Index

Bynner, J. 177, 260
Byrnes, J.P. 82, 84, 254

cabalistic 53
Calvin, J. 97
Campbell, C.M. 167, 258
Cannatella, H. 67, 68, 252
capability approach 13, 14
Capitini, A. 16, 30, 249
Carlos, J.P. 203, 263
Carnevale, A. 175, 260
Carofiglio, G. 39, 40, 41, 251
Casa Circondariale Don Bosco 51
Casey, E. 70, 252
Casteel, J.D. 141, 145, 147, 257
Cattaneo, L. 161, 258
Center for Disease Control (CDC)
  CE Study 195
Chandler, P. 72, 252, 256
chaotic home environment 196
Chapman, A.R. 161, 258,
Chapman, R. 117, 256
character education 100, 134, 138,
  148, 153, 200, 257
Chardin, T. 9, 249
Child, I.L. 256
Children's Community School
  (CCS) 193 - 203, 269
Chiu, L.F. 175, 260
Chodorow, N. 190, 260
Chomsky, N. 40
chronic stressors 195
Cognitive Behavioral Therapy 158,
  217, 269
cognitive distortions 165
cognitive reappraisal 158
cognitive restructuring 155, 158,
  166
Cohen, E.G. 90, 254
Cold War era 88
Coleman, J. 176, 260
Colzi, G. 43, 251
Commission of the European
  Community 17, 249

community engagement 231, 240,
  241, 242, 243
community support (partnerships)
  210
connectedness 182
conscientisation 178
consequential statement 146
consumption 13, 36, 44
contaminated social language 54,
  55
conventional absurdity 40
cooperative learning 99, 101, 185,
  256
Corbett, C. 185, 260
core classroom instruction 206
Corina, D. 254, 82

Cortelazzo, M. 42, 251
Covey, S.R. 155, 156, 169, 258
creative writing 49, 107, 108, 209
Crispi, E.L. 256, 262
critical thinking 84, 91, 93, 112,
  115, 138, 141, 143, 178, 188, 257
Cromwell, R.R. 2, 59, 252, 266
Crossley, N. 252
cultural diversities 47
cultural norms 183, 186
Curtis, A.M. 35, 36, 251

Dallago, L. 251, 56
Danaher, G. 71, 253
Danilo Dolci maieutic method 49
Davis, M. 259
deep breathing relaxation 160
Deer, C. 72, 252
Del Sarto, G. 251
Delpit, L. 91, 254
democratic state structure 38
Descartes, R. 36
DeSherebenin, P. 136, 258
Developmental Assets Profile 263
Dewey, J. 3, 96, 97, 104, 105, 113,
  134, 227, 255, 257, 264

Dewing, R. 117, 255
Diamond, J. 22, 249
Dillow, S.A. 187, 262
disempowerment 27, 181
divergent goals 162
diverse communities 82
Dolci, A. 57, 251
Dolci, D. 16, 30, 49, 50, 57, 249, 251
dominant exploitative ideology 181
doxa 72, 252
Dugan, J.P. 167, 258
Dunn, K. 96, 255
Durmowicz, M.C. 187, 261
Dutchess County Children's Services Council 207, 263

Easterbrooks, S.R. 138, 257
Edwards, A. 140, 257
egocentric self-fulfillment 43
Eibl-Eibesfeld, I. 19, 250
Einstein, A. 175, 219, 262
Eisner, E.W. 75, 76, 77, 252
Élan Vital 9, 29
Ellis, A. 158, 164, 166
Elovainio, M. 262
Emmett, J. 136, 257
emotional intelligence 155, 157, 158, 168, 170, 259, 260
emotional resources 195, 197
empathy 37, 41, 42, 137, 155, 156, 200, 204, 205, 212, 243, 252
empowerment (for school children) 195, 202
Epictetus 157
Erevelles, N. 77, 252
etico-pratica 41
expressive writing 159
Eye to Eye 207, 211
Eyler, J. 229, 264

Fabbri, M. 56, 251
Facilitator 24, 49, 97, 98, 114, 230 - 235, 236, 238, 239, 240, 242, 243, 245

Fallout Shelter Problem 143, 257
Fanning, P. 165, 259
federal poverty level 194
Feinstein, L. 175, 262
feminist professionalism 182
film spray 55, 56
Fingerhut, R. 155
Fisher, C. 263
Fitzgerald, M. 2, 81, 205, 264, 267
Flowers. C. 187, 260
Fountas and Pinnell Benchmark Assessment 199
Freire, P. 17, 87, 178, 191, 250, 254, 260
Freud, S. 97, 183, 184, 261
Friedman, J. 15, 250
Fromm, E. 9, 250
Frondizi, R. 129, 130, 257
Furedi, F. 46
functional plans of analyses (FBAS) 207

Galimberti, U. 45, 46, 251
Ganz, M. 31
Gardner, H. 120, 255
Gary, S. 102, 255
gender biases 185
gender related expectations 173, 186
General Systems Theory 15
generational poverty 193
Genung, P. 61, 253
Ghiani, G. 44, 251
Giles, D.E. 264
Gilligan, C. 182, 184, 185, 261
Giroux, H.A. 182, 184, 185, 261
Giusti, S. 57, 251, 252
Givone, S. 36, 251
global engagement 224
globalization 43, 45, 46, 47
goal attainment 98, 115, 153, 156, 161, 162, 163

Index

Goldberg, K. 148, 257
Goldin-Meadow, S. 82, 254

Golding, W. 97, 255
Goleman, D. 155, 168, 258
Gordon, T.T. 59, 68, 69, 252, 268
Gorman, S.T. 261
Grameen Bank 14, 30, 189
Green, A. 177, 261
Greenstone, M. 175, 262
Grosvald, M. 82, 254
Gurak, D.T. 180, 262
Gutierrez, E. 82, 254
Gutierrez, R. 103, 255

habitus 70, 71, 72, 265
Hall, V.C. 255
Hand, Judge W. Brevard 148, 257
Harari, Y.N. 19, 250
Harris, N.B. 195
Hart, B. 83, 87, 196, 254, 264
Hartman, A. 148, 257
Havemann, W. 175
Heath, S.B. 63, 253
Hegemony 180
Heidegger, M. 59, 91, 66
Heifer International 92
Heyes, C. 37, 251
Hicks, D. 27, 31, 250
hierarchy of values 129
Higgins, J.A. 175, 261
Hill, C. 185, 260
Hirsch, E.D. 83, 254
Hoff, E. 83, 254
Hofstede, G.J. 20, 21, 250
holistic 3, 13, 14, 22, 23, 30, 100, 101, 123, 245, 246
homestay 231, 237, 238, 239, 240, 247
hostile environment 91
Howe, L.E. 141, 258
Hudson, G.R. 137, 258

imitation mechanisms 37

inequality 75, 178, 186, 231
informed dialog 86
inner voice 48, 133, 135, 149, 153
inquiry projects 90, 93
instinct 40, 96
Institutional Review Boards 132
instrumental values 128, 129
intensive language instruction 198
intensive targeted intervention 207
intercultural engagement 234, 235
International Center for Research on Women (ICRW) 174, 175, 179, 186, 261
intimate partner violence 179, 261
intransitive actions 37
intrinsic ability 101, 133
introjected values 133
Istituto Lorenzo de' Medici 225
Istituto Penitenziario Mario Gossini 50

Jackson, P. 97, 255
Jenkins, K.L. 186, 261
Jewkes, R.K. 179, 261
Johnson, A.D 196, 264
Johnson, S.K. 170, 259
Jourard, S.M. 133, 257
Jung, C.G. 133, 257

Kajiado, W.E. 175, 261
Kanna, P.K. 100, 255
Kashf Foundation 189, 261
Kelman, H.C. 27, 250
Keltikangas-Jarvinen, L. 262
Kenkel, D.S. 175, 261
Keysers, C. 37, 251
Kiernan, K.E. 175, 261
King, J. 176, 261
Kirschenbaum, H. 135, 136, 141, 143, 257, 258
Kirschenbaum, R. 186, 261
Kivimaki, M. 262
Koestler, A. 11, 250

Kohlberg, L. 183, 184, 253, 261
Komives, S.R. 167, 258

Kristof, N.D 22, 189, 190, 250, 261
Kritz, M.M 180, 262
Kucan, L. 83, 254
Kuhn, M.R. 83, 254

Labby, S. 155, 168, 259
Ladson-Billings, G. 89
LaFata, V. 251
LaGrange Middle School 204, 205, 210, 212, 213, 267
Laird, G. 117, 256
language acquisition 37, 82, 93, 196, 253, 266
Lantolf, J.P. 61, 253
Lazarus, A. 157, 164
learning contracts 101, 106, 107, 115
learning disabilities (LD) 77, 211
Lee, B. 66, 253
Leigh, J.P. 174, 262
Leino, M. 262
Lerner, R. 263
Levin, J.B. 179, 261
liberational education 178
lifelong learning 17, 249
lifespan development 170
Lightsey, O. 157, 259
linguistic contamination 34
literacy 2, 3, 81 - 93, 162, 174, 188, 194, 254, 260, 264, 267, 268
low literacy level 194
low proficiency 63, 83, 87, 89
Looney, A. 175, 262
Lunenburg, F.C. 155, 168, 259
magister vitae 34
maieutic 10, 17, 18, 29, 38, 49, 50, 56, 57, 251
Makinwa-Adebusoye, P. 180, 262
Marhaban, S. 27
Martin, A. 264
Maslow, A. 11, 98, 155, 169, 250

Maturana, H.R. 9, 250
Maynard, E. 116, 117, 256
McClelland, A. 88, 254
McGhee, K. 264
McKay, G. 264
McKay, M. 165, 259
McKee, A. 168, 258
McKellar, D. 188, 189, 262, 263
McKeown, M.G. 83, 254
Melenyzer, B.J. 180, 181, 182, 262
mental health 133, 256, 289, 259, 263
Merang, C. 176, 262
Meyer, R.E. 115, 158, 256
Mezirow, J. 29
Mid-course correction 121, 122
minority students 87, 176, 201
Mirable, M.E. 9, 250
mirror neurons 2, 35, 37, 42, 251, 252
modus agendi e sentiendi 38
moral development 148, 184, 185, 253, 261
moral dilemmas 71
Mosconi, J. 136, 257
Montessori, M. 18, 30
Mullings, L. 250
Murphy, S.E. 170, 259
Murray, M.T. 160, 259
Myers, S.B. 155, 158, 259

Namara, N 174, 177, 178, 262
Naraghi-Anderlini, S. 26, 250
Nardi, B.A. 61, 253
National Girls Collaborative Project (NCGP) 188
National Policy of Education (NPE) 174
National Policy of Empowerment of Women 174
National Science Foundation (NSF) 88, 187
Nencioni, G. 44
negative language 36, 37, 61

negative view 96, 97, 124
neurosis 154

New Hope Manor 138, 139, 140
New York Dignity for All Students Act 206, 264
Newman, J.H. 61, 62, 253
NICHD (National Institute of Child Health and Human Development) 83, 254
Nietzsche, F. 46
Noddings, N. 182, 185, 262
Nosek, B. 159, 259
Nowell, I. 182, 262
null curriculum 76
Nussbaum, M. 18, 23, 250
NYS Education Department 264

Obama, B. 159, 177, 188, 254, 259
O'Keefe, E. 157, 166
Oglala Sioux Community College 116, 117, 256, 270
Ohlde, C.D. 144, 257
Omega Point 9
open classrooms 97, 110
optional learning projects 119, 120

Pajares, F. 104, 256
parental involvement 91, 201
Pasolini, P.P 46, 47, 48, 251
Passeron, J.C. 72, 252
Patriarchy 180
Payne, R.K. 160, 193, 194, 195, 197, 206, 259, 264
Penn-Kekana, L 179, 261
Petrill S.A 264
Phenomenology 41, 42, 43, 63
Piccardo, C. 56, 251
Pine Plains Central School District 211
Pine Ridge Reservation 116, 117, 119, 256, 270
Pinker, S. 19, 40, 250, 251
Pitman, C. 106, 256

Pizzorno, Jr, J.E. 160, 259
Plato 38
Popick, V. 155, 259
Porta, L. 49, 57, 251
Positive Behavioral Intervention-Support Program (PBIS) 205, 207
post-secondary education 179
Praszkier, R. 42, 252
Preston, J. 177, 261
prosocial orientation 137
progressive education 96, 104, 105, 124
progressive relaxation 160
psychological faculty 40
public narrative 28, 31
Pulina, G. 42, 252
Pulkki, L. 175, 262
Putnam, R. 21, 250
Putton, A. 55, 252

Quinn, E. 1, 3, 153, 169, 173, 259, 269

Randolph A. 203, 263
Raths, L.E 141, 258
Rational Emotive Therapy 166
Regan, J. 256, 262
reinforcing desired behavior 164
remedial interventions 83
resilience 157, 197, 198, 200, 204, 216, 226, 227, 240
Responsive Classroom model 199
Rhizomatic 43
Risley, T.R. 83, 87, 196, 254, 264
Rogers, C.R. 97, 98, 133, 258
Rokeach, M. 128, 129, 130, 131, 132, 258
Roskes, E.M. 187, 261
Rousseau, J-J. 97
Rubin, D.L. 223, 265

Sabates, R. 175, 177, 261, 262
Sadker, D.M. 185, 262

Index 277

Sadker, M.P. 185, 262
Sarbin, T.R. 113, 256
Schakel, L. 158, 260
Scheetz, N.A. 138, 257
Schirato, T. 71, 253
Schlozman, K.L. 177, 263
Schmidt, K. 159, 259
Schmiede, A. 264
School for International Training 31, 270
School of the New Community of Chicago 105, 106, 256
school psychologist 4, 205, 211, 212, 213, 219, 267
school reform 78
school without walls 109
Schunk, D.H. 255, 256, 257
Scileppi, J.A. 1, 3, 95, 96, 98, 104, 106, 113, 115, 118, 127, 148, 166, 167, 255, 256, 258, 259, 262, 269
Search Institute 193, 199, 208, 263
secondary intervention 204, 206, 211
self-actualization 155
self-assessment 98
self-awareness 106, 133, 134, 153, 155, 219
self-direction 89, 90, 135, 153
self-empowerment 34, 193, 198, 203
Selinker, L. 66, 253
Sen, A.K. 12, 13, 14, 250,
sensory neurons 37
Seymour Smith Elementary School 211
Shakeshaft, C. 182, 262
Simon, J. 246, 265
Simon, S.B. 136, 141, 142, 143, 144, 145, 147, 258
single-sex classroom 'better for girls' 187, 263
Skelding, M. 96, 255
Skinner, B.F. 164, 259
Slate, J.R. 155, 168, 259
Slattery, S.P. 187, 261

Smith, M. 83, 167, 254, 258
Snyder, T.D. 187, 262
social language 34, 36, 42, 46, 51, 53, 54, 55
social values 84
social-emotional developmental 196
socialization 23, 96, 97, 98, 113, 124, 159, 253, 256
societal inequalities 180
socio-economic status (SES) 86, 87, 91, 196
Socrates 10, 29, 38
Spring, J. 88, 254
St. Rose, A. 185, 260
Stahl, R.J. 141, 145, 147, 257
Stahl, S.A. 83, 254
Stakeholders 73, 78, 168
STAR (Student Teacher Achievement Ratio) 201
Stein, E. 41, 252
Steiner, R. 18, 30
STEM 88, 89, 134, 135, 186, 187, 188, 261
student-controlled places 69
study abroad 4, 24, 223 - 247, 264, 265
subconscious self 36
Sullivan, A.M. 101, 256
Sutton, R. 223, 265
Sweeney, A.C. 155, 259
symbolic violence 72, 75, 78
synergy 115

Tagore, R. 18, 30
teacher-controlled places 69
Teed, E.L. 113, 166, 167, 176, 256, 259, 262
terminal values 128, 129, 130
The XL Program at Saint Xavier College in Chicago 113
Thijs, M. 158, 260
Thompson, D.G. 137, 258
Titchener, E. 42

Todorov, T. 19, 250
Tormey, R. 174, 177, 178, 262
Tosolini, A. 57, 252
toxic words 34, 36

transformative learning theory 10, 29
transitive actions 37
trauma spectrum disorder 195
Tuan, Y.F. 65, 70, 253

Ubuntu 11, 29, 30
UNESCO (United Nations Educational, Scientific, and Cultural Organization) 37, 81, 91, 246, 254, 255
U.S. Department of Education 74, 87, 134, 253, 258, 265
U.S. Preventative Services Forces Guide to Clinical Preventative Services (UPSTF) 204

valuing set 138, 139, 140, 141, 144, 145
Van der Zee, K. 158, 260
Varela, F.J. 9, 250
Verba, S. 177, 263
Viikari, J. 262
Vinitsky, M.H. 144, 257

Wacquant, L. 252
Walker, L. 184, 263
Wallace, W.R. 174
Wasik, B.A. 82, 84, 254
Webb, J. 71, 253
Wei, X. 137, 258
Wesley, K. 155, 256, 259
West, M. 187, 263
Williams, D. 82, 254
word consciousness 86
World Learning Institute 31
WuDunn, S. 189, 190, 261

Yousafzai, M. 173
Yrigaray, L. 42, 252
Yunus, M. 30, 189

Zafar, R. 189
Zakaria, F. 1, 173, 249
Zerillo, V. 96, 255
Zigler, E. 96, 256
Zimmerman, B.J. 255, 257
Zittleman, K. 185, 262
Zolli, P. 42, 251
Zuo, H. 137, 258

www.ingramcontent.com/pod-product-compliance
Lightning Source LLC
Chambersburg PA
CBHW020746160426
43192CB00006B/262